WOMEN OF THE BLUE & GRAY

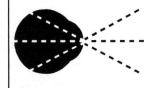

This Large Print Book carries the
Seal of Approval of N.A.V.H.

WOMEN OF THE BLUE & GRAY

TRUE CIVIL WAR STORIES OF MOTHERS, MEDICS, SOLDIERS, AND SPIES

MARIANNE MONSON

THORNDIKE PRESS

A part of Gale, a Cengage Company

GALE
A Cengage Company

Farmington Hills, Mich • San Francisco • New York • Waterville, Maine
Meriden, Conn • Mason, Ohio • Chicago

Copyright © 2018 by Marianne Monson.
Continuation of this copyright page can be found on pages 427–28.
Thorndike Press, a part of Gale, a Cengage Company.

ALL RIGHTS RESERVED
Thorndike Press® Large Print Popular and Narrative Nonfiction.
The text of this Large Print edition is unabridged.
Other aspects of the book may vary from the original edition.
Set in 16 pt. Plantin.

LIBRARY OF CONGRESS CIP DATA ON FILE.
CATALOGUING IN PUBLICATION FOR THIS BOOK
IS AVAILABLE FROM THE LIBRARY OF CONGRESS

ISBN-13: 978-1-4328-5997-8 (hardcover)

Published in 2019 by arrangement with Deseret Book Company/Shadow Mountain

Printed in Mexico
1 2 3 4 5 6 7 23 22 21 20 19

CONTENTS

5

INTRODUCTION

During the Victorian era, when photography exposures were painfully long, it was common practice to take photographs of children by placing them on the laps of their mothers, who were completely obscured by a veil. The intent, of course, was to keep a squirmy child calm during the thirty-second-long camera exposure. To modern viewers, these "Hidden Mother" images appear more than a bit creepy, with the shadowy outline of a woman or a pair of disembodied hands lurking like ghostly imprints behind the infant.

Though they seem rather macabre to viewers today, the photos, on a metaphorical level, are apt representations of a woman's role throughout history — all too often she has been relegated to the background, presented as no more than an obscured figure supporting others, unseen for her own merits. Historians, thankfully, are beginning to remove that veil, allowing her to step forward and speak of her own experience in her own words — turning his-story into their-story — bequeathing to us all a truer, fuller, richer version of events.

Walk through any Civil War museum of this country, and you'll find army uniforms, battle flags, percussion rifles, Colt revolvers, war medals, and photographs of soldiers. Here and there, tucked into corners, you may be lucky enough to find displays featuring a handful of women who contributed to the war effort. You would never guess from looking at such presentations that the vast majority of people impacted by this conflict were not male military leaders but civilians, whose perspectives describe a large part of what this country endured in the long years that stretched between 1861 and 1865.

And yet, behind the objects held within display cases of glass, many stories of women are waiting to be told. This straw hat, worn by a soldier to his death, was crafted by the hands of his sister; that mending kit, carried by another soldier, was cut and sewn from the fabric of his sweet-heart's dress; the ammunition cartridges on display were rolled by female factory work-ers. Women designed and created the flags men carried into battle; they braided gold epaulets for uniforms, while black female hands helped pick the cotton that clothed the entire nation. Female nurses cared for soldiers who fell on battlefields, then sent locks of hair and personal items to comfort mourners. Survivors cherished these items and, in many cases, donated the majority of them to museums to preserve their loved ones' memories.

But beyond the war stories we've heard most often, women also fought in the war disguised, recorded central events in journals, counselled generals on strategy, worked in factories, engaged in acts of espionage, smuggled medicines across enemy lines, organized, fundraised, and helped finance the war. In post-war years, women cared for the veterans who returned home, buried those who didn't, and listened to male survivors talk about their service. To support these veterans, they held ceremonies, erected monuments, and persuaded legislatures to declare holidays. These dedicated women might have accurately been called business consultants, philanthropists, medical personnel, event coordinators, and psychologists; and in later generations, they would have been properly compensated.

Throughout my research for this book, many people asked me, and some rather anxiously, "Are you writing about the War from the perspective of the North or the South?" My reply was always, "I'm telling it from the *women's* perspectives — North, South, black, white, Native American, immigrant, and other." The stories we tell matter, and these need to be told in order to achieve a clearer understanding of the conflict which is, in many ways, at the heart of our identity as a nation.

I believe the anxiety I often sensed was due to the fact that, without a doubt, deep divides remain in this country. The events of the Civil War are intrinsically connected to debates that continue to this day: whether it's the presence of the Confederate flag or the removal of Confederate monuments. The intensity of these debates is a tribute to the power of storytelling and its ability to influence the collective knowledge of a nation.

The stories we tell are powerful. And they matter.

If you, like I did, grew up in the North or were raised on the Northern view of the war, you may find yourself growing uncomfortable that the Southern view is allowed room in these pages at all. This is a natural reaction given the fact that during the era of post-Reconstruction, many in the South wielded their view of the conflict and of slavery as a way to justify ongoing racial prejudice in the country. The "Lost Cause" narrative allowed powerful white males on both sides to reconcile after the war, while erasing many of the initial gains that had been made toward racial equality.

For this reason, there is understandable sensitivity toward anything that smacks of defending the Confederate cause. And yet, from a conflict resolution standpoint, the women of the South simply experienced the war in an entirely different manner than did their sisters in the North. The level of violence, destruction, and loss they endured is unparalleled by the women whose front yards never became a battlefield. The Southern women's stories must be told from the framework of their own perspective, with a few essential departures from the Lost Cause narratives — most important, of course, being the reintroduction of minority voices to acknowledge the loss, destruction, and violence endured by those who were enslaved.

The original premise of the war, from the perspective of the United States, was a belief in the unity of this nation. They fought for the very idea that if the Confederacy formed a separate nation, something would be lost to *all* sides. There is no question that our modern nation has landed firmly on the side of the North on the issues of slavery and freedom for all. Yet the South's emphasis on local government and strong communities continues to play a fundamental role to this day. The African American culture adds a narrative of a people wrenched from their roots yet determined to draw strength and overcome. As a nation, we are better off for the unity of *all* of these values, taken together, taken in balance.

Throughout this book, I've tried to stay true to the story and perspective of each woman's view of the war — attempting to treat each story in turn as she would wish it to be treated. I believe the fissures in our country are destined to remain until we as Americans face our past and listen deeply to perspectives too long ignored and overlooked — finding from the history a way to step forward together, fully entitled to our stories as well as to our futures.

Women of the Blue and Gray gives voice to the women who endured this country's greatest conflict. It is an attempt to rescue from the shadowy corners of war incredible stories of women that remain relevant to our world today. So listen now, as the veil is pulled aside, and she begins to speak.

CHAPTER 1
REBELS, INCITERS, AND ALL-AROUND REVOLUTIONARIES

Harriet Beecher Stowe

"Times been changing ever since I come in this world. It is the people cause the times to change."
— Ellen Vaden,
slavery survivor, Arkansas

Looking back now at the years before the Civil War, it's easy to find indications that, like the slow but steady creep of a glacier, changes were coming, and words like "liberty" and "morality" would no longer mean what they had meant before. Slippery too was the role the federal government was expected to play for those living within its borders. Though the changes can be traced, identifying the events and people that formed the central pivots is far more difficult. Americans prior to the Civil War, much like Americans today, were varied and vast in their outlooks, and the nation remained deeply divided as it approached the elections for the sixteenth president of the United States.

However, in the tumultuous years leading up to the South's secession from the United States, the vast majority of the white populace of the country — North and South — believed slavery was a fact of life and that people of African descent were inferior to whites in terms of intellect and nature.

16

Throughout the 1700s, twelve million Africans had been forced onto ships bound for the West Indies and English, French, and Portuguese colonies, transported aboard filthy, overcrowded ships where one in six people would die of disease and exposure before touching land. Though the United States officially discontinued the importation of slaves in 1808, in the following decades, the slave population exploded from several hundred thousand to four million.

Though some religious arguments were raised against the practice, many other Christian sects claimed Africans were better off living enslaved in the western world, where they would be converted to Christianity, than with their family members who remained in Africa, living a "pagan" lifestyle.

At some point, these ideas gradually reversed. Not all at once, and not in entirety, but eventually the majority of people changed their minds about these previously accepted ideas. The shift happened, at least in part, as thinking, compassionate people considered these issues and took risks to speak out against popular opinion in spite of social hazards and the real potential for violence.

In the early 1800s, women were not supposed to hold views on political topics. By and large, they were expected to allow voting men to do this for them. But some of the women who helped bring about the aforementioned transformation in thinking didn't particularly care about the gender social code either. The "American Moses," Harriet Tubman, risked death in order to escape from slavery, then returned in secret no fewer than nineteen[1] times to lead other families and friends to freedom along the Underground Railroad. Harriet Beecher Stowe, author of *Uncle Tom's Cabin*, became the book club sensation of 1852, selling 10,000 copies of her book in the first week and 300,000 in the first year.[2] The novel was said to have caused Queen Victoria to weep, and it allegedly led Abraham Lincoln to exclaim upon meeting Stowe, "So you are the little woman who wrote the book that started this great war."[3] Louisa May Alcott and Sojourner Truth also eschewed societal norms to raise both their pens and voices to speak out for freedom.

Other women, just as fundamental to this growing revolution in the North, have had their names forgotten in dusty pages buried deep in the library. The Grimké sisters, Sarah and Angelina, were born in South

Carolina to a father who was a successful judge, owned numerous slaves on a cotton plantation,[4] and did not believe women should receive more than a cursory education. Sarah rebelled against the slave system by teaching her handmaid to read at night until her father caught her. Sarah longed to be a lawyer, but her parents would not consider such a thing. Sarah and Angelina were thirteen years apart, but their desires for equality united them. The sisters moved to Philadelphia in the 1820s and entered the national spotlight when Angelina authored a letter to an abolitionist paper. This was followed by a series of pamphlets urging the South to end the scourge of slavery. The Grimkés' hometown of Charleston took the most popular of these pamphlets, addressed to Southern Christian women, and publicly set them ablaze. Even Philadelphia, a relatively progressive Northern city, found the sisters' abolitionist positions too outlandish. They were kicked out of the Quaker sect to which they belonged and cursorily evicted from their housing.

Instead of backing down, Angelina and Sarah agreed to a nine-month speaking tour in sixty-seven cities across the Northwest on behalf of the abolitionist cause. Their speaking events were met with a mixture of fascination, admiration, and disgust, as it was unheard of for women to speak publicly on any subject, much less on a political one. The sisters began by addressing all-female audiences, but men soon began sneaking in to hear them. Though the idea of women addressing a "mixed audience" scandalized conservative society, the sisters' presentations on the realities of slavery held their audiences spellbound. Speaking in clear and persuasive language, their presence was a daunting one. As the Grimkés' popularity grew, so did the opposition. The Council of Congregationalist Ministers publicly warned all churches in the state about these "dangerous females."[5] Garish cartoons mocking Angelina circulated in the streets, and the press referred to her as "Devil-ina."[6]

The final speaking event of the tour in February of 1838 was delivered to the Massachusetts state legislature. Sarah was scheduled to speak, but when she fell ill, Angelina went in her place, thereby becoming the first US woman to ever address a legislative body. The sisters' fame preceded them, and would-be listeners packed the gallery and the staircases of the State House until they finally had to be turned away. The overwhelming crowds inspired a senator from Salem to ask drolly for a committee to examine the building's foundations "to see whether it will bear another lecture from Miss Grimké."[7]

Addressing the legislative body and the assembled and waiting crowd, Angelina's voice echoed through the imposing hall: "Because it [slavery] is a political subject, it has often tauntingly been said that women had nothing to do with it. Are we aliens, because we are women? . . . Have women *no* country? . . . I hold, Mr. Chairman, that American women have to do with this subject . . . because it is *political,* inasmuch as we are citizens of this republic and as such our honor, our happiness, and well-being are bound up in its politics, government and laws. . . . I stand before you as a southerner. . . . As a moral being I feel that I owe it . . . to my country and to the world to do all that I can to overturn a system of complicated crimes, built upon the broken hearts and prostrate bodies of my countrymen in chains."[8]

Though the sisters had plenty of detractors, their speaking events won over many listeners to the abolitionist cause. During a period of nine months, Angelina and Sarah spoke against slavery to more than 40,000 people in eighty-eight separate meetings. Of forty-four petitions sent to Congress from

Massachusetts calling for the abolishment of slavery, no less than seventy-seven percent of them came from towns where Angelina or Sarah had spoken.[9]

Like many abolitionists, the Grimké sisters believed the cause of emancipation to be inextricably connected with women's rights. Angelina asked, "Can you not see that women could do, and would do a hundred times more for the slave, if she were not fettered?"[10] Angelina's lecture to the legislature, which took place a full ten years before the Seneca Falls convention, inspired many of the key figures in the approaching women's movement.

Lydia Maria Child was among those seated in the audience that day when Angelina addressed the Massachusetts assembly. Lydia began her career publishing the kind of literature proper young ladies of her day could write while still keeping their reputations intact.[11] A series of popular children's books, a few historical novels, and three volumes of domestic-advice books helped Child develop a name and a following in the 1820s. She also edited the country's first children's magazine, and became one of the most popular female writers of her day. Her poem "Over the River and through the Wood" is still sung around holiday tables.

Then, in the 1830s, at precisely the time when Child's career and mainstream following began guaranteeing her both financial success and recognition, Lydia chose to address her audience on a far more divisive issue.

In quite a departure from her work addressing women on the subjects of cooking and childcare, Child published *An Appeal in Favor of that Class of Americans Called Africans,* the first scholarly examination of the history of slavery in the United States. In it, Child blamed both the North and the South

Lydia Maria Child

for maintaining and profiting off this "institution," and she called for its immediate abolition, along with a plea for equality and intermarriage between the races, a radical idea by almost any standard of the day.

To say that there was a public outcry over Child's change in subject matter is a little like saying the war was bloody. Though extreme abolitionists applauded her boldness, the majority of Child's previous followers were horrified that she, a woman of society, had dared address such a charged political topic in print. Sales of her traditional offerings plummeted, and many people boycotted anything with her name on it. So many magazine subscriptions were cancelled that Child was forced to resign her editorial post. Former friends stepped aside when they met her in the street, and Lydia found herself in the uncomfortable, and financially precarious, role of social outcast. Though she anticipated some of these reactions, it hardly made it any easier. In the preface to her book, she said, "I am fully aware of the unpopularity of the task I have undertaken; but though I *expect* ridicule and censure, I do not *fear* them."[12]

Child may have privately struggled with her choice of stepping into the world of politics, but instead of acquiescing, she became openly involved with the American Anti-Slavery Association and went on to publish dozens of additional anti-slavery texts intended "to familiarize the public mind with the idea that colored people are *human beings* — elevated or degraded by the same circumstances that elevate or degrade other men."[13] Though her name remained controversial and she never regained her former popularity, her books won many supporters for the cause of abolitionism. Taking the public ridicule in stride, Child later proclaimed, "Literary popularity was never a paramount object with me, even in my youth; and, now that I am old, I am utterly indifferent to it."[14]

Nothing turned the spotlight on Child's work, though, like the events at Harpers Ferry, West Virginia. Slave revolts had long been an indication of tensions simmering below the surface of an economic system built on forced labor. Most slave rebellions were put down in violent and gruesome ways to serve as warnings to the remaining slave population to toe the line. But as the enslaved population exploded to nearly four million people,[15] many Southern communities held black majorities, and white slave owners lived in constant fear of an uprising.

In 1831 in Southhampton County, Virginia, Nat Turner led a band of seventy disgruntled slaves who went from home to home, managing to murder fifty slave owners in their beds before they were apprehended.[16]

Eight years later, men on the ship *Amistad* had been kidnapped by Portuguese slave hunters and were being shipped to the Caribbean when they broke out of their chains and surprised their oppressors, successfully killing the crew and seizing control of the ship. Though the *Amistad* slaves were incarcerated once they touched ground, the United States Supreme Court eventually ordered their freedom.[17] Stories from these incredible uprisings and others were passed through slave quarters in whispers.

Then in the 1850s, in Kentucky, a religiously fervent white man named John Brown became increasingly annoyed with the lack of measurable progress towards abolition. "These men are all talk," he reportedly claimed. "What we need is action — action!"[18] Brown believed it was his own personal destiny to abolish slavery through the use of violence. In 1859, he attempted to seize the federal arsenal in Harpers Ferry, where he planned to use confiscated weapons to arm slaves before marching South, declaring freedom as he went. Some seventy people[19] knew about the plan ahead of time, including Harriet Tubman, who helped garner support for Brown and offered her logistical knowledge of the region.[20] Brown's rebellion met an abrupt end when US troops led by Robert E. Lee arrived to put down the insurrection, killing two of Brown's sons and capturing Brown, who was arrested, tried, and finally sentenced to death by hanging.

Though Lydia Maria Child did not condone John Brown's use of violence, she was one of many people captivated by Brown's determination to end slavery immediately. His final words, in her view, seemed particularly prophetic: "I, John Brown, am now quite certain that the crimes of this guilty land will never be purged away but with blood."[21]

Child wrote a letter to the governor of Virginia, offering to care for John Brown during his imprisonment, which the Governor rebuked: "I could not permit an insult even to woman in her walk of charity among us, though it be to one who whetted knives of butchery for our mothers, sisters, daughters and babes. We have no sympathy with your sentiments of sympathy with Brown."[22] Child and the governor exchanged more correspondence, and, hoping to embarrass her, Governor Wise sent their letters to the press; both the *New York Tribune* (in the North) and the *Richmond Examiner* (in the South) reprinted the full correspondence to their respectively captive and horrified audiences.

Child's eloquent response echoed Brown's words: "In this enlightened age, all despotisms *ought* to come to an end by the agency of moral and rational means. But if they resist such agencies, it is in the order of Providence that they *must* come to an end by violence. History is full of such lessons."[23]

Read by the light of candles, passed from hand to hand, Lydia's letters became so popular they were eventually reprinted in a tract that circulated 300,000 copies.[24] Child concluded the tract with William Allingham's poem "The Touchstone," which compared John Brown's burned body to ashes, sure to be scattered on the wind, each piece destined to flame and fan the revolt he had begun.[25]

As Child predicted, John Brown's execution in December 1859 made him a martyr of the abolitionist cause. Though his raid had failed abysmally in its military objectives, the aftermath galvanized the opposing sides — while Southerners saw some of their greatest fears realized in the event, Northerners watched John Brown's trial and execution with increasing horror.

A popular camp revival song, its lyrics repurposed, was lustily bellowed from street corners and fields: "John Brown's body lies a'mouldering in the grave. His soul is marching on!" Once war broke out, there was no tune more popular, and Union troops marched to the singing of "John Brown's Body," complete with a verse about hanging Jefferson Davis to a sour apple tree. The Southern army sang it too, though they changed the words, and hanged Lincoln instead. Soon after this, Julia Ward Howe penned a more refined version, and "The Battle Hymn of the Republic" rang out from Union parlors and war fundraising events.[26] Christians in the North embraced the ideas presented in Howe's lyrics, which reframed the growing conflict in religious terms: "I have seen him in the watch-fires of a hundred circling camps; . . . As he died to make men holy, let us die to make men free."

On the other side of the Mason-Dixon line, however, Confederate supporters also claimed religious ideals to support their own cause. In the years prior to the Civil War, the Southern economy ranked seventh in the *world.* For the last time in history, the products of the farm — cotton, tobacco, rice, and sugar — were worth more than the products of industry. The wealth of the Southern states rivaled the strongest economies around the globe, and the vast majority of that wealth, two billion dollars of it, was invested in imported and purchased slaves.[27] Though it's hard to fathom today, the value of the slaves of the South was worth more than the entire *land holdings* of the Southern states combined. By 1860, more riches resided in the slaves of the United States than in the entire nation's railroads, factories, and banks. While the North may have been more industrialized, the South created the raw materials used to fuel the North's industrialization. Dignitaries from all over the world flocked to the prosperous cities of Savannah, Charleston, Richmond, and New Orleans to meet with influential business leaders in lavish antebellum mansions at dinner parties and balls. In an era of strong state identity, the Southern states were proud of what they had created, though that creation depended largely on the labor and suffering of enslaved Africans.

As the cultural shift continued to widen, white Southerners became increasingly frustrated that the government in Washington did not seem to represent their interests.

While the North didn't mind using slave-made Southern wealth through taxation, the money was mainly used to fund projects that benefited Northern interests.

Meanwhile, the world was slowly evolving into a place where slavery would not be an acceptable practice *anywhere* much longer, but the South refused to admit this. Those progressive enough to see change coming wondered: how could such a powerful economy transition away from its dependence on enslaved labor? As recognition of the cruelty and inhumanity of the slave trade spread, country after country outlawed the sale and slavery of humans, beginning with Denmark in 1803, Spain in 1820, and France in 1848; emancipation spread from Scandinavia through Europe, and finally to North and South America. Britain experimented with compensated emancipation, where the government paid restitution to slave owners for the loss of their property. Former slaves in Portugal were subject to twenty-year apprenticeships as they transitioned to freedom.[28] Though the United States was fairly early in officially shutting down the trans-Atlantic slave trade in 1808, the black market value of internationally imported slaves remained high, and the internal slave trade grew in both the North and the South, through births and sales across state lines.

With so much power and wealth on the line, the battleground became the new states to the West, where pro- and anti-slave factions fought to determine whether newly created states would permit or outlaw the practice. Border states like Kansas and Missouri became violent bloodbaths as mobs sought to gain the majority. Complicating the debate were the hundreds of slaves each year who successfully breached the wall of freedom in the North, spinning tales of horrific abuse.

As Northern communities read firsthand accounts of slavery, such as *Incidents in the Life of a Slave Girl,* written by Harriet A. Jacobs in 1861, many Americans caught a glimpse of a cruel, inhumane system that appeared to flaunt the very principles espoused by the United States Constitution. Jacobs had been born into slavery and endured ongoing sexual abuse at the hands of her white master, who threatened to sell her children if she refused to allow him his way. Eventually she took refuge in a swamp, then hid in her grandmother's attic for *seven years* before making a narrow escape on board a ship bound for Pennsylvania. Jacobs was one of the first to openly write about the sexual abuse enslaved women too often experienced, and her candor horrified the sensibilities of her Victorian audience (see chapter 8).

When Jacobs and other runaway slaves arrived in the North, Southern slave owners demanded the return of their "property" and managed to pass the Fugitive Slave Act in 1850, making it illegal to harbor or help any slave who had escaped. Though this law was a compromise, in some ways it inflamed the issue, as Northerners who found slavery morally objectionable did not want to have to force an enslaved person to return to a situation where he or she was obviously not keen to go. Regardless, few white Americans, even in the North, were ready to consider allowing anyone of African descent to vote or become a citizen, nor were they particularly eager to fight a war over the issue.

This was the state of the debate fragmenting the nation when the highly controversial candidate Abraham Lincoln managed to win the presidential election but failed to win the popular vote. Many of Lincoln's contemporaries, both North and South, ridiculed him as uncouth and far too extreme, though Lincoln himself refused to identify as an abolitionist.

In one of the original "Not My President!" demonstrations, the announcement of Lincoln's election inspired the immediate secession of seven states, who declared themselves the Confederate States of America. By the time of Lincoln's inauguration a few months later, the tensions at Fort Sumter in Charleston, South Carolina, were at a boiling point. The fort was clearly located in the South, and the Confederacy demanded that Lincoln leave it in Southern hands. If Lincoln ordered the fort to be resupplied, the Confederates said they would deem it an act of aggression. When Lincoln persisted, the Confederates opened fire, each side calling the other the instigator of the violence. As soon as the new President called for Northern volunteers to take up arms, four additional states joined the Confederacy, including Virginia, hunched on the very border of the nation's capital.

Lincoln was now president over a country literally coming apart. Crucial border states hung in the balance, their populations deeply divided. If Maryland also seceded, as many of its residents clamored to do, Washington, DC, would find itself surrounded by hostile forces and would now be located in the middle of the Confederacy.

Women like Anna Elizabeth Dickinson, Anna Ella Carroll (see chapter 5), and Mary Shadd Cary (see chapter 9) stepped into this quagmire and became incredibly important in holding the nation together. As popular figures, they could influence public opinion in a way that Lincoln and other politicians could not.

Anna Elizabeth Dickinson began her oratory career when she was still a teenager; she published her first essay at age thirteen. Raised in a Quaker family that believed in the education of women, Anna's childhood home was a stop on the Underground Railroad. In her twenties, she spoke to 5,000 people at the Cooper Institute in New York City and earned a standing ovation for an impassioned speech she made on the floor of the House of Representatives before President Lincoln and other military leaders in 1864. Anna became the first woman to speak before Congress, addressing the wrongs of slavery, the political strife of the nation, and the rights of women.[29] Those who heard Dickinson speak seldom forgot the sight of a young, eloquent girl who could speak for two hours at a time using few notes. Eventually Anna became one of the highest paid speakers of her day and dedicated her wealth to supporting family and charitable causes.

In 1862, William Lloyd Garrison invited Dickinson to give a series of lectures to foment the abolitionist movement prior to the anticipated release of Lincoln's Emancipation Proclamation, hoping her speeches would create a climate where the controversial proclamation might be accepted. Mark Twain, who was once seated among Dickinson's audience, said, "Her vim, her energy, her determined look, her tremendous earnestness, would compel the respect and the attention of an audience, even if she spoke in Chinese — would convince a third of them, too."[30] Passionate and undaunted in her views, Anna became known as a modern Joan of Arc, a woman she often referenced in her speeches. The Republicans hired her a second time during the war to help Lincoln win reelection, inspiring one Republican newspaper editor to write, "This woman is sent from on high to save the state."[31]

Dickinson recruited soldiers for the United States Colored Troops during the war and applauded their war-time contributions.

After the war, Dickinson turned her attention to women's rights, dress reform, and racial equality, pushing the nation toward its future with the words: "In olden time, with the Red Sea in front, and the hosts of Egypt behind, God's voice was heard bidding the children of Israel go forward. Eternal advance — everlasting growth — is the price of life to every nation."[32]

South of the Mason-Dixon line, white women fought on the other side of the growing ideological battle, rallying around the cause of Southern independence and the belief that the Constitution allowed states the right to withdraw from the union in peace. In the pivotal state of Maryland, the Cary sisters, Hetty and Betty, argued that the Confederacy was continuing the work of the American Revolution by taking up arms against Northern invaders. When Maryland remained in the Union and Northern troops descended on the city, Hetty smugly waved a Confederate flag from a second-story window, risking arrest for her actions. The sisters chose to abandon their home, smuggling drugs and clothing to aid troops as they fled South. The pair took refuge in Richmond with their cousin Constance, and the three were deemed the "Cary Invincibles" for their bold actions on behalf of the Confederacy.

When the Confederate national flag, the "Stars and Bars," became too difficult to distinguish from the Union flag during battle, the Cary women designed a new banner, made from repurposed silk. This flag, which they designed and sewed by hand, is the one most people today associate with the Confederacy, though it was technically never its national flag. The Cary Invincibles made and presented three of these battle flags to Generals Beauregard, Johnston, and Van Dorn. Constance sent hers with a written note: "An earnest prayer that the work of my hand may hold its place near him as he goes out to a glorious struggle — and, God willing, may one day wave over the re-captured batteries of my home."[33] Trading in her sewing needle for a pen, Constance then began writing articles in support of Southern secession; she insisted, however, on publishing them under the pseudonyms "Refugitta" and "Secessia," as she felt it was improper for a woman's name to appear in print. Meanwhile, her sister Jennie Cary set a popular poem, "Maryland," to a catchy tune, creating the famous Confederate battle song, "Maryland, My Maryland."[34]

Other Southern women served "cotton diplomacy" missions in Europe, soliciting England and France to enter the conflict on the side of the Confederacy, which they very nearly did. One of the most notable emissaries was nineteen-year-old Belle Boyd, the infamous spy fresh from a Yankee prison, who was invited by Confederate Secretary of State Judah P. Benjamin to beseech Canadian, French, and British heads of state for the rebel cause. Belle charmed European society, and the French press referred to her as "La Belle Rebelle."[35] Rose Greenhow, also a spy turned ambassador, traveled to Europe on a blockade runner, successfully delivering letters from President Jefferson Davis to influential French and British leaders, raising much needed funds to aid the South (see chapter 4).[36]

The lines were drawn. With the fervor mounting in the North matched only by the indignation of the South, the conflict had begun.

Further Reading

Catherine Clinton. *Harriet Tubman: The Road to Freedom.* Boston: Little, Brown, 2004.

Jennie M. Day. *The Cary Sisters.* Chicago: A. Flanagan Co., 1903.

J. Matthew Gallman. *America's Joan of Arc: The Life of Anna Elizabeth Dickinson.* New York: Oxford University Press, 2006.

Lori J. Kenschaft. *Lydia Maria Child: The*

Quest for Racial Justice. New York: Oxford University Press, 2002.

Mark Perry. *Lift up Thy Voice: The Sarah and Angelina Grimké Family's Journey from Slaveholders to Civil Rights Leaders.* New York: Penguin Books, 2001.

Harriet Beecher Stowe. *Uncle Tom's Cabin.* Boston: J. P. Jewett and Company, 1853.

Notes

Epigraph: *FWP: Salve Narrative, Vol. 9.* Retrieved from the Library of Congress, https://www.loc.gov/resource/mesn.027/?sp=7.

1. This number is debated by historians; some set it at nineteen trips and more than 300 slaves; others indicate it was closer to twelve trips and 60 to 70 persons brought to freedom. See Laurel Thatcher Ulrich, *Well-Behaved Women Seldom Make History* (New York: Vintage Books, 2007), 118.

2. Ulrich, *Well Behaved Women,* 113.

3. See Barbara Anne White, *The Beecher Sisters* (New Haven, Conn.: Yale University Press, 2003), 92.

4. Gerda Lerner, *The Grimke Sisters from South Carolina: Pioneers for Women's Rights and Abolition* (North Carolina: The

University of North Carolina Press, 2004), 12.

5. Lerner, *Grimke Sisters from South Carolina,* 5.
6. Lerner, *Grimke Sisters from South Carolina,* 7.
7. Lerner, *Grimke Sisters from South Carolina,* 8.
8. Lerner, *Grimke Sisters from South Carolina,* 8.
9. Ulrich, *Well-Behaved Women,* 135.
10. In Scott J. Hammond, *Classics of American Political and Constitutional Thought, Volume 2: Reconstruction to the Present* (Indianapolis: Hackett Publishing 2007), 6.
11. The grandfather's house featured in Lydia Child's song has been restored and still stands in Medford, Massachusetts.
12. *Letters of Lydia Maria Child with a Biographical Intro by John G. Whittier* (New York: Houghton Mifflin, 1882), ix.
13. Lydia Maria Francis Child, *The Oasis* (Boston: Benjamin C. Bacon, 1834), vii.
14. Lydia Maria Child, *A Lydia Maria Child Reader,* ed. Carolyn L. Karcher (Durham, N. C.: Duke University Press, 1997), 252.
15. http://www.civil-war.net/pages/1860_census.html.

16. See Stephen B. Oates, *The Fires of Jubilee: Nat Turner's Fierce Rebellion* (New York: HarperCollins, 2009).

17. Marcus Rediker, *The Amistad Rebellion: An Odyssey of Slavery and Freedom* (New York: Penguin Books, 2013).

18. In John Spencer Bassett, *A Short History of the United States* (New York: The Mac-Millan Company, 1915), 502.

19. Karen Whitman, "Re-evaluating John Brown's Raid at Harpers Ferry." *West Virginia History* 34, no. 1 (October 1972): 46–84.

20. Judith E. Harper, *Women During the Civil War: An Encyclopedia* (New York: Routledge, 2004), 380. Legend has it that Tubman planned to participate in the raid herself, but this fact has not been verified by historians. See also W.E.B. DuBois, *John Brown* (Philadelphia, 1909), 293.

21. In Stephen B. Oates, *To Purge This Land with Blood: A Biography of John Brown,* Amherst, MA: University of Massachusetts Press, 1970), 8.

22. In Michael P Johnson, *Reading the American Past, Selected Historical Documents, Volume 1: to 1877* (Boston: Bedford/St. Martin's, 2012), 279.

23. In *Correspondence between Lydia Maria*

Child and Gov. Wise and Mrs. Mason of Virginia (Boston: American Anti-Slavery Society, 1860), 26. Digitized by the Library of Congress, https://archive.org/details/correspondencebe00lcchil. Last accessed February 8, 2018.

24. *Letters of Lydia Maria Child: with a biographical introduction by John G. Whittier,* xix. https://archive.org/stream/lettersoflydiama00chil_0/lettersoflydiama00chil_0_djvu.txt.

25. *Letters of Lydia Maria Child,* xix.

26. Library of Congress, Teachers, "John Brown's Body, The Battle Hymn of the Republic," found at http://www.loc.gov/teachers/lyrical/songs/john_brown.html. Last accessed February 8, 2018.

27. Bruce Catton, *The Civil War,* 7.

28. Henry Hobhouse, *Seeds of Change: Six Plants that Transformed Mankind,* 111.

29. Joseph Duffy, "Anna Elizabeth Dickinson and the Election of 1863." *Connecticut History Review,* no. 25 (1984): 22–38. www.jstor.org/stable/44369224.

30. In "Mark Twain, New York Correspondent," Walter Blair, *Essays on American Humor: Blair through the Ages* (Madison, WI: University of Wisconsin Press, 1993), 147.

31. "In 1863, Anna Dickinson Takes New England by Storm," *New England Historical Society,* January 18, 2016, http://www .newenglandhistoricalsociety.com/in-1863-anna-dickinson-takes-new-england 46.-by-storm/. Last accessed February 8, 2018.

32. "The People's Party: Miss Anna E. Dickinson's Lecture at Cooper Institute," *New York Tribune,* April 20, 1872, 8.

33. *Refugitta of Richmond: The Wartime Recollections, Grave and Gay, of Constance Cary Harrison,* ed. Nathaniel Cheairs Hughes, Jr, (Knoxville: University of Tennessee Press, 2011), 42.

34. She set the poem, originally written by James Ryder Randall, to the tune "Lauriger Horatius." *Refugitta of Richmond,* 39.

35. https://www.civilwar.org/learn/biographies/maria-belle-boyd.

36. http://docsouth.unc.edu/fpn/greenhow/menu.html.

CHAPTER 2
THE BEARDLESS BRIGADE
CIVIL WAR SOLDIERS

White Mountain rangers, ca. 1861

"If some few Southern women were in the ranks, they could set the men an example they would not blush to follow."
— Sarah Morgan Dawson,
New Orleans

In the early days of the war, nineteen-year-old Sarah Morgan from Baton Rouge, Louisiana, lamented, "*O!* if I was only a man! Then I could don the breeches, and slay them with a will!"[1] Unbeknownst to Sarah and many other Americans, women *were* serving in the ranks of both armies, using male clothing and aliases.

Determining the precise numbers of female soldiers who shouldered weapons and assumed male identities is a puzzle unlikely to ever be solved. If a soldier stayed successfully hidden, she either fulfilled her military assignment and returned home or found a final resting place beneath a grave marker etched with her adopted male name, like Private Lyons Wakeman, whose family once knew her as Sarah Rosetta Wakeman.[2] Most historians place the number of female Civil War soldiers somewhere between 400 and 1,000,[3] but these women had strong motivation to guard their secrets well. When one anonymous Union soldier's gender came to light, her tentmate attempted to rape her. She shot him at close range in the face, which kept her safety intact, but not her secret.[4] If discovered, women risked potential sexual abuse and exploitation by their fellow soldiers and military leaders, followed by discharge and a loss of income, which was a frequent motivation for enlistment in the first place. While communities welcomed returning male soldiers with honor and gratitude, a female soldier often returned home to ridicule and scorn.

The belief that female soldiers were rare, but not unheard of, is supported by primary documents, wherein soldiers responded to the discovery of female soldiers with mild surprise and humor rather than shock or disbelief. In one letter from the Historic New Orleans Collection, a soldier wrote his brother about several fairly mundane events before mentioning that "the cavalry boys bring in guerillas most every day, the other day they brought in about 40 of them, one of them a woman dressed in men's clothes, she was paroled, promising not to [take up] arms against the United States." After this brief comment, he returns to musing over how much longer the war could last, offering no indication he believed the situation to be unique.[5] Without exact numbers, it is still fair to say that hundreds of women fought, bled, and died on Civil War battle-fields.

In some ways, the Civil War was one of the easiest wars for women to gain entry to: desperate for recruits, army doctors performed farcical physicals that often involved nothing more than a brief visual appraisal. Frances Louisa Clayton passed the initial examination by wearing one of her husband's suits and pasting a false moustache and goatee to her face. If you could walk, you were probably accepted. Lack of communication eased matters too. If a woman was discovered by one regiment, she could easily enlist in a different location with another unit. A woman's insufficient military training scarcely set her apart in a nation of civilians turned soldiers overnight. Working-class women accustomed to long hours of farm or millwork quietly disappeared into an army of "amateurs led by amateurs."[6] Inadequate meals and harsh marching conditions probably eliminated many of the challenges that came with menstrual cycles, and most soldiers bathed separately and slept fully clothed. A stubborn dearth of facial hair could be blamed on youthfulness, as everyone knew the minimum enlistment age of eighteen was more of an overlooked guideline than any-

Frances Clayton

thing else. The Victorian perception of women as too frail for battle also helped female soldiers to hide in plain sight, as many men believed women patently incapable of the physical demands of war.

Women enlisted for reasons as wide as those that motivated any soldier. Some, like Mary Ann Clark of Kentucky, left to escape an abusive husband,[7] while others, such as Harriet Merrill, used the army as a way to escape prostitution.[8] Like soldiers before and after them, many women were drawn to the army by desperate circumstances. At a time when few occupations permitted women, those toiling for survival-level wages in the factories of the North for as little as $4 per month found the promise of $13 a month plus army rations far too appealing to resist. For many women living in financial desperation, soldiering provided a solid, dependable income, and many found it exhilarating to earn a decent wage for the first time in their lives. Sarah Rosetta Wakeman wrote to her family, "I have enjoyed my self the best since I have been gone away from home than [I] ever did before in my life. I have plenty of money to spend and a good time assoldier[ing]."[9] Wakeman clearly found the risks of military service worth the freedom they bought her. After serving two years in the Union army, she wrote to her family from Louisiana: "I am as independent as a hog on the ice. If it is God's will for me to fall in the field of battle, it is my will to go and never return home."[10]

Patriotism and love of country also influenced soldiers on both sides to serve. Frances Elizabeth Quinn of Illinois followed her fourteen-year-old brother into battle and wrote, "My dear Brother . . . I volunteered in the Army because I wished to have a part in the defense of my country's flag. I think I love my country as well as you do, and by sufficient drilling I think I may learn to shoot just as straight as you can."[11]

Freedom and safe passage induced former slave Maria Lewis to join the 8th New York Cavalry when they passed through her town, emancipating slaves as they rode. The seventeen-year-old disguised herself as a "darkly tanned" white male calling herself George Harris, a character from *Uncle Tom's Cabin*, who escaped slavery by passing himself off as a Spanish gentleman. Though Lewis initially planned to use the ruse only to travel North, she found she enjoyed soldiering, and she stayed on with General Philip Sheridan's cavalry unit in the Shenandoah Valley for an additional eighteen months. Lewis distinguished herself in service and became a member of the honor guard chosen to present seventeen captured Confederate flags to Secretary of War Edwin Stanton.[12]

A woman's desire to remain near those she loved often drew her to battle, particularly if she had few other family members at home. One woman from Ohio, alias Private Joseph Davidson, enlisted with her father and fought beside him until he was killed in the Battle of Chickamauga; she stayed on with the army, serving for a total of three years.[13] Melverina Elverina Peppercorn, drawn from the wild mountainous regions of Tennessee, refused to be separated from her brother, Alexander the Great Peppercorn, who went by the slightly less ostentatious nickname, Lexy. The sixteen-year-old twins enlisted for the Confederate army and fought side by side until Lexy fell in battle. Melverina rescued her brother and escorted him to a field hospital, where she nursed him to a full recovery.[14]

Some women preferred to go to war rather than face a long, uncertain separation from their husbands. Newlywed Lucy Gauss served beside her husband in the 18th North Carolina. A true soldier, Gauss adopted the motto: "Hold your head up and die hard." The couple fought together at the First Battle of Bull Run, where Lucy was wounded in the head. She made a complete recovery and returned to the field two months later. When her husband was killed in Richmond several years later, Lucy informed her commanding officer that she was pregnant, obtained a hasty discharge, and took her husband's body home for burial.[15]

When Martha Parks Lindley's husband decided to join the war effort in Pittsburgh,

Martha refused to be left behind. She later wrote, "I was so anxious to be with my husband that I resolved to see the thing through if it killed me." The couple entrusted their two children to Martha's sister and enlisted together, assuring fellow soldiers they were "chums."[16] In disguise, Martha cast her vote for Lincoln's reelection decades before women had the right to vote. Both Martha and her husband survived the war, and after being discharged, they returned to fetch their children. Martha refused to talk to the press about her army experience, but her children loved to listen to their parents recount their war adventures. Martha's uniform and pistol were passed down as family treasures for generations.[17]

Keith and Malinda Blalock have the distinction of being the only known couple to fight for both the South *and* the North. The couple were staunch Unionists, which put them at odds with their Confederate North Carolina community. Though he didn't want to join the army, having no love for the Confederate cause, Keith knew he would face persecution if he didn't enlist. Malinda passed herself off as Keith's younger brother "Sam," and together the couple drilled, marched, fought, and dug fortifications. Eager to desert and join the North, Keith rolled around in poison oak so vigorously he was able to convince the physician he might have smallpox or swamp fever. Malinda revealed her gender, and the couple took off for Union lines, where they joined the guerilla warfare raging in the mountains of North Carolina. In this deeply divided and remote area, the war played out in feuding bands that burned and pillaged. The Blalocks served as scouts and guides through the mountains, leading raids and destroying railroads and bridges to hasten the Confederate defeat. Malinda stopped these activities briefly to have a baby; two weeks later, she left the child with relatives and returned to the field. After the war, the couple picked up their child and returned to farming and storekeeping.[18]

Regardless of what drew women into the army, once there, they made substantial contributions. Five women are known to have fought at Gettysburg: two for the Union and three for the Confederacy.[19] One of the women on the Confederate side was shot in the leg and was removed to a military hospital, where her gender was revealed as they prepared to amputate her leg. Two other women fell in Pickett's charge as they rushed with their comrades across that infamous field. At least three women were incarcerated in the dreaded Andersonville prison, including Florena Budwin, who enlisted with her husband and was captured by his side.[20] Jennie Hodgers, alias Private Albert D. J. Cashier, served among the Union troops who lay siege to Vicksburg. Captured on a mission of reconnaissance, Cashier escaped by seizing one guard's gun and outrunning the others.[21] Like the majority of soldiers, women found war a sobering, intense experience that eluded all explanation. Sarah Rosetta Wakeman wrote to her family: "I was under fire about four hours and laid on the field of battle all night. There was three wounded in my Co. and one killed."[22]

Many times, the secret of a soldier's gender was revealed when she died or became wounded during battle. Union soldier James L. Dunn said after the Battle of Peachtree Creek, they "found several women in mens clothes also among the killed."[23] Eight known women fought in the battle of Antietam, including one from New Jersey who earned a promotion for her performance despite being in the second trimester of pregnancy![24] Though her name has been lost, she earned recognition for being "a real soldierly, thoroughly military fellow."[25] Not long after earning this honor, her commanding officer wrote a shocked letter explaining to his superior that the "corporal was promoted to sergeant for gallant conduct at the battle of Fredericksburg — since which time the sergeant has become the mother of a child."[26]

The discovery of a female soldier's identity through childbirth was more common than one would imagine; there are actually several recorded accounts of women pausing from soldiering to deliver a baby. A female corporal in the 6th New York Heavy Artillery went into labor while walking the picket line, and her sergeant, Herman Weiss, wrote, "What was our surprise when . . . we heard that the corporal had been taken very sick so that the doctor had send him right off to the division hospital and that then and there . . . this good looking corporal had been relieved of a nice little boy."[27] Though many in the regiment were entertained by the surprise, military leadership found the event less amusing. General William S. Rosencrans of Tennessee sent the following telegram: "an Orderlie Sergent . . . was to day delivered of a baby — which is violation of all military law and of the army regulations. . . . You will apply a proper punishment in the case, and a remedy, to prevent a repetition of the act."[28] Though his outrage is apparent, the laws and regulations he referred to are as unclear as his recommended remedy, as no recorded military law forbade soldiers having babies.

When female soldiers occasionally served side by side, did they see through one another's disguises? Some accounts seem to indicate they may have exchanged covert gazes and sometimes revealed their identities if they felt it was safe to do so. In the uniform of a male soldier, Sarah Emma Edmonds administered medical relief after Antietam, when a severely wounded patient sought out her attention. Beckoning Edmonds closer, the soldier whispered: "I am dying. . . . [I] am a female . . . and have remained undiscovered and unsuspected. . . . I have neither father, mother, nor sister. My only brother was killed today. . . . I have performed the duties of a soldier faithfully. . . . I wish you to bury me with your own hands, that none may know after my death that I am other than my appearance indicates."[29] Never certain whether the young woman had guessed her own hidden identity, Edmonds held the hand of this wounded soldier as she slipped from life, then buried her in an unmarked grave beneath a mulberry tree.

The fear of discovery compounded the trauma of injury for female soldiers like Mary Galloway, who was shot in the neck while fighting in the battle of Antietam. She lay in a ditch for thirty-six hours before being transferred to a field hospital, where a male surgeon tried to assist her; each time he approached, she cried out in distress and refused to allow him to touch her. The baffled surgeon finally summoned nurse Clara Barton, who succeeded in calming the soldier so the bullet could be removed. Once alone with Barton, Mary revealed her identity, confiding that at age sixteen she had joined the army when her sweetheart and all male members of her family enlisted. Injured and far from home, she was distressed at no longer knowing her lover's whereabouts. Barton not only kept Galloway's secret, but she also located the sweetheart, who was recovering from an arm amputation in Fredericksburg. After Galloway recovered from her own wound, she traveled to be reunited with him; the couple later married and named their first child Clara Barton Barnard.[30]

While the majority of female Civil War soldiers had to disguise themselves as males in order to enlist, a small number of openly female militias formed as the war progressed and absorbed all available male recruits. One of the most impressive local female militias came from LaGrange, on the western border of Georgia. Calling themselves the "Nancy Harts" in tribute to the Georgian heroine who had defended her home against the invasion of British soldiers during the Revolutionary War, these women trained regularly for three years.[31]

When the males of LaGrange left for battle, Nancy Morgan grew concerned about the lack of protection for the town, which lay at the crossroads of railroad lines. As Morgan spoke with her friend Mary Heard about what they could do, Nancy suggested forming a female military company.

"Did you ever hear of a military company of women?" Mary asked.

"No, but that doesn't matter," Nancy responded.

"I've got my grandfather's old flint-lock fowling piece," Heard offered.

"I've got an old rifle," said Nancy.[32]

The women enlisted an older veteran for lessons in marksmanship and training, and met twice a week at a schoolhouse to drill and train. They wielded a rather pathetic array of leftover firearms, but rounded up every "old musket, squirrel gun, and fowling piece" the men had not taken off to war.[33] None of the women had experience with firearms, and early practice sessions were dicey. One woman accidentally shot a nearby bull in pasture, and another took down a hornets' nest. But the militia continued to train until they could handle their weapons with ease. Following the pattern of home militias, the group nominated Nancy Morgan to serve as captain and Mary Heard as first lieutenant. At each meeting, they guided the recruits through a series of practices and drills, then boldly "marched through the streets with guns on our shoulders and banners flying"[34] to remind the town they were not without protection.

In 1863, LaGrange, Georgia, was designated a Confederate Hospital Zone, and most public buildings housed wounded soldiers. In addition to their soldiering, these remarkable women nursed the wounded, cared for their families, and ran their farms, even as they continued training.[35]

The Nancy Harts' years of practice finally paid off in 1864 when Sherman and his generals marched through Georgia, capturing nearby Fort Tyler. Confederate soldiers brought word of an advancing Union army dispatched from West Point, tearing up miles of railroad tracks, pillaging and destroying as they came. The women assembled at the home of First Lieutenant Mary Heard to form ranks and prepare to meet the enemy. Fleeing Confederate soldiers advised the women: "Go into your homes and bar your doors; the Federals are upon us."[36] But the Nancy Harts did not retreat, for as Leila Pullen later recounted, "We had made up our minds to dare or die."[37] When the Union army, led by Colonel Oscar LaGrange, came into sight, the Harts met them, lined up across Broad Street, armed and dangerous, fully prepared to do battle if needed to keep their homes from being torched. They also perhaps looked a tad comical, as many of the women wore every dress they owned in order to save their wardrobes from potential fire.

Taken aback by the sight of the assembled and armed women, Colonel LaGrange called his army to halt and asked to be introduced to the militia's leader. Confederate prisoners of war marching at the front of the Union army recognized many of their own sweethearts and family members among the brave militia members.

Colonel LaGrange promised Captain Nancy Morgan that no harm would come to the town if the militia allowed the army safe passage. Nancy graciously invited Colonel LaGrange to dine at her home, and, in turn, LaGrange paroled the prisoners of war so they could return to their beds for the night. Though the army destroyed military facilities, thanks to the bravery and determination of the Nancy Harts, private homes and property in LaGrange remained unscathed.[38]

When the war drew to a close and soldiers returned to their homes, both women and men struggled to resolve the shifting gender roles evoked by the conflict.

Though some soldiers resumed their female identities, others did not. Several years before enlisting for the Union, Jennie Hodgers had assumed the identity of Albert D. J. Cashier in order to earn a fairer factory wage. She fought with the 95th Illinois infantry and participated in more than forty battles during three years of enlistment without being discovered, and then she retained her male identity for an additional fifty years afterward. When Hodgers was injured in 1910, a doctor learned she was female but agreed to keep her secret. In 1913, due to the onset of dementia, Jennie was sent to a state hospital, where employees revealed her gender to the media and forced her to wear a dress for the first time in more than fifty years.[39] Many of her former military comrades protested the abusive treatment and successfully petitioned for Hodgers to retain her military pension. When she died in 1915, they also ensured that she was buried with full military honors laid to rest under a stone marked with her male identity and military service.[40] Hodgers's story illustrates the risks women continued to live with, years after completing their service. Pension, respect, and comradery with those they had served — all this was vulnerable if their true gender became known.

By the end of the war, the idea of a woman disguised and engaged in battle had become a popular tale, inspiring numerous newspaper articles and novels such as *The Lady Lieutenant,* published in 1862, or Sarah Edmonds's *Nurse and Spy in the Union Army,* which sold 175,000 copies.[41] By 1865, *The United States Service Magazine* bemoaned: "No editor can turn over a morning's 'exchange papers' without encountering . . . some fair and fast Polly or Lucy who, led by the spirit of patriotism, love, or fun, has donned the blue breeches and follows the drum."[42] Though some reporters deemed female soldiers "brilliant," "virtuous," "gallant heroines," and carried stories of their exploits, others accused women soldiers of mental illness and insanity. Wisconsin newspapers covered the story of Rebecca Peterman's military service by interviewing her stepfather, who said his daughter's "wild, erratic course" was a cause of embarrassment to the "staid, respectable" family. He concluded by saying, "The girl is perfectly uncontrollable."[43]

Married women tended to receive more favorable press than their single counterparts, though almost all had to endure extensive commentary on their dress and assessment of their beauty. Women's reasons for joining were held up to stringent scrutiny, such as an Ohio newspaper that claimed women enlisted "[for] profit, not patriotism, or love, as is the case with the girls that go into the United States service disguised as men."[44] In addition to the rigors of war, female soldiers faced additional attention and commentary, both positive and negative, from the larger community.

Regardless of their reactions, the generation that lived through the war knew many women had served among the army's ranks. Because of the popularity of Civil War stories that circulated about women disguised in battle, the government received regular requests for information about these hidden soldiers. Well into the twentieth century, however, the US army specifically denied having records or documents of females engaged in battle, despite significant evidence to the contrary. In a typical response from 1909, the Records and Pension Office stated: "I have the honor to inform you that no official record has been found in the War Department showing specifically that any woman was ever enlisted in the military service of the United States . . . at any time during the period of the Civil War."[45] This statement is patently untrue. In fact, the Adjutant General's Office maintained files on several of the best documented female soldiers, as well as correspondence from military officials citing discovery of females serving in their ranks.[46]

The reason for routine denial is unknown, but many petitions for women's suffrage specifically cited women's military service as evidence they deserved the vote.[47] In the post-war environment, Americans fought to reestablish gender norms that had been disrupted by the conflict, intentionally obscuring women's wartime achievements to erase many of the advancements combat facilitated. In a similar vein, governmental positions that had been extended to women during the war were routinely withdrawn and replaced with male workers.

Tragically, the military's official statements contributed to the loss of collective memory about these brave and heroic veterans, many of whose names would have been familiar to their contemporaries but whose lives are rarely commemorated in Civil War museums or battlefields today. These are stories of unsung veterans whose lives have been rediscovered through the modern renewed interest in women's history, and their riveting accounts need to be rescued from the attics and basements to which they were once relegated, dusted off, and told once more.

Further Reading

DeAnne Blanton and Lauren M. Cook. *They Fought Like Demons: Women Soldiers in the American Civil War.* Baton Rouge: Louisiana State University Press, 2002.

M. R. Cordell. *Courageous Women of the Civil War: Soldiers, Spies, Medics, and More.* Chicago: Chicago Review Mask, 2016.

Laura Leedy Gansler. *The Mysterious Private Thompson: The Double Life of Sarah Emma*

Edmonds, Civil War Soldier. New York: Free Press, 2005.

Elizabeth D. Leonard. *All the Daring of the Soldier: Women of the Civil War Armies.* New York: W W Norton, 1999.

Anita Silvey. *I'll Pass for Your Comrade: Women Soldiers in the Civil War.* New York: Clarion Books, 2008.

Notes

Epigraph: Sarah Morgan Dawson, *A Confederate Girl's Diary* (Boston: Houghton Mifflin Company, 1913), 21.

1. Dawson, *Confederate Girl's Diary,* 21.

2. Wakeman was buried without discovery, but her story and letters were preserved by her family.

3. Due to a deliberate attempt on the part of the military to suppress these stories, as discussed later in this chapter, accurate figures were not kept.

4. DeAnne Blanton and Lauren M. Cook, *They Fought Like Demons: Women Soldiers in the American Civil War* (Baton Rouge: Louisiana State University Press, 2002), 148–49.

5. Franklin S. Twitchell to his brother, Connecticut Volunteer after the Battle of Labadieville, December 3, 1862, The Historic New Orleans Collection, Accession

Number MSS 282 (86-48-L).

6. Bruce Catton, *The Civil War* (New York: Houghton Mifflin, 2004), 27.

7. M. R. Cordell, *Courageous Women of the Civil War: Soldiers, Spies, Medics, and More* (Chicago: Chicago Review Mask, 2016), 29.

8. Blanton and Cook, *They Fought Like Demons,* 36.

9. In Elizabeth D. Leonard, *All the Daring of the Soldier: Women of the Civil War Armies* (New York: W. W. Norton & Co., 1999), 194.

10. Judith E. Harper, *Women of the Civil War: An Encyclopedia* (New York: Routledge, 2004), 401.

11. Cordell, *Courageous Women of the Civil War,* 16.

12. Anita Silvey, *I'll Pass for Your Comrade: Women Soldiers in the Civil War* (New York: Clarion Books, 2008), 87.

13. Blanton and Cook, *They Fought Like Demons,* 33.

14. Blanton and Cook, *They Fought Like Demons,* 33, 34, 38.

15. Silvey, *I'll Pass for Your Comrade,* 89.

16. Donald C. Caughey and Jimmy J. Jones, *The 6th United States Cavalry in the Civil War: A History and Roster* (Jefferson,

N. C.: McFarland & Co, Jefferson, 2013), 18.

17. Silvey, *I'll Pass for Your Comrade*, 87–88.

18. Silvey, *I'll Pass for Your Comrade*, 20–23; Blanton and Cook, *They Fought Like Demons*, 33–34, 184.

19. Blanton and Cook, *They Fought Like Demons*, 15.

20. Silvey, *I'll Pass for Your Comrade*, 81.

21. Blanton and Cook, *They Fought Like Demons*, 16.

22. Sarah Rosetta Wakeman, *An Uncommon Soldier: The Civil War Letters of Sarah Rosetta Wakeman, alias Pvt. Lyons Wakeman,* ed. Lauren Cook Burgess (New York: Oxford University Press, 1994), 71.

23. Blanton and Cook, *They Fought Like Demons*, 19.

24. Her name remains unknown, but she also fought while pregnant in the Seven Days' Battle; Blanton and Cook, *They Fought Like Demons*, 14.

25. Blanton and Cook, *They Fought Like Demons*, 15.

26. Blanton and Cook, *They Fought Like Demons*, 15.

27. Blanton and Cook, *They Fought Like Demons*, 105.

28. Blanton and Cook, *They Fought Like Demons,* 105.

29. Silvey, *I'll Pass for Your Comrade,* 67–68.

30. Blanton and Cook, *They Fought Like Demons,* 14, 32, 94–95.

31. The famous historical artist Mort Kunstler, who painted more than 150 paintings depicting the Civil War, was captivated by the story of the Nancy Harts and created one final painting portraying the encounter. LaGrange vs. LaGrange, https://www.mortkunstler.com/html/store-limited-edition-prints.asp?action=view&ID=984&cat=152.

32. Thaddeus Horton [Mrs.], "The Story of the Nancy Harts," *The Ladies' Home Journal* (November, 1904): 1.

33. F.C. Johnson, III Troup County Historical Society, 2015, 7.

34. Mrs. Leila C. Morris, nee Pullen, Personal Recollections of the War, Girl Confederate Soldiers, 1986, Troup, Georgia County Archives, 3.

35. Thaddeus Horton [Mrs.], "The Story of the Nancy Harts," *The Ladies' Home Journal* (November, 1904): 14.

36. *Confederate Veteran Magazine,* Vol. XXX (1922): 466.

37. *Personal Recollections of the War, Girl Confederate Soldiers, December 17th, 1896, by Mrs. Leila C. Morris, nee Pullen,* Troup County Archives, 5.

38. Horton, "The Story of the Nancy Harts," 14.

39. Jean R. Feedman, "Albert Cashier's Secret," in *New York Times* (January 28, 2014). https://opinionator.blogs.nytimes.com/2014/01/28/ albert-cashiers-secret/.

40. Leonard, *All the Daring of the Soldier,* 185–91.

41. Carl Senna, "The Lives of Emma Edmonds," *New York Times* (April 21, 2014). https://opinionator.blogs.nytimes.com/2014/04/21/ the-lives-of-emma-edmonds/.

42. Blanton and Cook, *They Fought Like Demons,* 146.

43. Blanton and Cook, *They Fought Like Demons,* 153.

44. Blanton and Cook, *They Fought Like Demons,* 155.

45. DeAnn Blanton, "Women Soldiers of the Civil War," *Prologue Magazine* 25, no. 1 (Spring 1993), retrieved from National Archives, https://www.archives.gov/publications/prologue/1993/spring/women-in-the-civil-war-1.html. Accessed February 9, 2018.

46. Blanton, "Women Soldiers of the Civil War."

47. "It was a fact that women had actually enlisted and fought in our late war, until their sex was discovered, when they were summarily dismissed." Elizabeth Cady Stanton, Susan B. Anthony, and Matilda Joslyn Gage, *History of Woman Suffrage, Vol. 3* (1887), 8.

CHAPTER 3
SUSIE BAKER KING TAYLOR
UNION NURSE, TEACHER, AND AUTHOR

"There are many people who do not
know what some of the colored women
did during the war."
— Susie Baker King Taylor

Of the thousands of African American
women who served the Union armies in
countless capacities on both sides of the
Mason-Dixon line, we have the firsthand
account of one alone: Susie Baker King Taylor. *Reminiscences of My Life in Camp with
the 33rd U.S. Colored Troops, Late 1st South
Carolina Volunteers* is a remarkable story
told by a woman who escaped a life of slavery in time to serve as a nurse and an
educator on behalf of the Union cause.

Prior to the Civil War, half the wealth of
the thriving Georgia economy resided in the
enslaved population, which had reached
close to half a million people in the early
1860s. To maintain control over this potentially volatile populace, the white community kept careful guard over their most
potent weapon of all — knowledge. As long
as slaves remained illiterate, they could be
separated from their families and denied
further means to communicate. Without last
names and the ability to write them, slaves
could be sold at will to a new master, their
pasts erased in the process. Without literacy,

the enslaved could be kept from new political debates fomenting dangerously in the newspapers of the North. A slave who was discovered writing often had the tips of his or her thumbs cut off. In Georgia, if a white person was caught teaching an enslaved person to read, they were fined $500. If a black person was caught, they were fined $100 *and* received up to thirty-two lashes of the whip.[1]

Though Susie was born in Georgia in 1848 to the desperate world of plantation slavery, she had a powerful weapon on her side: a grandmother who believed in the power of education and desired freedom for her descendants. Dolly Reed lived forty miles from her daughter's family but visited her grandchildren in the ironically named Liberty County a few times each year. Dolly hired a wagon for these trips so she could haul supplies from town to trade in the country; she returned home laden with farm goods to sell in the city. When Susie turned seven, Dolly invited Susie and her younger brother and sister to join her household in Savannah. Compared with rural Georgia, the city of Savannah seemed like a bastion of opportunity for enslaved individuals. Savannah housed a thriving black community with churches and a wide variety of enterprises — some legal, and others not. Dolly Reed also enjoyed an unusual amount of latitude. It's unknown whether Dolly was freed or enslaved, but through her trade enterprise and work in town, Reed saved thousands of dollars and managed her own household.[2]

Shortly after Susie's arrival in Savannah, Dolly took Susie to meet Mary Woodhouse, a local seamstress who ostensibly apprenticed children interested in learning her trade. Woodhouse's twenty-five to thirty pupils entered her kitchen one at a time, but once the doors shut behind them, they got down to their real business: clandestine learning. A network of these secret schools ran a circuitous route through the city of Savannah. The black population referred to the institutions as "bucket schools" because the children carried their schoolbooks at the bottom of buckets, wrapped in paper or covered with wares to keep the contraband textbooks safe from prying eyes.

In 1860, six to seven of these secret schools operated around Savannah. Julien Fromantin pretended to teach his students carpentry while actually teaching them reading, writing, and arithmetic. Catherine DeVeaux and her daughter Jane also ran a successful bucket school for years, but the dangers were very real. James Porter, a talented musician and teacher who taught a more advanced curriculum, built a trapdoor in his house to hide the children in case of a raid.[3] When Porter's school was discovered, he was forced into temporary hiding. When James Simms was discovered, authorities made an example of him and sentenced him to a public whipping. Simms resumed teaching after his release, until threatened with further fines and arrest. He fled to Boston to wait out the war.[4]

Fully aware of the dangers of seeking out an education, Susie nonetheless became an eager and voracious pupil. After working with Ms. Woodhouse for two years, Susie continued her studies with Mary Beasley. By the time Susie turned eleven, Ms. Beasley told Dolly that she "had better get some one else" who could teach the girl more.[5] Many would have said Susie knew far more than a slave would ever need to know, but Dolly wanted to help her eager granddaughter, so, in spite of the dangers, she sought out new resources.

Meanwhile, Susie turned to another potentially risky source to find the knowledge she desired: white children. A wealthy family that lived down the street had a daughter, Katie O'Connor, who was close to Susie's own age. The girls became friends, and Susie begged Katie to share her books and lessons. Katie's mother reluctantly agreed as long as they kept the meetings strictly secret, particularly from Katie's father. For four glorious months, the girls met for clandestine lessons, but the meetings came to an abrupt close when Katie entered a convent.

Eager for more knowledge, Susie noticed James Blouis, their landlord's teenaged son. James attended the local high school and drilled with the local Savannah Volunteer Guards; Susie begged him to share his books and lessons. Hesitantly, Blouis agreed as long as Susie promised not to tell his parents. They also met together for a few months, until the approaching war derailed further lessons and James's volunteer unit was called up for service in 1861.

By this time, Susie was thirteen years old; she was lively and smart, with a voracious appetite for learning. Even as the war moved closer and closer to Georgia, Baker used her literacy skills to aid Dolly and her friends' work towards approaching emancipation. Dolly was involved in the city's black resistance movement, and her smart, literate granddaughter was an essential asset to the work. Though a city curfew prevented blacks from traveling at night, Susie forged passes so Dolly and other members of the community could attend and organize political meetings held in churches and deserted buildings. As the political situation intensified, police raided a church where Reed and the rest of the congregation were singing the hymn "We shall all be free." Though Dolly's white guardian intervened and she escaped punishment, Susie was sent back to the plantation — for her own safety — for the first time in six years.[6]

In the spring of 1862, the Union army laid siege to Fort Pulaski off the coast of Georgia. Fort Pulaski's fall, relatively early in the war, created a sanctuary for former slaves seeking to escape bondage. While the white Confederate populace fled away from the advancing US army, much of the enslaved population fled *toward* the troops, seeking the immediate freedom guaranteed by the military's presence. The Fugitive Slave Law technically required that escaped slaves be returned to their owners, but Northern military leader Benjamin Butler argued that if the slaves were, as the Confederates claimed, property, they would therefore be subject to confiscation during warfare like any other property. Butler coined the term *contraband* to justify the legal seizure and liberation of these escaped slaves, success-fully twisting Confederate logic to the Union's advantage.[7]

While white evacuees fled inland in droves, Susie and her family decided to try for the freedom waiting behind enemy lines. They traveled to Pulaski and joined a boatload of refugees bound for one of Georgia's Sea Islands. Landing safely on the soil of St. Catherine's Island, Susie's family proclaimed themselves contraband of the war and turned themselves over to the Union army.

The Sea Islands, which housed some of the most renowned cotton plantations in the South, provided much needed supplies for Northern troops; their capture early in the war meant Union armies could use the islands' soil to plan and launch incursions into the Confederate-held mainland. Thousands of former slaves fled to the islands in desperate need of food and housing, and camps and makeshift tent cities sprang up overnight. Hundreds of volunteers, both black and white, came from the North to help the refugees transition to self-sufficiency.[8]

Within a few days of their arrival, Susie and her family were transferred to St. Simon's Island, a dot of land that already held a long history of slavery and resistance. In 1803, a slave ship from Africa had been bound for St. Simon's when the captives rose up and seized control of the ship, drowning their captors and grounding the vessel. When the mutineers reached the shore, hundreds chose to commit mass suicide in Dunbar Creek, opting for death by drowning over a life of enslavement.[9]

En route to the island, the captain of the ship Susie sailed on was amazed to learn that the girl claimed to be literate and educated. "Can you read? Can you write?" he asked. She proudly answered, "Yes, I can do that too." When he realized the extent of her education, he asked if she would be willing to run a school for other new arrivals. Thrilled by the idea of being a teacher, Susie said she would need books. A relief group in the North provided the schoolbooks within a few short weeks, and fourteen-year-old Susie went to work. "I had about forty children to teach," she wrote, "beside a number of adults who came to me nights, all of them so eager to learn to read, to read above anything else."[10]

Unexpectedly employed, Susie suddenly found herself surrounded by family and friends, building a new life of freedom. On St. Simon's, on January 1, 1863, Susie first heard Abraham Lincoln's Emancipation Proclamation read aloud. The island celebrated the event with speeches, prayers, public readings, and singing — singing many of the same hymns that Dolly had been arrested for singing only months before. "It was a glorious day for all of us," Susie wrote of the occasion.[11] She read the proclamation to her students, and taught them to memorize it, sounding out the syllables: "all persons held as slaves" within the rebellious states "shall be then, thenceforward, and forever free."[12] The proclamation had been a controversial move — drawing upon hazy legality with ambiguous consequences at best. But for refugees so close to Confederate-held territory, with the outcome of the war still held in the balance, Lincoln's words meant Susie and her students on St. Simon's had moved one step closer to unthreatened freedom.

To guarantee that freedom, however, the war still had to be won. Lincoln's proclamation aligned the goal of victory with the end of slavery more clearly than ever before, and many of the newly released men and women longed to aid Union forces. Recruitment of the United States Colored Troops began in full force. Susie's brother and cousins eagerly enlisted in the First South Carolina

Volunteers of African Descent, later re-named the 33rd Regiment Infantry United States Colored Troops. A young carpenter named Edward King also enlisted with the regiment. Susie and Edward had known each other in Savannah, and they fell in love on St. Simon's, marrying sometime between 1862 and 1863.

Knowing so many people she cared about would soon depart for battle, Susie was determined not to be left behind. She followed her husband into the regiment and enrolled as a "laundress." In actuality, she "did very little of it" and spent far more time nursing, since white doctors rarely served soldiers from the members of the Colored Troops. Susie apprenticed under Union doctors and contributed to the health and well-being of the battalion.[13] During each conflict, King stood by to treat the wounded as they came in. In between, she prepared food and washed clothes, and also cleaned and reloaded guns. Susie wrote, "I learned to handle a musket very well while in the regiment, and could shoot straight and often hit the target."[14]

In 1863, the government offered the Colored Troops half the pay of their white counterparts. The 33rd Regiment, with several other units, refused pay entirely to protest this treatment, saying they would "rather give their services to the state"[15] until they were paid fairly. King recorded in her memoir, "A great many of these men had large families, and . . . no money to give them."[16] After eighteen months of boycott, the protest proved successful, and the United States government ordered a wage equal to white soldiers, plus back pay. This remedy was not extended to black nurses or laundresses, however, and Susie was one of thousands of women who gave her "services willingly for four years and three months without receiving a dollar."[17]

While Susie assisted at Beaufort hospital, Clara Barton — "Angel of the Battlefield" — came to review the nursing regiment. Administration officials led her through the white sections first, but Barton insisted on seeing the wards that housed the members of the Colored Troops, and she was introduced to King and her patients. Susie found Barton to be "very cordial" and paid tribute to her "devotion and care of those men."[18] Susie recorded details of her own grisly service, noting at times had to move decaying skulls out of her path to reach Fort Wagner. "It seems strange how our aversion to seeing suffering is overcome in war," she wrote, "how we are able to see the most sickening sights, such as men with their limbs blown off and mangled by the deadly shells, without a shudder; and instead of turning away, how we hurry to assist in alleviating their pain."[19]

In the winter of 1864, King traveled by boat with several other officers' wives, one of whom had a baby with her, when their vessel encountered stormy weather. After battling the storm, eventually the boat capsized, spilling the frantic passengers into the churning sea. For hours, the women clung to the mast of the overturned boat and screamed into the dark night for assistance. Finally, nearly four hours later, near midnight, the group was rescued. The baby and a soldier on board both drowned, pinned beneath the heavy shipping sails. Susie was miraculously pulled from the water, though she spent several months recovering her health and retained a fear of boats for the rest of her life.[20]

In February of 1865, King's 33rd Regiment marched into Charleston, South Carolina, on the retreating heels of the Confederate army that had set the city aflame before they departed. The black Union soldiers spent days fighting the fire, offering help to residents though the sullen Charlestonians were loath to accept help from former slaves. Susie marveled at the situation. "These white men and women could not tolerate our black Union soldiers, for many of them had formerly been their slaves; and although these brave men risked life and limb to assist them in their distress, men and even women would sneer and molest them whenever they met them."[21]

When the war at last came to a close, Susie and Edward King bid goodbye to their comrades and captain[22] and returned to Savannah with high hopes for the future. "A new life was before us now, all the old life left behind,"[23] Susie wrote. But she and Edward soon found the racial prejudices they had confronted their whole lives had, in fact, not shifted much at all. In spite of his skills, Edward was unable to find carpentry work and eventually accepted work as a laborer, while Susie started an academy for formerly enslaved children. Together they managed to eke out a livelihood. But in 1866, the situation grew even more dire: Susie was pregnant with the couple's first child when her beloved Edward was killed in a dock accident.

Death visited the family again the following year when Susie's father passed away, leaving Susie and her widowed mother to make ends meet while raising King's son.

Susie's school was forced out of business when the well-intentioned American Missionary Association opened a free institution nearby. Impoverished despite her education and intelligence, King joined the thousands of formerly enslaved women working as domestic servants. Leaving her young son in the care of her mother, Susie traveled North for the first time with her employers.

The relative open-mindedness of Massachusetts burst upon King like a revelation. In a period of personal renaissance, she trained as a chef and began earning prizes for her exceptional cooking. She landed a job working for the daughter of the former mayor of Boston and was at last able to financially provide for her mother and her son. At the age of thirty-one, Susie married Russell L. Taylor, a former Union soldier, in Boston. This happy union granted King time to work on projects to benefit the veterans of the 33rd Regiment, organizing reunions and documenting their service during the war. Susie spent a decade in Massachusetts and often marveled at the freedoms she felt there. She wrote in her memoir: "I have been in many States and cities, and in each I have looked for liberty and justice, equal for the black as for the white; but it was not until I was within the borders of New England, and reached old Massachusetts, that I found it."[24]

Meanwhile, Susie's son began performing with a traveling theater company. But in 1898, Susie received an urgent summons from him. He had become dangerously ill while on tour in Shreveport, Louisiana, and though Susie tried to buy him passage to Boston, he was too ill to make the journey. Instead, Susie traveled to be by his side, reentering the South for the first time in more than ten years. Forced to travel in a second-class smoking car, Susie stopped briefly in Shreveport, where she learned a black porter had been murdered for offering a white man a "saucy" response.[25] After spending so much time in Massachusetts, Susie found the persistent prejudice of the South deeply disturbing, where the early racial gains of the Reconstruction era had dissolved along with the Northern military occupation. Many original Confederate leaders had returned to power, driving African Americans out of office and ushering the region into the era of Jim Crow laws and alternative methods of keeping blacks from power.

When Susie finally reached her son, she found him dangerously ill. She tried to purchase a ticket in a sleeping car to bring him to better medical care but was denied because of her race. "It seemed very hard," she would later write, "when his father fought to protect the Union and our flag, and yet his boy was denied, under this same flag, a berth to carry him home to die, because he was a negro."[26] Tending to her son alone, Susie cared for him as he slipped from life, then buried him in one of Louisiana's many segregated cemeteries. As she traveled homeward, Susie witnessed the aftermath of a lynching in Clarksdale, Mississippi.[27]

Overcome by grief and despair for both her son and her country, Susie turned to writing to find relief from her frustration and pain. In light of all the sacrifices made to win the war, she was sickened by the overall lack of progress and of the prejudice that had not been eliminated but had only changed forms. "Was the war in vain?" King begged her readers. "Has it brought freedom, in the full sense of the word, or has it not made our condition more hopeless?"[28]

Writing from the perspective of several decades, Susie at last found the impetus she needed to complete her book about the war, documenting the wartime sacrifices of men and "noble women as well" — who had given so much to unify the country and emancipate those who had been enslaved. Susie placed the sacrifice of these veterans alongside the current reality of life in the South, raging against the hypocrisy of a nation that congratulated itself on having "one flag, one nation," while "in this 'land of the free,' we are burned, tortured, and denied a fair trial, murdered for any imaginary wrong."[29] Susie denounced women of the Daughters of the Confederacy who were opposed to performances of *Uncle Tom's Cabin* because of the "bad effect" it would have on children but who would not speak out against lynch law and racial segregation. Though Susie acknowledged that not all whites were to blame for the impact of those aligned with white supremacy, she called in no uncertain terms for racially motivated hatred and violence to cease.

After working for months on her manuscript, Susie sent the book to Thomas Wentworth Higginson, a war colleague who was now a well-respected editor and author. Higginson read *Reminiscences of My Life in Camp with the 33rd U.S. Colored Troops,* encouraged Susie's efforts, provided editorial feedback on the work, and assisted her with publication. Unique among Civil War accounts, the book is the only known firsthand account written by an African American woman embedded with the Union army. Susie lived until 1912, continuing her efforts to leave the world a better place until her death, when she was laid to rest in the sweet soil of Massachusetts she loved so well.

Susie Taylor's words remain more relevant today than ever before, echoing down generations, with the haunting reminder that the sacrifices of the Civil War were made in vain unless racial unity can be achieved in this reunited nation. In spite of great disappointment and heartache, Susie concluded her volume with the hope that future generations would continue this essential work of reconciliation: "I hope the day is not far distant when the two races will reside in peace in the Southland, and we will sing with sincere and truthful hearts, 'My country 'tis of thee, Sweet land of Liberty, of thee I sing.' . . . Justice we ask, — to be citizens of these United States, where so many of our people have shed their blood with their white comrades, that the stars and stripes should never be polluted."[30]

Further Reading

Ann Short Chirhart and Betty Wood, eds. *Georgia Women: Their Lives and Times, Volume 1.* Athens, GA: University of Georgia Press, 2009.

Susie King Taylor. *Reminiscences of My Life in Camp with the 33rd United States Colored Troops.* Susie King Taylor: Boston, 1902.

Notes

Epigraph: Susie King Taylor, *Reminiscences of My Life in Camp with the 33rd United States Colored Troops* (Susie King Taylor: Boston, 1902), 67.

1. Georgia Historical Society; see http://georgiahistory.com/education-outreach/online-exhibits/featured-historical-figures/mother-mathilda-beasley/educator-of-slave-children/.

2. Jacqueline Jones, *Saving Savannah: The City and the Civil War* (New York: Vintage Press, 2009), 55.

3. Jones, *Saving Savannah,* 55.

4. Walter J. Fraser Jr., *Savannah in the Old South* (Athens, GA: University of Georgia Press, 2003), 219.

5. Taylor, *Reminiscences of My Life,* 6.

6. Taylor, *Reminiscences of My Life,* 8.

7. Ron Chernow, *Grant* (New York: Penguin, 2017), 355–74.

8. Lisa Tendrich Frank, ed., *Civil War: People and Perspectives* (Santa Barbara, CA: ABC-CLIO, 2009), 100.

9. According to Gullah legend, the Ebo chief chanted, "The Sea brought me and the Sea will bring me home" before walking into the water. Though some historians have argued the story is more legend than fact, the story has been an important part of Gullah folklore and was recorded in various oral sources by the Federal Writers Project in the 1930s. See http://www.blackpast.org/aah/igbo-landing-mass-suicide-1803 and http://www.glynncounty.com/History_and_Lore/Ebo_Landing/.

10. Taylor, *Reminiscences of My Life,* 8, 11.

11. Taylor, *Reminiscences of My Life,* 18.

12. Emancipation Proclamation, Jan 1, 1863. Accessed online: https://www.archives.gov/exhibits/featured-documents/emancipation-proclamation.

13. "Susie King Taylor," by Catherine Clinton, in *Georgia Women: Their Lives and Times, Volume 1.* Ann Short Chirhart and Betty Wood, eds. (Athens, GA: University of Georgia Press, 2009), 138.

14. Taylor, *Reminiscences of My Life,* 26.

15. Taylor, *Reminiscences of My Life,* 16.

16. Taylor, *Reminiscences of My Life,* 15–16.

17. Taylor, *Reminiscences of My Life,* 21.

18. "Susie King Taylor," in *Georgia Women,* 139.

19. Taylor, *Reminiscences of My Life,* 32.

20. Taylor, *Reminiscences of My Life,* 38–39.

21. Taylor, *Reminiscences of My Life,* 42.

22. Of her white commander, Lt. Colonel C. T. Trowbridge, King had nothing but praise and said, "No officer in the army was more beloved" (*Reminiscences of My Life,* 46).

23. Taylor, *Reminiscences of My Life,* 54.

24. Taylor, *Reminiscences of My Life,* 63.

25. Taylor, *Reminiscences of My Life,* 73.

26. Taylor, *Reminiscences of My Life,* 71–72.

27. Taylor, *Reminiscences of My Life,* 74.

28. Taylor, *Reminiscences of My Life,* 61.

29. Taylor, *Reminiscences of My Life,* 61–62.

30. Taylor, *Reminiscences of My Life,* 62, 76.

CHAPTER 4
TALES OF SMUGGLING,
ESPIONAGE, AND
GENERAL SUBTERFUGE

Belle Boyd

"Hope, fear, the love of life, and the determination to serve my country to the last, conspired to fill my heart with more than feminine courage."

— Belle Boyd

Galloping wildly through the night to deliver a warning, secreting coded messages in the false handle of a parasol, concealing the movements of armies on parchment down the throat of a chicken — these are just a few of the many maneuvers employed by female spies that helped alter the course of Civil War battles.

The overall scope of the work carried out by female spies remains a mystery — the nature of the work itself depending, as it did, on stealth and covertness. Furthermore, informants were often situated in communities hostile to their own allegiances, which placed them at risk — socially, financially, and physically — if their identities were discovered. When the guns at last fell silent at the war's end, both sides systematically destroyed espionage records to avoid retaliation or government prosecution, making such records among the rarest of war documents. In spite of these challenges, it is clear from remaining records that espionage activity by women during the war had a significant impact.

In the early years of conflict, Victorian-era assumptions about gender made women distinctly suited to espionage work, as they were far less likely to be suspected and less likely to receive harsh punishments even if they were caught. The era's perception of "frail womanhood" proved one of the most valuable weapons of the spy, enabling her to remain daintily above suspicion. As the war progressed, and a handful of female spies attained notoriety, however, these traditional gender assumptions began to unravel, making it far more difficult for women to evade suspicion on the basis of gender alone.

BLOCKADE RUNNERS

The Confederacy controlled thousands of miles of coastline and border, and part of the Union's central strategy depended on sealing off their ports and borders. A deadly game of cat and mouse developed that depended on bold blockade runners and smugglers to supply the Confederacy with ammunition, medications, and machined goods to continue the struggle. Southern women acting as blockade runners concocted ingenious strategies for slipping through the lines. Many subverted Victorian sensibilities about gender codes for their own benefit, trusting they could depend on their status as a "lady" to protect them from thorough body searches. Military officials disliked finding themselves duped by swiftly batted eyelashes, which forced women to wax more creative as the conflict continued.

Betty Duval wound military dispatches into the elaborate curls of her hair, conveying top-secret communications embedded in her latest hairstyle.[1] Louisa Bruckner sewed a hundred ounces of quinine between the layers of her hoop skirts and curtseyed the much-needed medication all the way from DC to Virginia.[2] Playing the part of a Southern hostess, Elizabeth Harland concealed Union fortification maps inside the hollow bone of a ham, which she graciously delivered to Confederate army headquarters.[3] The daughter of General James Anderson carried her doll named Nina across the border many times, though she may not have known until she was older that Nina's hollow china head held quinine powder to aid sick soldiers.[4] Belle Edmondson fashioned a petticoat from gray wool, pinned dozens of hats and boots under her skirt, and loaded up her bodice with brass buttons — sporting enough supplies to make a dozen uniforms in one remarkable outfit. Finding it nearly impossible to walk under the weight of this load, Edmondson finally had to flag down a buggy in order to reach her destination.[5] Mary Carroll of Missouri wore Colt revolvers tied on ropes beneath her skirts, and filled each petticoat tuck with percussion caps. When Federals searched her wagon, she inquired politely if they needed her to dismount. Fortunately for her, they declined; she later confided, "I very much doubt if I could have moved as I was so heavily armed."[6]

The North also recruited Southern women to work the blockade whenever they could. Mary Ann Pitman relied on her Southern accent for protection as she traveled through the Missouri countryside pretending to purchase supplies for the Confederacy, while actually handing the names of suppliers over to Union officials. Though the details of Pitman's work are largely unknown, the War Department compensated Pitman a staggering $5,000, which they claimed was "a moderate compensation for her extended disclosures."[7]

ROSE GREENHOW

A widow with four children living in Washington, DC, Rose Greenhow became a formidable weapon in the Confederate's intelligence arsenal, daring to remain in the city in order to create a thriving spy network of Southern sympathizers in the enemy's very capital. "I am a Southern woman, born with revolutionary blood in my veins," the woman nicknamed "Wild Rose" once wrote.[8] A constant flow of information passed through Greenhow's home even after Allan Pinkerton, head of the Union Intelligence Service, set up observation of her activities. Rose employed an elaborate system of codes to continue her correspondence and planted objects to throw Federal officials off her track. Greenhow ensured the press reported her use of invisible ink, so the officials monitoring her movements would spend their efforts searching for mysterious documents instead of attempting to crack the encoded messages she actually used.

Greenhow became a Confederate hero thanks to her role in the Southern victory at the Battle of Bull Run. Sifting through the rumors that flew about the nation's capital prior to the battle, Rose passed on the accurate information to General Pierre Beauregard via the elaborate hairdo of courier Betty Duval. Once alone with the general, Duval took down her hair, undoing "the longest and most beautiful roll of hair [he had] ever seen."[9] Rose's note, sewed up in silk, read: "McDowell has certainly been ordered to advance on the sixteenth."[10] Beauregard telegrammed Jefferson Davis, requesting reinforcements, and, thanks to Rose, he departed for battle armed with the timing, size, and location of the Union troops. Years later, Jefferson Davis thanked Greenhow personally for her efforts by saying, "The Confederacy owes you a debt."[11] Rose called it "the proudest moment of my whole life."[12]

A month after Bull Run, soldiers searched Rose's home and found incriminating battle maps and coded messages. She was placed under house arrest and sent her oldest three children to stay with relatives for safety. When Greenhow continued passing essential information despite the presence of guards, officials incarcerated her in Old Capitol Prison along with her eight-year-old daughter, also named Rose. When they first arrived at the prison, Rose instructed her daughter, "My little darling, you must show yourself superior to these Yankees, and not pine." Little Rose replied, "O mamma, never fear; I hate them too much. I intend to dance and sing, 'Jeff. Davis is coming,' just to scare them!"[13] The pair needed every ounce of their determination, since their room at Old Capitol Prison was infested with mice and bedbugs, and the two rarely had adequate food. Little Rose later said her main memory from that time was "that I used to cry myself to sleep from hunger."[14]

In spite of the challenges, mother and daughter remained as dedicated to their cause as ever, occasionally flying a Confederate flag from their window and passing correspondence whenever possible. Rose pried loose a wooden plank of the floor so that little Rose could be lowered into the

Rose Greenhow and daughter

cell below, becoming perhaps the youngest spy of the war. The POWs below shared food and fresh news from beyond the prison. The two Roses spent more than five months imprisoned before they were banished in 1862 to Richmond, Virginia, a city that hailed them as heroes. Jefferson Davis rewarded Greenhow for her efforts, and in 1863 Rose sailed for Europe as an ambassador of the Confederacy. Her story came to a tragic conclusion, though, when she tried to return in 1864. Attempting to run the Federal blockade of Wilmington, North Carolina, her boat overturned and she drowned, allegedly weighed down by the gold sovereigns she carried in her skirts. She was buried with full military honors.

MARY JANE RICHARDS

More than 100 years after Mary Jane Richards[15] served her country as a Union spy, the United States Army inducted her into the Military Intelligence Corps Hall of Fame and called her "one of the highest placed and most productive espionage agents of the Civil War."[16] Mary was born into slavery as the property of the wealthy Van Lew family. Mrs. Van Lew and her daughter Elizabeth held relatively progressive ideas, and they allowed Mary to be baptized as a baby and sent to Philadelphia for an education. After Van Lew's father's death, Elizabeth convinced her mother to free the family's slaves, but the combination of Virginia law and her father's will made official manumission nearly impossible. Richards remained an ostensible slave while enjoying more than normal amounts of freedom.

From a very young age, Richards was known for her "more than usual intelligence."[17] At age fourteen, she traveled to Liberia to serve as a missionary, experimenting with the movement to colonize Africa with former US slaves. Richards decided not to stay in Liberia, though, and returned to the United States several years later, where she must have found the restrictions of the South galling after enjoying so much independence. Not long after Mary's return, Elizabeth's mother had to pay a fine for "permitting her slave to go at large" about the city.[18]

A Northern sympathizer in the center of the Confederate capital, Elizabeth Van Lew used her prominent social position to operate a vibrant spy ring, reporting information directly to General Ulysses S. Grant. When Varina Davis, wife of Confederate president Jefferson Davis, asked Van Lew for suggestions regarding the acquisition of house slaves, Elizabeth immediately thought of Mary.[19] Richards agreed to the dangerous assignment, working in the Confederate White House and relying on the Davis's perceptions of her abilities (or inabilities) as her greatest protection. Pretending to be illiterate, Richards was able to hide in plain sight, even as she quietly went about undermining the Confederate government's war efforts.

Assuming the air of an illiterate slave interested only in dusting, Richards gained easy access to battle plans and other correspondence. She also served as wait staff in Confederate Senate meetings, regarding each detail with shrewdness. Memorizing a constant stream of information, she passed this on to Van Lew using a variety of encryption methods, including invisible ink and secret compartments carved into the heels of shoes.[20] Elizabeth, in turn, dispatched three letters a week to General Grant and marveled at Mary's ability to unearth information: "When I open my eyes in the morning, I say to the servant, 'What news, Mary?' and my caterer never fails!"[21] With access to troop sizes, and confidential correspondence, Mary rerouted information into the hands of Union army officials.

As the war prospects grew increasingly grim for the Confederates, President Jefferson Davis urged discretion and wondered how the enemy seemed to know his plans before they had even been finalized. Davis knew there had to be a mole in the White House, but no evidence suggests he ever suspected Richards.

After the Confederate government went into hiding and the city of Richmond fell, Mary departed for the North, where she could travel and speak as she chose. She delivered popular lectures under the pseudonym Richmonia to protect herself from hostility from the Richmond community, who viewed her as a traitor because of rumors that connected her to the spy Elizabeth Van Lew. The Confederate Secretary of State burned all intelligence records shortly before the Union troops invaded Richmond, and Elizabeth Van Lew also destroyed her files to prevent retaliation. Further details of Richards's reconnaissance work and its impact turned to ash along with the city.

Mary founded a freedman's school in Georgia, and some of her few surviving words speak of this work: "I felt that I had the advantage over the majority of my race both in Blood and Intelligence, and that it was my duty if possible to work where I am most needed."[22] Like the skilled spy that she was, Richards disappeared from the public record after the war by using alternate names. Some evidence suggests she may have lived out her final years in the West Indies. Mary Jane Richards was inducted into the Military Intelligence Corps Hall of Fame, and Major General Benjamin Butler and General Grant both claimed the intelligence passed through Van Lew's network was instrumental to their success, deeming it "the most valuable information received from Richmond during the war."[23]

BELLE BOYD

Belle Boyd, one of the South's favorite war darlings, achieved near stardom for the aid she rendered General Stonewall Jackson in the Shenandoah Valley campaign. The seventeen-year-old had an incredible knack for eliciting information from those foolish enough to consider her harmless. In 1862, after learning that Union troops had been ordered to march, Belle rode fifteen miles under cover of darkness to inform General Jackson of the development. Weeks later, Boyd raced at full speed across a battlefield through a mélange of exploding Union bullets to bring Jackson word that it was the ideal time to advance on the city of Front Royal, Virginia. Those who watched her fly across the battlefield never forgot the sight, and Belle claimed: "The rifle balls flew thick and fast about me, and more than one struck the ground so near my feet as to throw the dust in my eyes. . . . I shall never again run as I ran on that day. Hope, fear, the love of life, and the determination to serve my country to the last, conspired to fill my heart with more than feminine courage."[24] Jackson used the troop positions Belle supplied to successfully reclaim the city, driving the army of the Potomac back toward Washington. The Southern press hailed Boyd as a hero, dubbing her "La Belle Rebelle" and "The Siren of the Shenandoah." At the conclusion of the battle, Jackson wrote to Boyd, "I thank you for myself and for the Army, for the immense service that you have rendered your country today."[25]

Belle was arrested several times but managed to sweet-talk her way out of incarceration until 1863, when she was locked up in the Old Capitol Prison in Washington. From her prison cell, the unfazed rebel sang "Dixie," blazoned a Confederate flag from the window, and continued to smuggle messages to the outside world. When she fell ill with typhoid, Boyd was released and banished south. Not long after her recovery, Belle boarded a ship bound for Europe, carrying important Confederate documents. The blockade run failed, though, and a Union vessel seized her ship. Boyd used the time before reaching port to charm her guard, Union naval lieutenant Samuel Harding. The handsome officer not only helped Belle escape; he then resigned his post and followed her to London, where the couple were married.[26]

Boyd is one of several female spies who went on to publish accounts of their wartime exploits. *Belle Boyd in Camp and Prison* and similar volumes have at times attracted criticism for embellishing the facts. However, postwar audiences of the 1800s enjoyed the recounting of sensationalized war tales in a way that deserves comparison to modern America's TV shows; veterans notoriously embellished their wartime service in a way their audiences understood as entertainment rather than deception. Memoirs such as Boyd's must be historically contexualized in this way, but at times they appear to attract undue hostility for their lack of historicity that other accounts by male veterans do not elicit.[27]

PAULINE CUSHMAN

Like Belle Boyd, Pauline Cushman built an identity and career around her work as a spy. Raised on a frontier trading post in Michigan, Pauline was taught by Native Americans to hunt, ride, and shoot while she was still a child. The dream of being an actress led Cushman to New York City at age seventeen, and soon she traveled the country to accept different roles. Pauline was performing in Kentucky, a border state that attempted to remain neutral during the war, when Confederate sympathizers offered her $300 to publicly toast the South. Cushman reported the offer to Union officials, who recognized the situation would make a perfect cover and told her to go through with the request. In a crowded theater, Pauline raised her glass and boldly proclaimed, "Here's to Jefferson Davis and the Southern Confederacy. May the South always maintain her honor and her rights!"[28] The theater erupted in response, and the horrified theater owners fired her at once, but the action established her as a darling among Confederates.

Established publicly as a Confederate, Pauline put her acting skills to work for her country. She adopted the part of a wealthy Southern gentleman, ferreting out details of treason plots over games of billiards at the local saloon. Adept in a variety of social settings, Pauline was equally at ease tracking guerilla networks as she was teasing confidences from people in high society. In one of her most well-known successes, Pauline foiled a plot to poison Union soldiers by gaining the confidence of those planning it. In another successful sting operation, Cushman masqueraded as a male army captain arranging to smuggle supplies behind Confederate lines; anyone willing to be her accomplice was immediately arrested.

A string of successes perhaps left Cushman feeling a bit overconfident, however. Trusted with a dangerous mission to obtain information regarding the size and position of Bragg's army of Tennessee, Cushman was warned by military personnel to memorize and destroy any intelligence she found. Pauline slipped behind enemy lines and managed to become acquainted with one of the engineers working on Bragg's plans. Pauline stole the papers and a horse, donned a man's suit, and rode into the woods, where she encountered a group of rebel guerillas. After a thrilling chase, Cushman escaped by firing a quick succession of shots so those following believed they were being led to an ambush.

Pauline Cushman

Convinced she had made a clean getaway, Pauline awoke in the early dawn's light to find herself surrounded by rebel scouts. She might have succeeded in charming her way out of the situation had the scouts not discovered the stolen papers. Cushman was convicted of espionage and sentenced to hang. Pauline spent five tedious days in a prison in Shelbyville, Tennessee, awaiting the gallows; when she fell ill, her captors granted a momentary reprieve before carrying out her sentence, which, as it turned out, saved her life. Union troops took control of the prison and freed Cushman just in time to prevent her death. She said of that day, "The roar of artillery and small arms gave me great strength, and as the stars and stripes floated by my window, I got up from my sick bed."[29] For her service to the United States, the Army named her an honorary "Major of the Cavalry," and thereafter she went by Miss "Major Pauline" Cushman. At the end of the war, she toured the country giving lectures on her exploits.

THE SANCHEZ SISTERS

While Belle Boyd and Pauline Cushman approached their espionage work as a serious career, other female spies found themselves drawn temporarily into the work by being at the right place at the right time. Such is the case with the Sanchez sisters — Lola, Panchita, and Eugenia — daughters of a Cuban immigrant in Florida. When Union officers stayed at their home, the sisters listened at an open window as the soldiers sat on front porch discussing plans for an upcoming gunboat attack. Recognizing the importance of the intelligence the officers offered up to the night air, Panchita and Eugenia diverted the soldiers' attention while Lola rode through the dark woods on horseback. At the Confederate lines, Lola asked to be taken to an officer immediately. The information she delivered allowed the Confederates to ambush and capture the gunboat, which they renamed *The Three Sisters* in honor of the Sanchez women.[30]

REBECCA WRIGHT

Rebecca Wright initially had no intention of becoming involved in espionage work either. In the spring of 1864, Confederate general Jubal Early and his troops caused terror and destruction in the area surrounding Washington, DC, threatening to advance on the capital city. The Lincoln family evacuated to their summer residence, while citizens and government officials waited, terrified by the thought of Early's troops swooping down upon them. With the war going so poorly, Lincoln's chances at reelection were looking slim. For him to have any chance of success at either the war or at the ballot, Confederate troops had to be pushed away from the capital. Lincoln discussed the situation with General Philip Sheridan, leader of the notorious Sheridan's Scouts, a cavalry corps that often adopted Confederate uniforms as they hunted down spies, gathered information, and battled guerilla units. Understanding exactly what was at stake, Sheridan followed General Early into the Shenandoah Valley, where key informants returned conflicting reports about the size of the enemy and expected reinforcements. Sheridan knew he could not proceed without more information.

From local sources, Sheridan heard of a Winchester teacher who had recently been fired from her teaching position for her Northern sympathies and public denunciation of slavery. Rebecca Wright lived in Winchester with her mother and pro-Confederate sister. Sending a message to Rebecca would be a long shot, but Sheridan trusted a black produce vendor named Tom Laws, who peddled his wares in town several times a week. Laws wrapped Sheridan's message in tinfoil before securing it in a corner of his mouth, ready for easy swallowing should he be apprehended. Laws knocked on Wright's door and requested a private consultation. Rebecca led the man into her study and watched, baffled, as Laws retrieved the message from his mouth and unrolled it on her desk. General Sheridan's request read: "I learn from Major-General Crook that you are a loyal lady, and still love the old flag. Can you inform me of the position of Early's forces, the number of divisions in his army, and the strength of any or all of them, and his probable and reported intentions? . . . You can trust the bearer."[31] Startled at the invitation from a prominent Union general, Rebecca knew that replying could quite literally jeopardize her life. Wondering if it might be a trap from hostile neighbors, Wright weighed how best to respond.

Only a day previously, a Confederate officer had called upon Wright, talking freely about his troops and their intended movements. By complete coincidence, Rebecca had the information Sheridan so desperately needed. Knowing the act might bring swift retaliation, she scrawled a response that began: "I will tell you what I know . . ." Wright described the infantry division and artillery battalion that had departed Winchester, confiding that the troops were not as large as the Confederates represented. Rebecca's information was more than Sheridan could have hoped for, and he now knew he could attack Early's forces without fear of being overpowered.

The third Battle of Winchester began three days later. From her home, Rebecca could hear the sounds of the cannon fire, uncertain if her note had precipitated the action. As the battle drew nearer, she recorded, "Houses about us were on fire, our own fence was burning, and shells fell so near that my mother and I went into the cellar for safety."[32] The Confederates were beaten back and forced to abandon the town after hours of fighting. As the sounds of war were quelled, Rebecca and her mother watched from their window as two men on horseback carried the American flag into town; they must have been shocked when the military officials dismounted before their front door. Generals Sheridan and Crook had come to personally thank Rebecca for her bravery, which she begged them to keep secret. The third Battle of Winchester became one of the most important skirmishes fought in the Shenandoah Valley, a turning point in the North's favor, and an essential win needed for Lincoln's reelection campaign.

Wright successfully hid her role in the conflict until 1867, when Sheridan sent her a letter and a pocket watch, saying in part, "It was on [your] information the battle was fought and probably won. . . . By your note I became aware of the true conditions of affairs, inside of the enemy's lines. . . . I will always remember this courageous and patriotic action of yours with gratitude."[33]

Along with the gift, Sheridan included a recommendation from Ulysses S. Grant for a position in the Treasury Department should Wright ever wish to have one.

Sheridan's thoughtful action had disastrous consequences for Wright, at first. When her Confederate sister found out about the incident and informed the local newspapers, the full fury of Southern wrath descended on Rebecca. Neighbors decried her as a traitor, spit on her as she passed in the streets, and removed her, once more, from her teaching post. The community successfully boycotted the Wright's boardinghouse until Rebecca and her mother were destitute. Forced to leave Winchester, the two women moved to Washington, DC, where Rebecca accepted the position Grant had offered her, serving in the Treasury Department for forty-seven years. At one point, a politician wanted the job and attempted to maneuver it away from her, but Wright had only to pen a brief letter to General Sheridan reminding him of the Battle of Winchester. She remained in her post.

NANCY HART

Nancy Hart, from the wilds of western Virginia, was fifteen years old when the war broke out, splitting up her family and her state, right along with the Union. Hart's brothers took up arms for the North, supporting the newly created West Virginia, while her brother-in-law and sister aligned themselves with Virginia and the South. Though she was opposed to slavery, Nancy's cultural background inclined her toward the Confederate cause. She had spent most of her youth learning to shoot and ride bareback and had a reputation as an excellent marksman. Though Hart's parents tried to persuade her to keep the house and tend her siblings, Nancy would have nothing to do with domesticity. Instead she joined a local guerilla gang called the Moccasin Rangers, who vandalized railroads, raided families sympathetic to the Union, and passed information to the Confederate army. The Rangers named themselves after the moccasin snake's tendency to strike quickly and without warning. Mostly along for the adventure rather than motivated by particularly strong political beliefs, Nancy proved invaluable as a spy and a guide, relying upon her extensive knowledge of caves, mountains, and trails in the region.[34]

In late 1861, Nancy took a break from guerilla warfare to visit her sister Mary, who was pregnant with her first child. When

Union soldiers arrived to search the house, Mary pretended to be confined to her bed by "womanly distress," and the soldiers apologized for disturbing her. Had they looked more closely, they would have found Nancy hidden behind her sister, tied up in a bolster. The soldiers insisted on taking Mary's husband, William, who had been known to aid Confederate troops, but they promised the two women he would soon return.

Two days later, Nancy found William's body riddled with bullets and hanged from a tree. Incensed by this act of violence, Hart swore revenge, vowing to do all within her power to aid the Confederate cause. Soon her name was infamous as the only woman tough enough to ride with the Moccasin Raiders, each escapade more daring than the last. Hart escaped capture several times by pretending to be an innocent farm girl; but the Union put out a reward for her arrest, and eventually someone recognized her from a reward poster. Nancy and the girl-friend who was hiding her whereabouts were captured and imprisoned.

Jailed in Summersville, the two women were kept under constant surveillance. Late one night, Nancy began conversing with the guard outside her door, claiming she couldn't sleep. Exuding innocence, she expressed interest in the design of his gun and asked sweetly if she could see it; when he complied, she turned and shot him through the heart. Hart stole a horse that was tied up outside and galloped bareback into the dark woods. She rode hell-bent toward the Confederate lines, where she mustered recruits in exchange for information about the enemy's position.

A week later, Nancy returned to Summersville accompanied by 200 cavalry soldiers who had ridden by her side for two days through tortuous mountain passes. The unit surrounded the headquarters where she had been imprisoned, inspiring a few lucky soldiers to flee out the back window in their undergarments while Nancy rescued the friend who had been left behind. The Confederate cavalry captured a Union colonel, a captain, two lieutenants, and other soldiers, who were all immediately sent off to Libby Prison. In the raid, the Confederates made off with valuable horses, mules, ammunition, and armaments, while Hart had her revenge. She continued aiding the Confederacy as a spy and a guide for the rest of the war. When it was all over, she married a member of the Moccasin Rangers and gave birth to two sons.[35]

HARRIET TUBMAN

Harriet Tubman's name would be etched in history books if only for her remarkable escape from slavery and subsequent return trips to the South — dozens of them — carried out with great stealth as she led family and friends north via the Underground Railroad. But the CIA praised Tubman's lesser-known, yet no less incredible role, as "one of the Civil War's most daring and effective spies."[36] Tubman's father, an avid hunter, taught Harriet essential survival skills as a child, guiding her through the forests of Maryland, teaching her which plants were edible and how to navigate by the stars. He unwittingly prepared his young daughter for a lifetime of clandestine efforts in support of freedom. As a young girl, Tubman learned to creep soundlessly through the forest, crawling at times on her belly, practicing over and over until she could surprise even her father.

Harriet never doubted the cruelty of bondage; she was sold at the age of six to a family who did not feed her and sent her home months later, dangerously ill. Tubman's mother nursed her back to health, only to see her daughter sold again, this time to a family who whipped Harriet so cruelly she bore the scars for the rest of her life. When Tubman attempted to escape, her owners beat her close to death, loaded what was left of her on a wagon, and sent her home. Another master threw an iron weight at Harriet's head when she assisted an escaping slave; the attack fractured her skull and rendered her prone to narcolepsy and vivid dreams, which she often deemed prophetic. In 1849, after one of these night visions warned her she would soon be sold again, Harriet fled north, navigating the ninety miles to Philadelphia. After stepping across the state line that divided her from freedom, Tubman said, "I looked at my hands to see if I was the same person. There was such a glory over everything; the sun came like gold through the trees, and over the fields, and I felt like I was in Heaven."[37] Harriet would soon return — traversing that line again and again in search of family and friends, her soft song carrying through slave cabins, beckoning anyone ready to try for freedom. Harriet rescued a niece and her two children days before they were scheduled to go to the auction block; she also freed her brothers and their wives and smuggled her elderly parents out of town in a wagon.

Shifting routes and becoming intimately familiar with every creek and thicket, Tubman used songs as important signals for those she guided. "Swing Low, Sweet Chariot" meant it was time to depart, while "Go Down, Moses" meant there was danger afoot and runaways should stay hidden. In somewhere between ten and nineteen trips, Tubman rescued between seventy and three hundred slaves, guiding them from Maryland to Pennsylvania and, after the passage of the Fugitive Slave Law, into the safety of Canada.[38] Harriet's fame grew, and people began calling her the American Moses, a newly born prophet who had come to lead her people out of bondage. Southern governments posted reward posters and placed a bounty on her head, which would eventually climb as high as $40,000, while the United States government responded by inviting her to work as a scout and spy. To elude bounty hunters, one of Tubman's favorite disguises involved dressing as a harmless old slave woman, playing on people's expectations that she was unintelligent and harmless. In this guise, and in numerous others, Tubman spoke with every slave and former slave she could around the coast of South Carolina, amassing a powerful network of intelligence.

In 1863, General David Hunter invited Tubman to put her skills to use aiding a

Harriet Tubman

series of river raids to seize supplies, determine enemy positions, and attack key Confederate holdings. The most famous of these raids, the Combahee River Raid, was designed and guided by Tubman, who spent months preparing for the mission. By visiting contraband camps, gathering and training recruits familiar with the area, and scouting much of the land herself, Harriet determined key targets and strategy. The Confederates had secured deadly torpedoes in the muddy depths of the water to protect the important river highway. To learn the location of these weapons, Tubman visited slave cabins at night and spoke with the very men who had placed them in the water.

Under cover of darkness on June 2, 1863, three steamships slipped up the Combahee River, safely maneuvering around each of the torpedoes intended to prevent their passage. Tubman served as a lookout on the lead gunboat. Troops disembarked, setting fire to a bridge, sacking mills, storehouses, and plantations, and salvaging all the supplies they could carry while destroying the rest. Initially alarmed by the destruction, local slaves quickly realized the gunboats offered free passage to the North; they rushed to gather belongings and family members before the boats departed. One eighty-eight-year old man climbed aboard, saying he was "never too old [to] leave the land of bondage."[39] Harriet later recalled "children squalling, chickens squawking, and pigs squealing. They all come runnin' to the gunboats through the rice fields. They [reminded] me of the children of Israel coming out of Egypt."[40]

As the boats began to fill, pandemonium broke out among latecomers desperate not to be left behind. More people than could possibly fit grasped frantically for oars, pleading to be allowed onboard. Alarmed they might capsize the boats, Colonel Montgomery called to Tubman: "Come here and speak a word of consolation to your people."

At a loss for what to do, Harriet be[gan]
reply they weren't her people, and she
no more what to do than he; but the
she used on the Underground Railroa[d]
comfort people fleeing for their lives ro[se]
her lips. Relying on the music to calm
throng, her powerful voice carried thro[ugh]
the darkness: "Come along, come alo[ng]
Don't be alarm'." Her listeners joined
singing "Glory!" as they raised their han[ds]
and released the boats, which eased aw[ay]
from shore, and slipped safely into th[e]
night.[41]

Though she was loathe to leave anyon[e]
behind, Tubman freed more than 700 people that night, the single largest liberation of
slaves in US history. The raid dealt a staggering blow to already low Confederat[e]
reserves and garnered 200 new recruits fo[r]
the Union army. A Boston newspap[er]
praised Tubman and her allies, who, th[ey]
said, "dashed into the enemy's count[ry]
struck a bold and effective blow, destroy[ing]
millions of dollars' worth of commiss[ary]
stores . . . and striking terror into the h[earts]
of rebeldom . . . without losing a ma[n]
receiving a scratch. It was a glorious
summation."[42]

HIDING IN PLAIN SIGHT

The work done by female spies in the Civil War provides great insight into the shifting ground of gender roles as they evolved over the course of the conflict. Women deemed too frail and naïve to understand the world of politics proved instrumental in helping to pass state secrets for their respective governments, influencing the course of the war at its most basic level. Such actions caused a society still deeply enmeshed in Victorian era mores to reevaluate the capabilities of the "gentler sex," paving the way for women to move more boldly into their futures. Women of color, underestimated for both their race and their gender, were in some ways the most potent forces of all, wielding society's faulty assessment of their abilities as one of their most effective disguises, pitting intelligence and cunning against a power structure whose greatest weakness was its refusal to understand that strength is not always visible and the repressed are not as submissive as they may appear. These bold, brave, and daring espionage agents relied upon their arsenal of talents, using their abilities to impact not only the outcome of the war, but the evolution of the world.

Further Reading

Ann Blackman. *Wild Rose: Rose O'Neale Greenhow, Civil War Spy.* New York: Random House, 2005.

Ina Chang. *A Separate Battle: Women and the Civil War.* New York: Puffin Books, 1996.

M. R. Cordell. *Courageous Women of the Civil War: Soldiers, Spies, Medics, and More.* Chicago: Chicago Review Press, 2016.

Elizabeth D. Leonard. *All the Daring of the Soldier: Women of the Civil War Armies.* New York: W. W. Norton & Co., 1999.

H. Donald Winkler. *Stealing Secrets: How a Few Daring Women Deceived Generals, Impacted Battles, and Altered the Course of the Civil War.* Naperville, IL: Cumberland House, 2010.

Notes

Epigraph: Judith E. Harper, *Women During the Civil War: An Encyclopedia* (New York: Routledge, 2004), 41.

1. Elizabeth D. Leonard, *All the Daring of the Soldier: Women of the Civil War Armies* (New York: W. W. Norton & Co., 1999), 37–38.

2. Leonard, *All the Daring of the Soldier,* 72.

3. Leonard, *All the Daring of the Soldier,* 72.

4. "Nina the Smuggling Doll," display at The Museum of the Confederacy, Richmond, Virginia.

5. Leonard, *All the Daring of the Soldier,* 74–75.

6. M. R. Cordell, *Courageous Women of the Civil War: Soldiers, Spies, Medics, and More* (Chicago: Chicago Review Press, 2016), 53–54.

7. DeAnne Blanton and Lauren M. Cook, *They Fought Like Demons: Women Soldiers in the American Civil War* (Baton Rouge: Louisiana State University Press, 2002), 90.

8. Ann Blackman, *Wild Rose: Rose O'Neale Greenhow, Civil War Spy* (New York: Random House, 2005), 122.

9. Don Johnson, *Thirteen Months of Manasses/Bull Run: The Two Battles and the Confederate and Union Occupations* (Jefferson, NC: McFarland & Co., 2013), 51.

10. H. Donald Winkler, *Stealing Secrets: How a Few Daring Women Deceived Generals, Impacted Battles, and Altered the Course of the Civil War* (Naperville, IL: Cumberland House, 2010), 8.

11. Winkler, *Stealing Secrets,* 11.

12. Rose O'Neal Greenhow, *My Imprisonment and the First Year of Abolition Rule at Washington* (London, Richard Bentley, 1863), 19; see http://docsouth.unc.edu/fpn/greenhow/greenhow.html.

13. Greenhow, *My Imprisonment,* 216.

14. Blackman, *Wild Rose,* 208.

15. Mary Jane Richards married Wilson Bowser in 1861. She had resumed the name Richards by 1867, however, and because it appears she preferred that name, it is the one I have used in this chapter.

16. Ryan Ann Hunter, *In Disguise! Undercover with Real Women Spies* (New York: Aladdin, 2013), 59. (Ryan Ann Hunter is a pen name for Elizabeth G. Macalaster and Pamela D. Greenwood, who write together.)

17. In Lois Leveen, "A Black Spy in the Confederate White House," *New York Times,* June 21, 2012; at https://opinionator.blogs.nytimes.com/2012/06/21/a-black-spy-in-the-confederate-white-house/. Accessed February 18, 2018.

18. Leveen, "A Black Spy in the Confederate White House."

19. This was Van Lew's account of the situation; Varina Davis publicly denied the

entire event, probably due to embarrassment and from a desire to save face. See Lois Leveen, "Mary Richards Bowser (fl. 1846–1867)," *Encyclopedia Virginia,* at https://www.encyclopediavirginia.org/ Bowser_Mary_Richards_fl_1846-1867 #start_entry. Accessed February 18, 2018.

20. These strategies were known to be used in Van Lew's spy ring, though not specifically associated with Mary Jane Richards Bowser.

21. In Leveen, "A Black Spy in the Confederate White House."

22. Leveen, "A Black Spy in the Confederate White House."

23. In Winkler, *Stealing Secrets,* 84.

24. Harper, *Women During the Civil War,* 41.

25. In Leonard, *All the Daring of the Soldier,* 29.

26. Harper, *Women During the Civil War,* 42.

27. For an example, I would point to the controversy over Loreta Janeta Velazquez and her memoir, which inspired a whole volume devoted to allegedly disproving her notoriously sensationalized wartime account: William C. Davis, *Inventing Loreta Velasquez: Confederate Soldier Impersonator, Media Celebrity, and Con Artist* (Carbondale, IL: University of Southern

Illinois Press, 2016).

28. *The Times from Philadelphia, Pennsylvania,* July 3, 1898, 27.

29. Winkler, *Stealing Secrets,* 129.

30. Leonard, *All the Daring of the Soldier,* 67.

31. Winkler, *Stealing Secrets,* 137.

32. Winkler, *Stealing Secrets,* 139.

33. Winkler, *Stealing Secrets,* 140.

34. Winkler, *Stealing Secrets,* 160–61.

35. Winkler, *Stealing Secrets,* 159–66.

36. In Winkler, *Stealing Secrets,* 143.

37. Harriet Tubman, in "Harriet Tubman and the Underground Railroad," National Park Service; https://www.nps.gov/articles/harriet-tubman-and-the-underground-railroad.htm. Accessed February 18, 2018.

38. Laurel Thatcher Ulrich, *Well-Behaved Women Seldom Make History* (New York: Vintage Books, 2007), 118. Historians estimate Tubman's trips at somewhere between ten to twelve, with sixty to seventy persons rescued, though other contemporary sources place the numbers at nineteen trips with three hundred persons led to freedom.

39. In Cordell, *Courageous Women of the Civil War,* 63.

40. In Winkler, *Stealing Secrets,* 155.

41. In Cordell, *Courageous Women of the Civil War,* 64.
42. In Winkler, *Stealing Secrets,* 156.

CHAPTER 5
ANNA ELLA CARROLL
MILITARY STRATEGIST AND
POLITICAL ADVISOR

"We feel a pride that amid discordant tumults of public opinion, a star of no ordinary brightness has arisen in our firmament, to shed the rays of genius over our civic landscape."
— Horace Galpen, 1855, speaking of Anna Ella Carroll

On the battlefield of ideological warfare, few voices were as important a weapon in the Union's arsenal as Anna Ella Carroll. Though few Americans have heard of her, Anna's pen made hers a household name during the war years, and her writings proved to be some of the most effective ammunition raised in support of Lincoln's ideals.

A 2,000-acre tobacco plantation was an unlikely location for the beginning of a life dedicated to promoting the politics of the North; but this was where Anna was born. Her father served in the Maryland legislature and as governor beginning in 1829. He was extremely close to his oldest child, and Anna addressed him as "my precious father"[1] in affectionate letters she wrote to him when he traveled. By the age of three, Anna enjoyed listening to Shakespeare while sitting on her father's lap;[2] by eleven, she was reading Kant.[3] She cared nothing for the drawing, music, dancing, or sewing a girl of her day was expected to learn — she wanted only to study political science and law. In quite a progressive response, her father "viewed with delight her remarkable intelligence, and early made her his companion in the political interests in which he took such an active part."[4] By age twelve, Anna regularly assisted her father in his professional work, locating legal passages to serve as evidence for his legislative debates.

At age fifteen, Anna entered a boarding school in Annapolis, where teachers described her as animated and vivacious on any topic about which she felt passionate. In 1837, Maryland went through an economic depression, and the Carroll family lost a great deal of their fortune. They were forced to sell the family estate, along with most of their slaves, which they sold en masse, so families would not be divided. In an impressive display of independence that belied her privileged background, Anna left for Baltimore at the age of twenty-two and supported herself as a publicity writer and advertiser for seven years.

Carroll's first taste of notoriety arrived when she turned her marketing skills toward politics, authoring a series of political pamphlets and articles in support of Millard Fillmore, the "Know Nothing" candidate for United States president. Fillmore won the state of Maryland, though it was the only state he won. Millard proposed marriage to Carroll, but Anna felt politics were far more interesting than marriage, and she turned him down. Instead, she returned to the campaign trail on behalf of Governor Thomas H. Hicks. This time her candidate succeeded, and Hicks credited his victory to Anna's persuasive pen. Publishing two books on political topics brought Carroll more national attention and motivated Attorney General Edward Bates to call her "a person of superior mind, highly cultivated, especially in . . . American literature, political history, and constitutional law . . . a writer fluent, cogent, and abounding with evidence of patient investigation and original thought."[5]

To celebrate the election of Abraham Lincoln, Anna liberated the remainder of her own slaves. Jefferson Davis, also aware of Carroll's persuasive skills, wrote to her shortly after secession, requesting her support for the South and entreating her father to defect too. Anna claimed the Confederate president offered her father "any position he asks for," but neither would accept the offer, "Not if you will give him the whole

South."[6] Throughout the conflict, Carroll understood all that was at stake in the conflict, and a visitor in 1861 described Anna's preoccupation with the war: "Her room was lined with military maps, her tables covered with papers and war documents. . . . Her countenance would light up most radiantly as she spoke of the Union victories and the certainty that the great Nation must win an ultimate success. When fresh news from the army came in, she would step up to one of her charts and . . . begin thoughtfully to predict the result and suggest the proper move."[7]

In some ways, no state was a more important pawn in the conflict than Maryland. Virginia bordered Washington, DC, to the south, but north of the capital hunched Maryland, a deeply divided territory. While the western portions of the state's manufacturing towns aligned with the Union, people in eastern cities like Annapolis and Baltimore held significant slave holdings and were far more sympathetic to the Confederacy. In the presidential elections of 1861, Lincoln carried only two percent of the state's votes, and in some counties, he did not receive a single ballot. When Lincoln emerged as victor, some in Maryland even called for seizing control of the capital city by force to prevent his inauguration. Should Maryland topple towards secession, their departure would cut off Washington, DC, from the rest of the Union, stranding the capital in the midst of Confederate territory — in short, the war would soon be over.

To pacify voters, Maryland's political leaders walked a precarious balancing act, knowing how quickly the situation could turn to all-out anarchy. Representatives voted to stay in the Union but preserved slavery and forbade passage to any Union troops attempting to make war on their southern neighbors. Governor Hicks, a slave owner himself, waffled on the issue of secession. President Jefferson Davis sent 5,000 muskets to Maryland in April 1861, hoping the gift would persuade the state to rise up against Union forces, but when Anna Ella Carroll learned of the Confederate plan, she felt no ambivalence. Calling upon Hicks, who trusted Anna's opinion, Carroll persuaded him to confiscate the firearms and clarify his intent to remain in the Union. Hicks followed Anna's advice and held an emergency session of Congress in Frederick instead of the customary location of Annapolis, a city seething with Confederate support. Anna advised and assisted Hicks as he negotiated the compromise with

Congress that kept Maryland in the Union.[8]

Given the strategic position of the state, Lincoln saw no way to allow Maryland to remain neutral. The tensions erupted into violence in April 1861 when pro-Confederacy rioters attacked Union troops as they marched through the streets of Baltimore on their way to Washington DC. Riots continued for days across the city, leaving forty-two soldiers and twelve civilians dead.[9] In a bold and widely criticized reaction, Lincoln sent 1,000 Federal soldiers led by General Benjamin Butler to occupy Baltimore. Turning Federal guns upon the city, President Lincoln declared martial law and rescinded the right of *habeas corpus*. Southern sympathizers found themselves arrested at will, their lands confiscated as the United States Supreme Court chimed in to rule Lincoln's arrests unconstitutional. Rather than changing course, the president ignored the verdict and continued shutting down state newspapers and jailing reporters and other members of the press. Thousands of Confederate-inclined Marylanders fled south, including 25,000 soldiers who would join ranks with the Confederacy, while 60,000 Maryland men enlisted with Union forces.[10]

The volatility of the situation left public

opinion more fragile than ever before. As the daughter of a former governor and advisor to the current leader, Anna's opinions were already well-respected, and when she lifted her pen in behalf of abolition and Maryland's tenuous status as a Northern state, she was listened to. While the Confederacy claimed to be continuing the work of the American Revolution, Anna countered that the country's founders would, on the contrary, have kept the country together and worked toward peace. Carroll authored a series of pamphlets, which she published at her own expense, drawing on her extensive background in politics and Constitutional law to defend Lincoln's actions as extraordinary measures taken during times of war.

In the summer of 1861, John C. Breckinridge of Kentucky delivered a scathing speech on the floor of the Senate, claiming that Lincoln had violated the Constitution with his actions in Maryland. Anna was seated in the balcony as Breckinridge delivered his attack, and she wrote a pamphlet in response, using informed legal arguments to claim that Lincoln had acted within his role as commander-in-chief in order to preserve the unity of the nation. "By virtue of the express and implied powers of the Constitution," she wrote, "it is impossible to question the duty of the President to use every belligerent right, every instrument known to the law of war: — To annoy, to waken, to destroy the enemy, until its armies are overthrown and the civil authority is re-established."[11] The publication was so successful that the United States War Department distributed it to all members of Congress, and when Lincoln read it, he sought funding to publish 50,000 copies of the pamphlet. Governor Hicks later said that Anna's persuasive writing did more to ensure Maryland remained in the Union's hands than "all the rest of the campaign documents together."[12] Lincoln was so impressed that he invited Carroll to a private meeting at the White House, where he asked her to serve as an unofficial advisor and member of his Cabinet.

Under contract for the government, Anna wrote three additional pamphlets offering constitutional support for Lincoln's actions. These pamphlets were widely circulated throughout the North, influencing public opinion and aiding in the president's reelection, which was anything but certain and particularly vulnerable in a state as divided as Carroll's was. Engaging dramatic imagery, Anna aligned the work of unification with the broader spiritual destiny she saw for the country. She also clearly identified all she considered to be at stake in the debate, claiming that the actions of Breckinridge and other Confederate supporters "Thrust a knife into the ribs of the Constitution which is now pouring out its life's blood."[13] Carroll occasionally waxed sentimental in keeping with the writing style of her day, but insight, cogency, and reason formed the basis of her arguments. Governor Hicks expressed his appreciation for her support and assistance by saying: "Your moral and material support I shall never forget in that trying ordeal. . . . When all was dark and dreadful for Maryland's future . . . you stood nobly by and watched the storm and skillfully helped to work the ship, until, thank God, helmsmen and crew were safe in port."[14]

In the fall of 1861, the federal government invited Carroll to work as a secret agent to assess the feasibility of a Union invasion of Texas. Anna traveled the rivers and interviewed riverboat captains about a potential Union attack via the Mississippi River. Charles M. Scott advised that the plan could not work because sections of the river would need to be opened up to navigation before they could be invaded successfully. When Carroll asked about using the Tennessee and Cumberland rivers instead, the pilot provided technical navigation details which could make the idea viable. Thrilled by the prospect, Anna became convinced this approach would prove essential to winning the war. Carroll immediately authored a memorandum to the Assistant Secretary of War, recommending the army and navy change strategies and eschewing the Mississippi River in favor of the Tennessee. She presented the idea in Washington on November 30.[15]

This approach was successfully implemented in February of 1862, when the Union armies captured key forts in Tennessee and used the river to achieve victory in the war's western theater. As events unfolded, Carroll assumed that her recommendations had been instrumental to the successful campaign. Though she appears to have been the first to present the plan to Lincoln, who immediately adopted it, unbeknownst to either of them, several top Union military leaders had been considering the same strategy before Anna presented the concept.

In addition to the Tennessee plan, Carroll also worked with General Ulysses S. Grant on plans to attack Vicksburg, Mississippi, in 1863. Anna advised him to attack the city by land from the rear, a plan which Grant initially rejected as too difficult, since it involved leading men far behind enemy lines. Instead, Grant launched several unsuccessful attempts to take Vicksburg directly before accepting the need to adopt Carroll's advice and lay siege to the city from the rear. Anna's role as military strategist in both of these campaigns, essential to the outcome of the war, remains unparalleled among females of her day and demonstrated exceptional military acumen and insight. Her role in both efforts was originally kept secret to protect her continued work on covert intelligence activities.[16]

For the remainder of the war, Anna served as unofficial advisor to the Lincoln administration in an era when having a formal female Cabinet leader was unthinkable. Lincoln sought her advice regarding emancipation and how best to approach the issues of reconstruction. Carroll initially recommended the recolonization of former slaves, a solution which Lincoln seriously considered, though he eventually decided integration into United States society would be a better outcome. Anna also advised against issuing the Emancipation Proclamation, fearing that it would threaten the loyalty of border states. She correctly pointed out that

Lincoln did not legally have the right to free the slaves, except as a temporary war measure, and making emancipation permanent would require a constitutional amendment. Carroll considered the Constitution and law the ultimate authority on all matters. That Lincoln appreciated her input is shown in the words one of his administrators said to her: "Mr. Lincoln, with whom I have conversed, has, I know, the highest appreciation of your services."[17]

When she wasn't writing or advising, Anna spent the remainder of the war years engaged in humanitarian concerns, offering political and financial support to war widows and wounded soldiers. She lobbied for government positions for women who had lost relatives in the conflict and encouraged the Treasury Department to employ women as copyists. As an outspoken advocate for the advancement of women, Carroll argued: "The intellect of woman must then be cultivated — her first and last refuge is education."[18]

In the aftermath of the war and the chaos of Lincoln's assassination, the government Carroll had worked closely with suddenly shifted dramatically. Anna had footed the bill for printing and circulating many of her influential publications, and she claimed that Lincoln had agreed to compensate her for them but died before he was able to do so. For decades, Carroll unsuccessfully sought compensation for her work for the Lincoln administration; her open and vocal criticism of President Andrew Johnson's approach to Reconstruction surely did not help her case.[19] Anna had been paid $750 for her role as a secret agent in 1862, but regarding the remainder of her work, Assistant Secretary of War Thomas A. Scott wrote on her behalf: "No price was fixed, but it was understood that the Government would treat her with sufficient liberality to compensate her for any service she might render, and I believe she acted upon the expectation that she would be paid by the Government."[20] As Carroll's request languished in Congress, Scott paid her $1,250 out of his own pocket, agreeing that her role deserved far more recognition than it had received.[21]

At the urging of Senator Benjamin F. Wade, Anna petitioned Congress directly, asking for reparation for her wartime service. In 1871, a committee approved her claim, but Congress failed to pass the bill authorizing the expenses. Howard confided to Anna that former military officers did not want her to receive payment, and some key evidence may have been "accidentally" lost from her files. Though the claim was resubmitted a number of times, accompanied by numerous letters in support of her request, no bill was passed. In the 1880s Anna's petition garnered support among suffragists, who launched a campaign on her behalf. Meanwhile, Carroll's health had deteriorated, making the need for funds more urgent than ever. Finally, in 1881 Congress reviewed a bill that would have given Carroll compensation at the same rate as major generals, but the assassination of President Garfield put a stop to the debate, and Congress instead awarded her a pension of $50 per month for "important military service rendered by her during the late Civil War."[22] Carroll used the meager income to support herself and her sister Mary. Anna continued writing long after she was bedridden by old age, working from a room stacked with books, letters, and political maps.

In the wake of the battle over women's suffrage, Anna Ella Carroll's war contribution became associated with the suffragist movement, eliciting support or disparagement along these political lines. While Anna's supporters point out that males who played similar roles in the war were far more generously compensated for their efforts, detractors criticize Carroll's insistence that she deserved sole credit for the Tennessee Plan, and point out that she claimed credit for the strategy only years later when she needed money.[23]

All of this debate aside, reading through the letters to, from, and about Anna in the Library of Congress holdings is sobering and compelling. Four out of the five military committees who examined her claim before Congress voted in her favor. Senator Benjamin Wade and Assistant Secretary of War Thomas Alexander Scott both testified to Congress that Anna's involvement with the Tennessee strategy was intentionally kept secret in the interest of national security.

Governor Hicks, Carroll's lifelong friend, wrote during the war, "No money can ever pay for what you have done for the State and the country in this terrible crisis, but I trust and believe the time will come when all will know the debt they owe you."[24] Neither Anna nor Hicks could have possibly imagined just how long her story would have to wait to be told. As a contributor to politics and war strategy decades before women even had the right to vote, Carroll left an indelible mark on her state and her country. Perhaps artist Francis B.

Carpenter's homage to her is the perfect symbol of Anna's neglected contribution. When asked in 1864 to paint Lincoln and his Cabinet signing the Emancipation Proclamation, Carpenter painted an empty chair surrounded by maps and notes similar to the ones Carroll was known to carry. Some believe this was the artist's tribute to the member of Lincoln's cabinet whose service went largely unrecognized.[25] In 2012, a popular portrait artist, Laura Era, was commissioned to replicate Carpenter's famous painting — with Anna returned to her place in the empty chair. The new work is entitled "Maryland's Version of the First Reading of the Emancipation Proclamation."[26] Though many details surrounding Carroll's contributions are unclear, the fact remains that long before women could vote in this country, she was involved in politics in an unprecedented manner and played an essential role in the crisis of this nation.

Further Reading

Sarah Ellen Blackwell. *A Military Genius: Life of Anna Ella Carroll, of Maryland, the "Great Unrecognized Member of Lincoln's Cabinet."* Washington, DC: Judd & Detweiler, 1891.

Sylvia Bradley. "Anna Ella Carroll, 1815–1894: Military Strategist — Political Propagandist," in *Notable Maryland Women,* ed. Winifred Gertrude Helmes. Cambridge: Tidewater Publishers, 1977.

C. Kay Larson. *Great Necessities: The Life, Times, and Writings of Anna Ella Carroll, 1815–1894.* Philadelphia: Xlibris, 2004.

Notes

Epigraph: In Anna Ella Carroll, *The Great American Battle, or the Contest Between Christianity and Political Romanism* (New York: Miller, Orton & Mulligan, 1856), xi.

1. Sarah Ellen Blackwell, *A Military Genius: Life of Anna Ella Carroll, of Maryland, the "Great Unrecognized Member of Lincoln's Cabinet"* (Washington, DC: Judd & Detweiler, 1891),

2. Blackwell, *A Military Genius,* 14.

3. Blackwell, *A Military Genius,* 15.

4. Blackwell, *A Military Genius,* 14.

5. Blackwell, *A Military Genius,* 25.

6. Blackwell, *A Military Genius,* 28.

7. Blackwell, *A Military Genius,* 28.

8. Blackwell, *A Military Genius,* part 4.

9. Kevin Conley Ruffner, *Maryland's Blue and Gray: A Border State's Union and Confederate Junior* (Baton Rouge: LSU

Press, 1997), 34.

10. See http://americancivilwarinstitute
.blogspot.pt/2013/08/maryland-in-civil-
war.html.

11. Anna Ella Carroll, in Judith E. Harper,
*Women During the Civil War: An Encyclope-
dia* (New York: Routledge, 2004), 60.

12. Janet L. Coryell, *Neither Heroine Nor
Fool: Anna Ella Carroll of Maryland* (Kent,
OH: Kent State University Press, 1990),
55–64.

13. *Southern Unionist Pamphlets and the Civil
War,* edited by Jon L. Wakelyn (Columbia,
MO: University of Missouri Press, 1999).
20.

14. In Blackwell, *A Military Genius,* 38, 39.

15. Coryell, *Neither Heroine Nor Fool,* 55–
64.

16. Sylvia Bradley, "Anna Ella Carroll,
1815–1894: Military Strategist — Political
Propagandist," in *Notable Maryland
Women,* ed. Winifred Gertrude Helmes
(Cambridge: Tidewater Publishers, 1977),
62–70.

17. R. J. Walker (Representative in Congress
and later Secretary of Treasury under
President Polk) to Anna Ella Carroll, May
22, 1862, as quoted in Blackwell, *A Military
Genius,* 45.

18. Carroll, *The Great American Battle,* 19–20.

19. Johnson did not support former slaves voting and opposed civil rights for African Americans. Carroll spoke out in favor of Johnson's impeachment, criticizing his role in returning former Confederate leaders to their former posts, actions which she felt were in direct opposition to Lincoln's original intentions regarding the Reconstruction era. Her criticism led in part to the impeachment proceedings begun against Johnson. For more, see http://www.friendsofannaellacarroll.org/aboutanna.php#9.

20. Thomas A. Scott, January 28, 1863, Petition of Anna Ella, Library of Congress, RPO 454155.

21. See http://www.friendsofannaellacarroll.org/aboutanna.html.

22. See http://msa.maryland.gov/msa/educ/exhibits/ womenshall/html/carroll.html.

23. C. Kay Larson, *Great Necessities: The Life, Times and Writings of Anna Ella Carroll, 1815–1894* (Philadelphia: Xlibris, 2004), 477–99.

24. Thomas H. Hicks to Anna Ella Carroll, Sept 22, 1861, Anna Ella Carroll Papers, Library of Congress, RPO 454155.

25. This, like everything else about Carroll's

contribution, is debated. See also Sylvia Bradley, "Anna Ella Carroll, 1815–1894: Military Strategist — Political Propagandist," in *Notable Maryland Women* (Cambridge: Tidewater Publishers, 1977), 62–70.

26. See http://talbotspy.org/troika-gallery-displays-historic-painting-with-lincoln's-secret-female-cabinet-member/.

CHAPTER 6
INK OF THE CENTURIES
THE DIARISTS

Sarah Dawson

"Need I say how dear you are to my heart, how essential to my existence?"
— Sixteen-year-old Clara Solomon of New Orleans speaking of her diary

On brittle sheaves of parchment, yellowed and spotted with age, written in fading ink and looped handwriting, the reality of a nation at war can be experienced again through the diaries of those who lived it. Turning the pages of these diaries creates a rush of air — a soft exhale of the past — as the ghosts of conflict arise, speaking across the years. The Civil War inspired more men and women to keep journals than any other event in United States' history.[1] As they watched the world transform before their eyes, many writers sensed the importance of the sights they documented, but as time and resources dwindled, the seemingly simple act of journal keeping became increasingly difficult. Maria Lydig Daly of New York City wrote, "I have so much to do and think of that I forget my diary, which, in such momentous times, is a *crime* against myself."[2]

Particularly in the South, the lack of paper, ink, or safety caused many diarists to break off mid-account, often leaving stories whose only resolutions would be etched on tombstones. Cornelia Peake McDonald wrote from Winchester, Virginia: "Paper being very difficult to get, any that could be made available was used."[3] Some women repurposed old account books, while others wrote on strips of wallpaper taken from walls damaged by shells. Those wealthy enough to have private libraries laid claim to blank spaces and the margins of printed volumes. Paper, that rare and valuable commodity, was scrawled across, turned, and written over again, creating labyrinths of text many layers deep. War refugees, preparing to leave homes behind, wrenched journal pages from their bindings and sewed sheaves between the layers of their skirts. As Union armies approached, Catherine Devereaux Edmondston of North Carolina recorded: "And now, old friend, you my Journal, for a time goodbye! You are too bulky to be kept out, exposed to prying Yankee eyes and thievish Yankee fingers. You go for a season to darkness & solitude & my record must henceforth be kept on scraps of paper, backs of letters, or old memorandum books which I can secrete."[4]

Even as they fled, some managed to continue their records, clinging to the final remnants of a world swiftly crumbling to dust. Beyond creating an account of historical significance, a woman's diary was often also the very key to her psychological survival, the only place of surety in a swiftly changing world. Sixteen-year-old Clara Solomon of New Orleans confided to her written page, "Need I say how dear you are to my heart, how essential to my existence?"[5]

The majority of Civil War diaries that have been preserved come from white, well-educated, upper-class women, who had higher literacy rates and more resources to draw upon. Working class or African American perspectives are much harder to come by, while female Native American and Mexican-American perspectives are sadly believed to be nearly nonexistent.[6] Beyond the accounts that have been published, more records remain, tucked into boxes in county historical societies and stowed away in attics. The voices that speak from these brittle pages offer haunting testaments of the day-to-day reality of war.

THE NORTH

The Cormany Diaries are some of the most unique of the war, as they come from a middle class family, and because both husband and wife kept diaries, preserving the two perspectives (see chapter 13). One of the most famous Northern diaries from the conflict was written by Maria Lydig Daly. Married to a prominent judge from New York, Daly gathered firsthand knowledge of the political scene in Washington, such as the story of a senator who expressed a common enough sentiment before violence broke out: "There is no danger of civil war. It will all be over in six weeks."[7] Because of Maria's position, she witnessed many significant events and watched from the upper gallery of the Senate when Louisiana senators announced their secession. "It was a very sad sight to see the stars fading away out of our banner one by one,"[8] she wrote. Later Daly recorded a senator from Texas say he hoped "to see this Union split into as many pieces as cannon could split glass." Never mincing her own commentary, Daly confided: "I should like to have hurled something at him myself."[9] Maria captured the complexity of the conflict, blaming England for sowing discontent between the North and South and criticizing Massachusetts "firebrands" for setting torch "to the smouldering discontent of the South."[10] Though opposed to slavery on principle, Daly recognized the economic complexity of abolition and suggested: "Let those who feel so concerned for the slaves at the South and who ask such sacrifices from slave-owners to each buy one and then liberate them by degrees."[11]

After the attack on Fort Sumter, Maria said even those who didn't care for Lincoln rallied together. "All feel that our very nationality is at stake," she recorded, "and to save the country from anarchy . . . that every man must do his best to sustain the government, whoever or whatever the President may be."[12] The political discussions in Washington took a far more personal turn when her husband began practicing with the home guard. "I suppose it is right that every man should know how to use a bayonet," she wrote, "but it seems as if my heart strings tighten whenever I hear him speak of the war. I know he would like the excitement of it. I thought him more of a philosopher."[13]

Despite her fears, Maria's husband, Charles, did not see a battlefield, and her brother, who did serve in the army, survived to return home. Four years later, Daly recorded: "Last night at midnight we heard an extra called. . . . 'Surrender of Lee's army, ten cents and no mistake,' said the boy all in one breath (a true young American). . . . Glory be to God on high; the rebellion is ended! Phil, my brother, is uninjured, and peace soon to descend to bless the land again. . . . I hope the animosity that has so long reigned will now pass away. May God comfort and change the hearts of our so long vindictive foes!"[14] Safe in New York, secure in her own economic prosperity, Daly's life more or less could return to normal, though she acknowledged that "Mrs. Young tells me that we have no idea of the destitution of the South; that most of the men . . . were driven into the Confederate Army because their families would else have starved."[15]

THE SOUTH

Eliza Frances Andrew of Georgia, on the other hand, needed only to look through her window to see the destitution and suffering of which Daly heard rumors. Shortly after the surrender, Eliza wrote: "The poor wounded men go hobbling about the streets with despair on their faces. There is a new pathos in a crutch or an empty sleeve, now, that we know it was all for nothing."[16] Emma LeConte also watched the devastation unfold in South Carolina in 1865 as cities in the South burned to charred skeletons of their former glory, set alight by advancing Union troops and retreating Confederates. "Imagine night turned into noonday," LeConte wrote, "only with a

blazing, scorching glare that was horrible —
a copper colored sky across which swept
columns of black, rolling smoke glittered
with sparks and flying embers . . . while
every instant came the crashing of timbers
and the thunder of falling buildings."[17]

Winchester, Virginia, a staunchly Confederate stronghold in the Shenandoah Valley,
changed hands dozens of times during the
war,[18] as the strategic location was sheltered
by hills, and centered at the crossroads of
seven major thoroughfares. Each time the
Union army gained control of the town, the
occupiers felt the wrath of women whose
husbands and sons were fighting and dying,
at times only hundreds of yards away. "The
men are all in the army, and the women are
the devil," Secretary of State Edwin Stanton
told Lincoln of Winchester. A remarkable
number of women in the town recorded
their experiences during the war, and they
became collectively known as "the devil
diarists of Winchester." Mary Greenhow
Lee was one of the most strident of these
devil diarists. She carefully disobeyed every
edict of Union generals occupying the town,
until General Sheridan finally exiled her in
1865.[19] Her vibrant record captures life in
an occupied town. "The Yankees advanced
this evening to within one mile of our lines

and are now encamped three miles from town . . . the idea that by this time tomorrow night we may be in their hands, is too terrible for my mind to grasp. . . . I still cling to the conviction that it will not be permitted. . . . Oh, it is terrible to be listening for the cannon, now in the dead hours of the night . . . horsemen are dashing by continually; why do they ride as if the enemy were pursuing them. May the God of battles have mercy on us."[20] Cornelia Peake McDonald was another of the Winchester devil diarists; she kept an extensive record of her efforts to help her nine children survive the conflict after her husband enlisted with the Confederate army (see chapter 7).

Mary Ann Loughborough, wife of a Confederate officer, made a brief visit to see friends in Vicksburg, Mississippi, when Union troops laid siege to the city. The visit that was planned to last a few days turned into weeks of confinement for Loughborough and her baby. Cannons opened fire upon the town, and Mary Ann joined Vicksburg residents sheltering from the barrage in nearby caves. With her baby in tow, Loughborough recorded the events of the siege from an earthen cave that shook with the reverberations of falling shells. "How blightingly the hand of warfare lay upon the town!" she wrote. "Even in the softening light of the moon — the closed and desolate houses — the gardens, with gates half open, and cattle standing amid the loveliest flowers and verdure! This carelessness of appearance and evident haste of departure was visible everywhere — the inhabitants, in this perilous time, feeling only anxiety for personal safety and the strength of their cave homes."[21]

One of the most famous Southern diarists of the war, Mary Boykin Chesnut, recorded events from her rural plantation home in South Carolina. Mary survived the deaths of numerous loved ones and countless acquaintances over four years of battles. "I know how it feels to die," she wrote. "Some one calls out, 'Albert Sydney Johnston is killed.' My heart stands still. I feel no more. I am . . . without sensation of any kind — dead; and then, there is that great throb, that keen agony of physical pain. . . . The ticking of the clock begins, and I take up the burden of life once more."[22]

As the difficulties and challenges of the war increased, food grew scarce and casualties mounted; some Southern communities lost more than a quarter of their male populace. Food shortages affected the most vulnerable people disproportionately, and it was much more difficult for them to flee as the wealthy could. Too often slave owners directed their increasing anger over the conflict at their own workers. One female slave in Missouri pled with her husband serving in the Union army: "[The slave owners] are treating me worse and worse every day. Our child cries for you. Send me some money as soon as you can for me and my child are almost naked."[23]

Children in the South, many of whom couldn't even remember their lives prior to the conflict, were forced to shoulder responsibilities beyond their years. Carrie Berry, a ten-year-old girl living in Atlanta, Georgia, faithfully kept her diary under siege: "We can hear the canons and muskets very plane [sic]," she wrote, "but the shells we dread. One has busted under the dining room which frightened us very much. . . . We stay very close in the cellar when they are shelling."[24] A few days later in a rather heartbreaking entry, she recorded: "This was my birthday. I was ten years old, but I did not have a cake times were too hard so I celebrated with ironing. I hope by my next birthday we will have peace in our land so that I can have a nice dinner."[25]

In pages where words are frequently

scribbled and blotted out, Carrie described her longing for normal life: "I feel so lonesome I cant stay at home. I wish it was so that I could go to school."[26] A determined little patriot, her lines of complaint are often followed by reminders to be brave: "I dislike to stay in the cellar so close but our soldiers have to stay in ditches."[27] The departure of newly freed servants meant more of the household tasks fell on her small shoulders, and one day she wrote, "Mary [their servant] went off this evening and I don't expect that she will come back any more. . . . I will have to go to work to help Mama."[28] Carrie elaborated on her new tasks a week later: "I helpt to wash till dinner time and then I got dinner by myself. It made me very warm and tired but I supose I will have to learn to wirk."[29] When her mother gave birth to another baby, Carrie's life again took on new challenges. "I had a little sister this morning at eight o'clock and Mama gave her to me," she wrote. "I think its very pretty. I had to cook breakfast and dinner and supper."[30]

With the fall of Atlanta and the Union occupation of the town, Carrie's anxiety mounted. Friends and relatives departed, and her parents struggled with uncertainty over their own living situation. She wrote:

"Papa came and told us that Gen. Sherman had ordered us to move. It broke into all our rangements."[31] Seeing the potential move as more exciting than the adults did, Carrie confessed, "The citizens all think that it is the most cruel thing to drive us from our home but I think it would be so funny to move. Mama seems so troubled and she can't do any thing. Papa says he don't know where on earth to go."[32]

In the weeks that followed, Carrie recorded the destruction of Atlanta: "I took a walk to see how the soldiers had torn down the fine houses"; "Mama and Papa . . . say that they never saw a place torn up like Atlanta is"; "Some mean soldiers set several houses on fire in different parts of the town. I could not go to sleep for fear that they would set our house on fire."[33]

As food grew scarce, Union soldiers often made off with the family's supplies, and Carrie feared her family would soon have nothing to eat: "We lost our last hog this morning early. Soldiers took him out of the pen. Me and Buddie went around to hunt for him. . . . We will have to live on bread."[34] On December 22, 1864, she wrote of a rare holiday tradition unchanged by the presence of war: "We went to get our Christmas tree this evening. It was very cold but we did not feel it we were so excited about it." Only four days later, though, the war was once more foremost in her thoughts: "Papa left us this morning. He has gone to Macon to be tried for staying here with the Yankees. We are afraid they will put him in the army. We all feel very sad."[35] Carrie survived the war and the traumatic events of her childhood. She witnessed the rebuilding of Atlanta, where she would marry, raise four children, and live the remainder of her life.

Sarah Morgan Dawson, a few years older than Carrie when the war began, kept her own record of the conflict in a journal that deserves comparison to Anne Frank's account of World War II. Both are vivid accounts written by girls coming of age against the backdrop of battle. Fifteen months into the conflict, nineteen-year-old Sarah looked back at her childhood in Baton Rouge, Louisiana, and marveled at how much had changed: "Until that dreary 1861, I had no idea of sorrow or grief. . . . How I love to think of myself at that time! Not as myself, but as some happy, careless child who danced through life, loving God's whole world. . . . I can say it now, for she is as dead as though she was lying underground."[36]

Despite this opening claim, Sarah's early

accounts in 1861 describe "parties, rides, and walks" with "pleasant officers." Sarah confessed that she "did not think for a moment that trouble would grow out of it."[37] But the Morgan family, like many in Louisiana, were hit hard by the events of the next four years. Sarah's older brother sided with the Union, while her three younger brothers joined the Confederacy. Feisty and defiant, Sarah sided with the South, enthusiastically describing how bottles of liquor were poured into the street and bales of cotton burned so they would not fall into enemy hands: "Each sent up its wreath of smoke and looked like a tiny steamer puffing away. . . . The cotton floated down the Mississippi one sheet of living flame, even in the sunlight."[38]

Union general Benjamin Butler occupied Baton Rouge and ordered "all devices, signs, and flags of the Confederacy" banned from the streets. Sarah devoted all the red, white, and blue silk she could find to the manufacture of Confederate flags, and she confided to her journal: "As soon as one is confiscated, I make another."[39] On more than one occasion, Morgan pinned a flag to her shoulder and went into town, disregarding her family's concerns over this "unladylike display of defiance."[40] Sarah lamented her gender, which prohibited her from joining the army, and her animosity toward the Yankees veered toward violence fairly regularly; on paper at least, she dared Northern soldiers to approach her, saying they would feel the sting of her hidden "pistol" and "carving-knife"[41] if they gave her occasion to use them.

Sarah's words reveal bravery and a determination to stay strong as the conflict ravaged her home, city, and loved ones. She recorded supplies growing scarce and often going hungry; friends fell in battle or came home deeply changed by what they had survived. Though Sarah claimed she would not "move one step, unless carried away," eventually she fled town with her mother and sister. Sarah recalled her mother screaming and the children "crying hysterically" as she gathered a few belongings, freed her pet bird, and took to the road "in the midst of flying shells."[42] Abandoning their home to looters, Sarah and her family joined the hordes of people fleeing the besieged city, noting the "women searching for their babies along the road, where they had been lost; others sitting in the dust crying and wringing their hands."[43]

Sarah, her mother, and two sisters squeezed themselves into one bedroom in

Clinton for a time, while food supplies went from scarce to nonexistent. Never losing her sense of humor, Sarah wrote: "Next time I go shopping, I mean to ask some clerk, out of curiosity, what they *do* sell. . . . shopkeepers actually laugh at you if you ask for: Glasses, flour, soap, starch, coffee, candles . . . in short, everything that I have heretofore considered as necessary to existence. If anyone had told me I could have lived off of cornbread, a few months, ago, I would have been incredulous; now I believe it, and return an inward grace for the blessing at every mouthful."[44] Union forces freed Sarah's house servants, but several opted to stay with the family through the remainder of the war.

During her time in Clinton, Sarah fell from a buggy when the horse bolted, badly injuring her back. Shortly thereafter, her mother became seriously ill, which was only compounded by stress and lack of food. Though the Morgan women hated to leave Confederate-held territory, eventually they made their way to the home of Sarah's Unionist brother. Before landing in New Orleans, the Morgans were forced to swear an oath of loyalty to the United States, though Sarah said she was "half-crying" and "heard not a word he was saying."[45]

While in her brother's home, word reached Sarah of the fall of Vicksburg, and soon thereafter, the devastating Confederate defeat at Gettysburg. Even more personal distress followed with the notice that her brother Gibbes had been taken prisoner and placed in Sandusky prison. Gibbes succumbed to his illness. In shock and grief, Sarah recorded: "My brain seems afire. Am I mad? Not yet! God would not take him yet! He will come again! Hush, God is good! Not dead! not dead!"[46]

Even as the family reeled from this shock, within the week, news from an army hospital arrived of another brother's death. Watching her mother deal with the loss of two sons, Sarah wrote: "I felt as though the whole world was dead. Nothing was real, nothing existed except horrible speechless pain. Life was a fearful dream through which but one thought ran — 'Dead — Dead!' "[47]

Sarah's journal entries grew brief after these twin tragedies, but she did pause long enough to pen: "Our Confederacy has gone with one crash — the report of the pistol fired at Lincoln."[48] In the final pages of her journal, Sarah claimed she could never remain in the Union after all she had witnessed; but once more, the events of her life belied her intentions, and somehow

Sarah persisted. In even the darkest moments of her account, her humor continued to be unquenchable. Even as she mourned the loss of her brothers, she still acknowledged the mercy and wisdom of God.

After the war, Sarah started over, carving out a new life for herself while trying to hold on to the ideals of her past. She fell in love with a British man named Dawson who had willingly left his own country behind to fight for the Confederacy; the couple married and had three children. In further testament to Sarah's strength, they both pursued successful careers as writers and journalists, inspired by the events they had witnessed during the conflict. Though Dawson left instructions that her personal papers should be burned upon her death, Sarah's son defied these instructions and published her war journal posthumously. He wrote in the introduction that "souls like unto hers leave their mark in passing through the world," and he testified of her remarkable resilience. "The Sarah Morgan, who as a girl, could stifle her sobs as she forced herself to laugh or sing, was the mother I knew in later years."[49]

Many years after finishing the account of her wartime experiences, Sarah returned to add a gracious postscript: "Reading this for the first time, in all these many years, I wish to bear record that God never failed me. . . . Whatever the anguish, whatever the extremity, in His own good time He ever delivered me. So that I bless Him today for all of life's joys and sorrows — for all He gave — for all He has taken — and I bear witness that it was all Very Good."[50]

THE END OF CONFLICT

When Lee at last surrendered, he did so in a South devastated and mutilated from four years of battle. Never again would the region regain the wealth it had previously enjoyed. Having watched as a world of seeming stability and plenty disappeared week by week, millions looked about, grasping to hold on to anything that remained familiar. Wrapped in grief at the devastation of her home and country, Mary Chesnut lamented all that had been lost. "There are nights," she wrote, "here with the moonlight, cold & ghastly, & the whippoorwills, & the screech owl alone disturbing the silence when I could tear my hair & cry aloud for all that is past & gone."[51]

Four days after Lee's surrender, the assassination of Lincoln shocked the entire nation, and thousands of hands recorded the event. Maria Lydig Daly wrote: "Just as we were rejoicing over the return of peace, everything once again in confusion. . . . God save us all. What may not a day bring forth!" Though she was not a supporter of Lincoln herself, Daly believed the event would "make a martyr of Abraham Lincoln, whose death will make all the shortcomings of his life and Presidential career forgotten in, as Shakespeare says, 'the deep damnation of his taking off.' "[52]

The African American community particularly mourned this president who many viewed as a liberator. Former slave Sarah Walker of Missouri had met Lincoln on one of his trips to the south. She remembered him standing "in all dignity and charm, and yet you had the feeling he was saying all the time, 'I am no better than you are.' "[53] Emilie Davis, a free black woman in Philadelphia, recorded the mourning of her home city: "The President Was assasinated by Som Confederate villain at the theathre die Saturday morning the 15 the city is in the Deepest sorrow."[54] Davis said it was the gravest funeral she had ever seen. Thousands thronged the streets to watch the procession pass by, waiting for hours to catch a brief sight of the beloved president's casket. Emilie stood among the crowds and wrote, "i got to see him after waiting tow

[two] hours and a half it was certainly a sight worth seeing."[55]

For white Southerners, worries about blame and retaliation compounded the shock of assassination. Devastated by the successive losses of her daughter, husband, stepsons, and home, Cornelia Peake McDonald confessed, "I cannot deny that when I first heard of the taking off of Lincoln, I thought it was just what he deserved; he that had urged on and promoted a savage war that had cost so many lifes; but a little reflection made me see that it was worse for us than if he had been suffered to live . . . he was disposed to be merciful. . . . no mercy was to be expected from a nation of infuriated fanatics."[56] Sarah Morgan Dawson, too, feared retribution for the event and prayed: "Let not his blood be visited upon our nation, Lord."[57]

Through these fragments of paper crossed with lines of ink, we hear the voices, fears, and hopes of women speaking across centuries, capturing the agony of war, entreating their readers to fight for peace. The experience of war for women was vastly different, depending on where they were born and the resources they had access to throughout the conflict. Many survivors used words to feel their way through the events unfolding around them. The firsthand accounts they left behind are testimony to the power of story and an invitation to create a path unwinding behind us, expressed in our own voices, laid down upon the earth, one sentence at a time.

Further Reading

Maria Lydig Daly. *Diary of a Union Lady, 1861–1865.* Edited by Harold Earl Hammond. Lincoln: University of Nebraska Press, 2000.

Sarah Morgan Dawson. *A Confederate Girl's Diary.* London: William Heinemann, 1913.

Charles East, editor. *The Civil War Diary of Sarah Morgan.* Athens, GA: University of Georgia Press, 1991.

Judith Giesberg, editor. *Emilie Davis's Civil War: The Diaries of a Free Black Woman in Philadelphia, 1863–1865.* Philadelphia: The Pennsylvania State University Press, 2014.

Kerry Graves, editor. *A Confederate Girl: The Diary of Carrie Berry, 1864.* Mankato, MN: Blue Earth Books, 2000.

Mary Ann Loughborough. *My Cave Life in Vicksburg.* New York: D. Appleton & Co., 1864.

Cornelia Peake McDonald. *A Woman's Civil

War: A Diary with Reminiscences of the War, from March 1862. Edited by Minrose C. Gwin. Madison, WI: University of Wisconsin Press, 1992.

James C. Mohr, editor. *The Cormany Diaries: A Northern Family in the Civil War.* Pittsburgh: University of Pittsburgh Press, 1982.

Andrew Ward. *The Slaves' War: The Civil War in the Words of Former Slaves.* New York: Houghton Mifflin, 2008.

C. Vann Woodward, editor. *Mary Chesnut's Civil War.* New Haven, CT: Yale University Press, 1981.

Notes

Epigraph: Clara Solomon, *The Civil War Diary of Clara Solomon: Growing Up in New Orleans, 1861–1862,* ed. Elliott Ashkenazi (Baton Rouge: Louisiana State University Press, 1995), 357.

1. Judith E. Harper, *Women During the Civil War: An Encyclopedia* (New York: Routledge, 2004).

2. Maria Lydig Daly, *Diary of a Union Lady, 1861–1865,* ed. Harold Earl Hammond (Lincoln: University of Nebraska Press, 2000), 298.

3. Cornelia Peake McDonald, *A Woman's*

Civil War: A Diary with Reminiscences of the War, from March 1862, ed. Minrose C. Gwin (Madison, WI: University of Wisconsin Press, 1992), 21.

4. Catherine Ann Devereaux Edmondston, *Journal of a Secesh Lady: The Diary of Catherine Ann Devereaux Edmonston,* ed. Beth G. Crabtree and James W. Patton (Raleigh, NC: North Carolina Division of Archives and History, 1999), 692.

5. Clara Solomon, *The Civil War Diary of Clara Solomon: Growing up in New Orleans, 1861–1862,* ed. Elliott Ashkenazi (Baton Rouge: Louisiana State University Press, 1995), 357.

6. Harper, *Women During the Civil War: An Encyclopedia,* 104. It should be acknowledged that the "diary" is very much a literary form centered in Western culture. The majority of American Indian tribes had their own ways of preserving women's perspectives, usually through oral storytelling. For more on their experiences during the war, see chapter 11 in this book. Similarly, enslaved African American women engaged in many other methods of storytelling to preserve their histories, including oral narrative poetry, quilt making, and song.

7. In Lydig, *Diary of a Union Lady,* 5.

8. Lydig, *Diary of a Union Lady,* 6.

9. Lydig, *Diary of a Union Lady,* 8.

10. Lydig, *Diary of a Union Lady,* 13.

11. Lydig, *Diary of a Union Lady,* 15.

12. Lydig, *Diary of a Union Lady,* 12.

13. Lydig, *Diary of a Union Lady,* 22–23.

14. Lydig, *Diary of a Union Lady,* 51–52.

15. Lydig, *Diary of a Union Lady,* 357.

16. Eliza Frances Andrew, in *A Day at a Time: The Diary Literature of American Women from 1764 to the Present,* ed. Margo Culley (Old Westbury, NY: Feminist Press, 1985), 136.

17. Emma LeConte, *When the World Ended: The Diary of Emma LeConte,* ed. Earl Schenk Miers (New York: Oxford University Press, 1957), 45–46.

18. Some sources say Winchester changed hands fourteen times, others say it was as many as seventy-two. Stanton stated this in March 1862 after visiting Winchester. Jonathan A. Noyalas, *Stonewall Jackson's 1862 Valley Campaign: War Comes to the Homefront* (Charleston: The History Press, 2010), 239.

19. Mary Greenhow Lee Papers, Winchester-Frederick County Historical Society; see http://www2.youseemore.com/handley/contentpages.asp?loc=591.

20. Mary Greenhow Lee Papers, March 11, 1862.

21. Mary Ann Loughborough, *My Cave Life in Vicksburg* (New York: D. Appleton & Co., 1864), 82.

22. Mary Boykin Chesnut, in Walter Sullivan, *The War the Women Lived: Female Voices from the American South* (Nashville, TN: J. S. Sanders & Company, 1995), 34.

23. In *Letters from Black America,* ed. Pamela Newkirk (New York: Farrar, Straus and Giroux, 2009), 9.

24. Carrie Berry, *A Confederate Girl: The Diary of Carrie Berry, 1864,* ed. Kerry Graves (Mankato, MN: Blue Earth Books, 2000), preface.

25. Berry, *A Confederate Girl,* August 3, 1864.

26. Berry, *A Confederate Girl,* October 4, 1864.

27. Berry, *A Confederate Girl,* August 14, 1864.

28. Berry, *A Confederate Girl,* September 7, 1864.

29. Berry, *A Confederate Girl,* September 14, 1864.

30. Berry, *A Confederate Girl,* December 7, 1864.

31. Berry, *A Confederate Girl,* September 8, 1864.

32. Berry, *A Confederate Girl,* September 10, 1864.

33. Berry, *A Confederate Girl,* October 2, 1864; October 23, 1864; November 12, 1864.

34. Berry, *A Confederate Girl,* November 8, 1864.

35. Berry, *A Confederate Girl,* December 22, 1864; December 26, 1864.

36. Sarah Morgan Dawson, *A Confederate Girl's Diary* (London: William Heinemann, 1913), 4.

37. Dawson, *A Confederate Girl's Diary,* 5.

38. Dawson, *A Confederate Girl's Diary,* 17–18.

39. Dawson, *A Confederate Girl's Diary,* 24.

40. Dawson, *A Confederate Girl's Diary,* 28.

41. Dawson, *A Confederate Girl's Diary,* 24.

42. Dawson, *A Confederate Girl's Diary,* 16, 39–43.

43. Dawson, *A Confederate Girl's Diary,* 46.

44. Dawson, *A Confederate Girl's Diary,* 212–13.

45. Dawson, *A Confederate Girl's Diary,* 383.

46. Dawson, *A Confederate Girl's Diary,* 426.

47. Dawson, *A Confederate Girl's Diary,* 433.

48. Dawson, *A Confederate Girl's Diary,* 440.

49. In Dawson, *A Confederate Girl's Diary,* xix.

50. Dawson, *A Confederate Girl's Diary,* 441.

51. Mary Chesnut, *Mary Chesnut's Civil War,* ed. C. Vann Woodward (New Haven, CT: Yale University Press, 1981), xli.

52. Lydig, *Diary of a Union Lady,* 353–54.

53. Andrew Ward, *The Slaves' War: The Civil War in the Words of Former Slaves* (New York: Houghton Mifflin, 2008), 11.

54. Emilie Davis, *Emilie Davis's Civil War: The Diaries of a Free Black Woman in Philadelphia, 1863–1865,* ed. Judith Giesberg (Philadelphia: The Pennsylvania State University Press, 2014), 193.

55. Emilie Davis, *Emilie Davis's Civil War,* 158.

56. McDonald, *A Woman's Civil War,* 235.

57. Dawson, *A Confederate Girl's Diary,* 440.

CHAPTER 7
CORNELIA PEAKE McDONALD
MOTHER AND DIARIST

"All the while the batteries thundered, and booming of cannon, the screaming of shells go shooting over our heads. . . . Donald, poor little four year old baby, hid his face on my knee and sobbed."
— Cornelia Peake McDonald

Cornelia Peake McDonald experienced the Civil War as a constantly shifting battle playing out in her literal backyard. Several contests were fought so close to her house that she and her children could feel the vibrations of exploding shells as they dropped from the sky. After such clashes, Cornelia helped care for hundreds of wounded soldiers who streamed to her door. In many ways, McDonald's story epitomizes the war experience of white women in the South — their fears, their losses, their grief. Cornelia's story further illustrates the way Civil War battlefields and home fronts were often one and the same, offering insight into the sentiment that can still be heard often in the South today: "There wasn't a war. There was an invasion."[1]

Cornelia spent her childhood in Alexandria, Virginia, where she read extensively and loved the poetry of Lord Byron. She often took long horseback rides into the mountains to sketch and paint. Her father was a doctor who owned slaves and moved his family to Palmyra, Missouri, in 1835, where several members of the family suffered from tuberculosis. Young Cornelia cared for her ill mother and spent long hours reading books by her side. When her mother passed away in 1837, Cornelia became even closer with her five older siblings. Not long after Cornelia's older sister married Edward McDonald, Edward's older brother, Angus, began courting Cornelia. Though Angus McDonald was a widower twenty-three years Cornelia's senior when he proposed marriage, she accepted.

Cornelia gave birth to her son Harry — the first of nine children born to the couple — the following year. Four sons were followed by a daughter; three additional sons were followed by a final daughter. Angus also had several children from his first marriage, so the household was a loud and boisterous one. Cornelia had a talent for visual art, and her children's earliest memories were of her sketching. The family settled at the north end of the Shenandoah Valley, a lush and fertile area that would become known as the "breadbasket of the Confederate army." Angus practiced law from their large home with ample gardens overlooking the town.

McDonald watched the approaching conflict with increasing concern. She later reflected, "The gentlemen, most of them . . . declared that once separated from the North we should have peace and prosperity to a degree before unknown."[2] Though Cornelia was raised around the system of slavery, she had misgivings about it from the time of her youth. This did not, of course, keep her from owning slaves and benefitting from the system. "I never in my heart thought slavery was right, and having in my childhood seen some of the worst instances of its abuse . . . I could not think how the men I most honored and admired, my husband among the rest, could constantly justify it."[3] More than anything else, Cornelia identified as a mother, and prior to the war, she accepted her role in Southern society and trusted the men around her to make political decisions. Her most fervent desire was to keep her family together in peace.

Virginia seceded, and when Angus became colonel of the 7th Virginia Cavalry in March 1862, her ordered world showed the first signs of change. To deal with the uncertainty, she began a journal. Even as drums beat out in the night and her husband rode off to an unknown fate, she sat at her desk and wrote: "Soon the heavy tramp of the marching columns died away in the distance. The rest of the night was spent in violent fits of weeping at the thought of being left, and of what might happen to that army before we should see it again."[4]

For a time, the war remained a distant thought as McDonald went about her days, tending to her home and children. But within a few months, the conflict arrived in Winchester. As the sounds of battle cascaded through town, Cornelia's oldest sons begged for permission to watch the skirmish from the top of a nearby hill. She told them they could go, but then realized how dangerous it might be. "I remained during all those miserable hours with my baby on my lap and the four little ones clustered round, listening to the dreadful storm of battle, and feeling, Ah! How bitterly, that at each shot some one . . . [was] being cut down like the grass."[5]

The next morning, a "worn and weary, ragged and hungry train of prisoners" entered the town. Civilians wanting to assist the wounded had been denied access to the battlefield, and the numbers of the suffering had reached critical proportions. "Every available place was turned into a hospital," Cornelia recorded. "The courthouse was full, the vacant banks, and even the churches. . . . The porch was strewed with dead men. Some had papers pinned to their coats telling who they were. . . . So pitiful they looked and so helpless."[6]

Like most women in Winchester, Cornelia left her children with servants and took turns nursing in the local hospitals, which were overwhelmed far beyond their capacity. Confronted for the first time with the human cost of war, she was completely overwhelmed by the endless rows of wounded soldiers. "Many, many poor sufferers were there, some so dreadfully mutilated that I was completely overcome by the sight. I wanted to be useful, and tried my best, but at the sight of one face that the surgeon uncovered, telling me that it must be washed, I thought I should faint. . . ." As Cornelia staggered toward the door, she brushed up against "a pile of amputated limbs heaped up near the door."[7] Overcome by the gruesome sights and smells, she had to stop and lean against the wall to keep from falling over. McDonald had to leave that day, but she returned, better prepared for what to expect, and, like many survivors, eventually grew able to tolerate the misery that followed each battle.

The Shenandoah Valley became a strategic location. As the Union and Confederate armies vied for control of the region, Winchester changed hands dozens of times. The staunchly Confederate town bristled each time the Union army occupied, and breathed a collective sigh of relief when the boys in gray regained control.

Often when the Union controlled Winchester, officers attempted to use the McDonald house as army headquarters. Fighting to keep her children alive during so much upheaval, Cornelia implored the soldiers to leave her family alone. One day in April, she found a US flag flying over her own front door and learned that a colonel had named her home his headquarters. Summoning her courage, McDonald asked the colonel if he could find quarters elsewhere, as her children were sick. He reminded Cornelia "that their presence would be a protection," and she saw "the wisdom of submitting." But though she might endure their presence, she refused to endure the flag: " 'You will confer a favor on me Col. Candee if you will have that flag removed from the front door if you must remain, as while it is there, I shall be obliged to enter at the back of the house.''[8] The colonel bristled at her statement, but by late afternoon, the flag had been moved.

Other officers were far less respectful to the home. When one regiment took over, the family awoke to find that "mud, mud, mud — was everywhere. Over, and on, and in everything. . . . Wet great coats hung dripping on every chair and great pools of water under them where they hung."[9] Cornelia did her best to live as normally as possible, though she was thrilled when the tide turned and Winchester again fell into Confederate hands. As they prepared to leave her house, one Union captain warned her, "I know that one Southerner is worth six Northern men in a fight, but we will win. . . . And, it will be a terrible day for you when we do."[10] Cornelia turned away, despising the man for his scare tactics. Soon after this conversation, the Confederate army marched down the street victorious and Cornelia described the celebration: "Old men and women, ladies and children, high and low, rich and poor, lined the streets . . . shouting for joy. . . . People in different spheres of life, who perhaps never before had exchanged a word, were shaking hands and weeping together."[11]

But Winchester's celebrations never lasted long. As the Union captain had warned, US soldiers reclaimed the town and took over the McDonald house once more. When paper grew scarce, Cornelia started keeping her diary in the margins of printed books pulled from her own library. Troops dug up Cornelia's garden to pilfer what they wanted and left the rest of the crops to spoil in the sun.

As the war entered its second year, its cost became very personal for the McDonalds. Cornelia's oldest son, Harry, left to join the Confederate forces, shortly before two of Cornelia's stepsons were killed in battle. Casualty lists poured in, sparing few families. "The whole town is in mourning," Cornelia recorded.[12]

Army camps that dotted Cornelia's land and the surrounding area harbored rampant diseases, and exposed the family to many dangers. When her youngest daughter, Bess, fell ill, Cornelia searched in vain for a doctor and medication to help the child, but with so many severely wounded soldiers to attend to, no medic had time to care for an ailing toddler. Bess grew sicker and sicker and finally died in her mother's helpless arms. "My sweet blue-eyed baby has left me forever," Cornelia wrote that night. "I held her night and day and I clung to her as if I could not give her up. . . . I held her in my arms, and as she breathed out her little life her eyes were fixed in my face. . . . The children stood around sobbing. . . . I could see or feel nothing but that it was only her lovely clay that I held, and that I must let go my hold."[13]

After the death of her daughter, Cornelia's journal became a place of mourning, a place to pour out her grief and to process all that had been lost since the conflict began. Some months later, she wrote: "When they gather at the fireside in the evening my precious little one is there, too, in my heart, and before my eyes often . . . and often her face fills the page of the book I am reading."[14] Though Bess certainly was a casualty of the war, she would not be counted as one of the fallen, revealing the way traditional war statistics fall far short of accurately measuring the true impact of conflict.

Christmas of 1862 drew near, and Cornelia considered how to observe the holiday in the midst of so much strife. She spent six dollars to hire a man to find them a turkey — a relatively large expense for such a time. Cornelia passed hours in the kitchen making cakes and biscuits for her children with the last of their flour. On Christmas Eve, some Union soldiers paid a visit, hoping to pilfer a holiday meal. Cornelia fought to hold on to the hard-won food, though the soldiers said she had no right to them since she was "secesh" — a slang term for secessionist. Determined not to let them make off with the holiday meal, Cornelia threatened to follow them back to camp and inform their commanding officer if they did not return the food. Her brave move succeeded, and the soldiers returned the turkey and most of the cakes.[15] As the Emancipation Proclamation had its intended impact,[16] slaves abandoned their posts and Confederate inflation soared. Cornelia found the demands of her household increasing every day, and she struggled to maintain normalcy with each slave's departure. Refugees fleeing toward freedom behind the lines of the Union army filled up the woods around Cornelia's home, and she was distressed by their suffering. "Women, and many children were killed in their flight through the streets, and thousands houseless, shelterless and starving are wandering in the woods, there to abide the frost and cold of the winter days and nights."[17]

A nurse who had looked after the McDonald children joined the migration with her own two children and attempted to flee toward the approaching Union army.[18]

Along the way, she ran out of supplies and was nearly starving when Cornelia encountered her. "When I saw her gaunt figure approaching the house with her poor baby on her arm . . . I could not believe the starved, forlorn creature could be my trim-looking, neat nurse. . . . She said she had had only three hard crackers in the three days past, and that she had turned back because she saw women drop by the roadside with their babies to die."[19] These passages offer a rare snapshot into the difficulties facing former slaves as they attempted to reach the safety of encroaching Northern lines.

During the second battle of Winchester in the summer of 1863, General Lee drove the Federals from the Shenandoah Valley, and Winchester remained under Confederate control. Casualties once more overwhelmed the town. The army appropriated the McDonald house for a makeshift hospital, leaving Cornelia and her children little space to exist in the middle of suffering and chaos. Wounded men were placed in every spare corner of the house, but more continued to arrive. "Crowd after crowd of men continued to pour into the porch till it was packed full. . . . Ambulances were backed up to let out their loads of wounded. . . . All the while the batteries thundered, and booming of cannon, the screaming of shells . . . go shooting over our heads. . . . Donald, poor little four year old baby, hid his face on my knee and sobbed."[20]

Overwhelmed by the magnitude of the destruction, Cornelia realized she would soon have to flee. She had no idea where to go, however, and every method of conveyance in town had been snatched up by either the army or refugees. After several days, Cornelia located a wagon and loaded her children and any remaining supplies inside. "Heavy-hearted I was," she wrote, "for I knew nothing of what was before me, and I felt that I had let go the only hold I had on anything."[21] A portion of her precious diary was lost in the chaos of flight.

Cornelia turned her wagon south to join family, but only a few days after their arrival, she received word that Angus lay ill in Richmond. She traveled to be by his side and was shocked by how much he had changed since she had last seen him. "I at first could not believe that wreck was my husband. Worn and emaciated, and with hair snow-white, he was unable to move from his chair."[22] The couple decided to travel the 140-mile distance to Lexington, where they had friends. In Lexington, Cornelia met a man who had a large home he was willing to rent in exchange for her teaching his children. In this way, she was able to secure both housing and employment. There, Cornelia cared for Angus while he convalesced. Not much is written of the intervening time between their arrival in Lexington in late summer 1863 and June 1864, but Angus eventually recovered enough to return to his army post.

Within a few months, Cornelia received news that Angus had disappeared. Desperate for information, Cornelia eventually learned that Angus had been captured and put in Atheneum prison in Wheeling, Virginia. He was very ill, and in November 1864, Cornelia received an urgent summons to come to his side.[23] Angus slipped from life a few hours before her arrival. Stricken by grief too large to contain, Cornelia wrote, "If I only had seen him to have spoken one word, I could have borne it better, but to have him go without one kind word or look, to be gone forever!"[24]

That same day Cornelia's sister also passed away. Shocked and distraught, she considered her prospects for the future. Well-meaning family members, who had traveled to her side, suggested splitting up the children among relatives, as they couldn't possibly imagine how Cornelia could manage on her own. She roused herself to consider their offer, then wrote, "I thanked all the family for their kindness . . . but told them I could not consent to part with the children, that they were all I had."[25]

Cornelia began teaching art and French classes to wealthy young ladies in town. Her older sons cut wood for the Confederate government and were allowed to keep some of it for their own use. In this way they survived the winter. The spring of 1865 carried "a dreadful certainty of disaster and defeat, knowing the end must be near."[26] Each day, Cornelia watched men walking away from the army and mourned her husband and stepsons who would never return.

Inflation soared and paper money became practically worthless. Two hundred dollars bought "a calico dress" and forty dollars "a pair of very coarse children's shoes,"[27] Cornelia recorded. It seemed to take every waking hour to find enough food to just keep her children alive, and she often subsisted all day on one roll and a cup of coffee. "I grew so thin and emaciated, and was so weak that I scarcely had strength to take my usual evening walk,"[28] she recorded.

The word of Lee's surrender, inevitable as

it may have been, struck each member of the family with a new sense of loss. "I felt as if the end of all things had come," Cornelia recorded, "at least for the Southern people. Grief and despair took possession of my heart, with a sense of humiliation that till then I did not know I could feel. The distress of the children was as great as mine . . . and each went about sad and dejected as if it was a personal matter."[29]

The events at Appomattox were soon overshadowed by the shot in Ford's theater, however, and Cornelia, like many Southerners, feared the retaliation of Northerners now that all hope for a separate country had melted away. "No mercy was to be expected from a nation of infuriated fanatics,"[30] she wrote.

Hoping that she and her children would be able to return to Winchester after the war, Cornelia sent her son to assess the situation, but he found the property completely uninhabitable. Though the conflict lay behind them, the McDonald family's situation was more dire than ever before. Starving and dealing with severe depression, Cornelia sought some way to continue living, though the desire to do so had left her long ago. Again, she turned to the pages of her journal to share her fear that God had forsaken her. As she wrote, her faith revived in "the remembrance of the goodness my God had shown me in the former dark hours I had passed through; how He had been near, my Heavenly Father, and how I had leaned on and trusted Him. . . . I got up, saying or trying to say . . . I trust me in my God."[31]

Feeling she had more friends among the dead than the living, Cornelia walked out through the night to the cemetery, where she sat alone and considered what should be done. Near the gate, she met a neighbor who said, "What can be the matter, you look so dreadfully?" In response, Cornelia burst out crying. Smothering her pride, she admitted, "We are starving, I and my children." This kind neighbor discreetly spread the word, and generous neighbors, who had far too little even for themselves, donated food supplies and money to help Cornelia and her children survive. The neighbor also told Cornelia there would be relief funds raised for widows and orphans of Confederate soldiers. Cornelia gathered strength to continue on.[32]

Slowly, things got better for the McDonalds. Cornelia continued teaching art and French lessons until 1873, when she was able to move into her own home in Louisville, Kentucky. Her sons eventually formed a successful architectural and construction company. As her children achieved careers and financial stability, they in turn took care of their mother, who had sacrificed so much on their behalf. The impact of the war years never completely left Cornelia. Books lost their appeal, for, as she said, "I had seen so much of real suffering, of conflict, danger and death, that for years I could read neither romance or history, for nothing equaled what I had seen and known. All tales of war and carnage, every story of sorrow and suffering paled before the sad scenes of misery I knew of."[33] In her final years, Cornelia began painting china, drawn to the art because the colors were permanent, "never fading or changing."

In Louisville, Cornelia completed her writings about the war, rewriting the lost portions from memory. After finishing the five-hundred-page record, she hand-wrote *eight* identical copies, one for each of her surviving children. In 1935, her son Hunter published his mother's account. The journal is a testament to a remarkable woman, whose life was shaken to its core by the casualties of war but who remained determined to survive, and equally determined to shelter her children from the worst of the conflict. In the diary's pages, we see Mc-Donald's relentless work for the future mingling with a longing for the past. In one of the rare moments of quiet in the midst of the conflict, when she allowed herself to look back and remember, she wrote: "The low moon is shining brightly, casting long black shadows on the ground. . . . I sit at the window late, late when every body else is asleep, to think of the past, and try to live over again the pleasant days that are gone."[34]

Further Reading

Stephen V. Ash. *A Year in the South: 1865: The True Story of Four Ordinary People Who Lived through the Most Tumultuous Twelve Months in American History.* New York: Palgrave Macmillan, 2002.

Cornelia Peake McDonald. *A Woman's Civil War: A Diary with Reminiscences of the War, from March 1862.* Edited by Minrose C. Gwin. Madison, WI: University of Wisconsin Press, 1992.

Notes

Epigraph: Cornelia Peake McDonald, *A Woman's Civil War: A Diary with Reminiscences of the War, from March 1862,* ed.

Minrose C. Gwin (Madison, WI: University of Wisconsin Press, 1992), 158.

1. I heard this sentiment several times on my research trip to the South in June of 2017, but perhaps most memorably from Bubba Bolm at the Vicksburg, Mississippi Old County Courthouse Museum, who also told me: "When the Yankees came through, they stole food and supplies from my grandmother and tried to burn her house. We still haven't forgiven them. But my grandmother used to always say, 'If it weren't for the Yankees, we wouldn't have any good stories to tell.' "

2. Cornelia Peake McDonald, *A Woman's Civil War: A Diary with Reminiscences of the War from 1862,* ed. Minrose C. Gwin (Madison, WI: University of Wisconsin Press, 1992), 247.

3. McDonald, *A Woman's Civil War,* 247.

4. McDonald, *A Woman's Civil War,* 23.

5. McDonald, *A Woman's Civil War,* 35.

6. McDonald, *A Woman's Civil War,* 36–37.

7. McDonald, *A Woman's Civil War,* 38.

8. McDonald, *A Woman's Civil War,* 28.

9. McDonald, *A Woman's Civil War,* 44.

10. McDonald, *A Woman's Civil War,* 56.

11. McDonald, *A Woman's Civil War,* 52.

12. McDonald, *A Woman's Civil War,* 67.

13. McDonald, *A Woman's Civil War,* 71.

14. McDonald, *A Woman's Civil War,* 116.

15. McDonald, *A Woman's Civil War,* 102.

16. Technically, the Emancipation Proclamation did not free any slaves, as it applied only to the states that were currently in rebellion. Lincoln could not free the slaves in the border states without risking more states joining the Confederacy. Therefore, the Emancipation Proclamation was largely a move intended to encourage slave revolt in the South.

17. McDonald, *A Woman's Civil War,* 99.

18. McDonald, *A Woman's Civil War,* 13.

19. McDonald, *A Woman's Civil War,* 65.

20. McDonald, *A Woman's Civil War,* 158.

21. McDonald, *A Woman's Civil War,* 165.

22. McDonald, *A Woman's Civil War,* 169.

23. McDonald, *A Woman's Civil War,* 214.

24. McDonald, *A Woman's Civil War,* 216.

25. McDonald, *A Woman's Civil War,* 217.

26. McDonald, *A Woman's Civil War,* 224.

27. McDonald, *A Woman's Civil War,* 210.

28. McDonald, *A Woman's Civil War,* 230.

29. McDonald, *A Woman's Civil War,* 232.

30. McDonald, *A Woman's Civil War,* 235.

31. McDonald, *A Woman's Civil War,* 242.

32. McDonald, *A Woman's Civil War,* 244–45.

33. McDonald, *A Woman's Civil War,* 231.

34. McDonald, *A Woman's Civil War,* 81.

CHAPTER 8
VOICES FROM SLAVERY

Harriet Jacobs

"After the reading [of the Emancipation Proclamation] we were told that we were all free, and could go when and where we pleased. My mother, who was standing by my side, leaned over and kissed her children, while tears of joy ran down her cheeks."
— Booker T. Washington

By 1862, casualties, destruction, and financial strain had brought the staggering costs of the war into sharp focus. Both the US and the Confederacy felt a need to make sense of the bloodshed. In some ways, it was easier for the white South to verbalize its reasons for fighting — as they believed their autonomy and existence were being threatened by an overbearing and corrupt federal government. Confederates could scarcely forget their very homes and families were at stake as the conflict played out in their own backyards. Much less clear was a picture of the world the white South would arrive in should they choose to surrender.

In the North, Lincoln had initially been careful not to identify slavery as the primary cause for waging battle, focusing instead on the preservation of the nation. But as the nation wearied of bloodshed, hazy platitudes about the unity of the country unraveled, and many began to feel it was time to let the South go their separate way. For Northerners farther removed from the scenes of the action, the only justification for the continued loss of life lay in viewing the war with a bolder goal than national preservation. As bloody months morphed into bloodier years, Lincoln recognized that, in order to continue, a new rallying cry was needed — one that would reframe the war as a struggle for freedom.

Lincoln believed such a shift was necessary to not only gain domestic support but to garner international favor as well. France and England were very close to officially recognizing the Confederate states' call for independence, just as a fledgling America had done fewer than a hundred years before. But no self-respecting European nation would raise arms in support of slavery; the practice had been successfully abolished on the other side of the Atlantic for decades. In a strictly literal sense, the Emancipation Proclamation accomplished exactly nothing: it freed only the slaves in rebel-held territory — that is, in exactly the areas where the United States government had no control or ability to implement such a policy. But in a larger sense, the Proclamation accomplished everything it hoped to and more. By successfully reframing the conflict as a fight against oppression, the measure held Europe at bay, and offered slaves in the South an even greater enticement to flee toward the North. Whether the war actually delivered on the Proclamation's promises is a different matter entirely, as many of the hopes raised for African Americans dissolved in the Reconstruction and Post-Reconstruction eras, the chains of slavery morphing into the bondage of Jim Crow.

Before, during, and after the war, most of the debate over slavery was engaged in by those who never directly experienced it. In the council rooms of the White House, in the chambers of Congress, and in local city halls, white men disputed, discussed, and deliberated the merits of a system they had perhaps seen but had never experienced — at least not from the point of view of the enslaved. First-hand accounts of slaves remain among the rarest documents of the war due to anti-literacy laws, the denial of legal marriage, the practice of withholding last names, and the constant rupture of families.

In the 1930s, recognition of the importance of survivors' voices led to the creation of *Born in Slavery: Slave Narratives from the Federal Writers' Project*. The collection includes more than 2,300 first-person accounts and 500 photographs from former slaves. Housed and digitized today by the Library of Congress,[1] the collection allows modern readers to read about slavery and the war from the perspective of those who lived through it. Lu Perkins of Texas described the war in vibrant terms: "I seen troubles in this land. I seen a big black wave of hating going on over the land and the folks getting poorer and poorer and starving for the childrens and the old."[2]

Anna Baker was eighty years old when she contributed to the Federal Writer's Project. She spoke of her mother, who had run away because the overseers "kep' a-tryin' to mess 'roun' wid her an' she wouldn' have nothin' to do wid 'em."[3]

Baker's mother returned after the war and told her former master she wanted her children. Anna admitted, "At firs' I was scared o' her, 'cause I didn' know who she was."[4]

While every person who once stood in chains experienced a different reality, the stories of Harriet Jacobs and Rachel Brownfield are more completely documented than most, and these two women's experiences illuminate in small part the lives of millions of women who existed under the oppressive system which was, at that time, sanctioned by law.

Harriet Jacobs would not have been surprised by Anna Baker's story. Jacobs was one of the first women to call national attention to the slave system's habit of depriving children of their mothers. In 1861, Jacobs published her autobiography, *Incidents in the Life of a Slave Girl,* under a pseudonym. Addressing her story mainly to white women in the North, Harriet described the devastation slavery wrought on women as individuals, wives, and mothers. Jacobs described women forced to watch their children be sold to far off destinations. Deprived of literacy, mothers and their children were rarely able to find the means to reunite, and families crumbled into farflung fragments. Pleading with readers to see slaves as people not unlike themselves, Harriet wrote, "[The slave mother] may be an ignorant creature, degraded by the system that has brutalized her from childhood; but she has a mother's instincts, and is capable of feeling a mother's agonies."[5] The book was one of the first to openly address the way women all too often found themselves trapped between a desire to avoid sexual exploitation and a commitment to protect their own children. It was a situation Jacobs knew all too well.

Born in Edenton, North Carolina, in 1813, Harriet Ann Jacobs's early years were relatively peaceful. Until the age of twelve, she rarely considered herself a slave, since her father was a self-supporting carpenter, and Harriet lived with her family in a residence separate from their owners. Jacobs worked for a mistress who taught her to sew and even write, but when the woman passed away, the true dangers of the slave system emerged from behind the façade.

Harriet found herself bequeathed to her mistress's daughter and sent off to work for Dr. James Norcom and his family. A few years later, Norcom began harassing Harriet, now age fifteen. Taking every opportunity to find her alone, Norcom whispered "words that scathed ear and brain like fire," telling the girl she was "made for his use, made to obey his command in everything; that [she] was nothing but a slave, whose will must and should surrender to his."[6] At first Jacobs tried to pretend she did not understand the meaning of these sexual overtures from a married man forty years her senior. When she responded with "indifference or contempt,"[7] he persisted. The doctor's wife soon began regarding Harriet with jealousy and suspicion, while the doctor threatened to kill her if she reported his advances. Despite her lack of power, Harriet remained adamant in her refusal, determining early on that though she might be "one of God's most powerless creatures," she was "resolved never to be conquered."[8]

Jacobs fell in love with a black free man, whom she requested permission to marry. Dr. Norcom refused to give consent and threatened to shoot the man if he stepped foot on his property. Fearing for her beau's life, Harriet encouraged him to go north; once he did, she found the loneliness and despair of life overwhelming. After a period of grieving, she entered into a relationship with a white man who treated her with affection, but they could not marry because of her slave status and the illegality of interracial marriages. Still, she wrote of this liaison: "There is something akin to freedom in having a lover who has no control over you, except that which he gains by kindness and attachment."[9] Though she undoubtedly cared for this man, she admitted that a large part of the attraction lay in asserting the small amount of control she had over an impossible situation — when she became pregnant, she hoped her lover would find a way to free both herself and her child.[10]

But when Jacobs informed Norcom she was pregnant, he flew into a rage and reminded her that all her future children would belong to him. Using physical force to punish Harriet for her refusal, Norcom held a razor to her throat, threw her down a flight of stairs, and shaved her head.[11] Still, she refused to give in.

Harriet gave birth to a son and, later, to a daughter. Though she adored her children, she could not help mourning their status as slaves, and swore to someday see them free. The children, meanwhile, provided Norcom with even more ammunition to wield against Jacobs; he often threatened to sell them if she didn't become his mistress. Finally Norcom sent Harriet to work at his son's plantation, saying that if she didn't comply with his wishes, he would see her "broken in" to work in the fields along with her children, some of the most physically demanding work that could be required of a slave. Realizing Norcom would never give up, Jacobs fled under cover of night. She sheltered in a snake-filled swamp while friends prepared a more permanent hiding spot — a tiny corner of Harriet's grandmother's attic. Harriet would inhabit this space for the better part of seven years as she waited for an opportunity to escape and redeem her children, who lived in the house below the attic.

Over the following years, Jacobs occasionally wrote letters to Mr. Norcom to confuse him about her location. Norcom made several trips to New York to find her but returned empty-handed, never realizing the woman he sought still remained a stone's throw from his own backyard. Eventually he sold Harriet's children to a slave trader, who in turn sold them to their father. Though their father did not immediately free them as he had promised, Jacobs felt a huge sense of relief, writing, "Whatever slavery might do to me, it could not shackle my children."[12]

During her long days in the attic, Harriet read and sewed, but her muscles atrophied from inactivity, leaving her in physical and psychological agony. As time passed and Norcom no longer searched for her as vigilantly, Jacobs found ways to regain muscle movement and strength. Harriet's children lived directly below her hiding place, and she could see and hear them often through the cracks in the floorboards, but she dared not reveal her location. After seven long years, relatives managed to obtain Harriet passage on a ship bound for the North. Jacobs revealed herself to her children, held them close, and told them she had always been near. She promised one day she would find a way to be with them again.

Harriet sailed into Philadelphia harbor, holding fast to the railing as she watched the sunrise "for the first time in our lives, on free soil."[13] Some months later she dispatched word to her family to send both her son and daughter north. "O reader, can you imagine my joy?" she wrote. "No, you cannot, unless you have been a slave mother."[14]

Incensed that Harriet had escaped, Norcom continued to search for her during occasional trips to the North, and her peaceful life was occasionally interrupted by the terror that he would reappear. Finally one of Harriet's employers reimbursed Norcom for the slave he had lost. Relieved and grateful to be released from the bonds of slavery after so long, Harriet wrote, "I laid my head on my pillow, for the first time, with the delightful consciousness of pure, unadulterated freedom."[15]

As Jacobs became involved in her new community in New York, friends encouraged her to write down her incredible life experiences. Though Victorian sexual mores often held women responsible for their own sexual abuse, Jacobs's narrative clearly established herself as the victim of the crime rather than the perpetrator. In a society just beginning to grapple with such issues, Harriet addressed the fear and shame that frequently accompanies abuse by admitting that "both pride and fear kept me silent."[16]

Harriet's memoir also revealed the use of religion within slavery as a tool of manipulation. Slave owners, she wrote, "seem to satisfy their consciences with the doctrine that God created the Africans to be slaves. What a libel upon the heavenly Father, who 'made of one blood all nations of men!' "[17] She recounted several tales of violence she had personally witnessed, saying, "It needs an abler pen than mine to describe the extremity of their sufferings, the depth of their degradation."[18] Released during the early years of the Civil War, her book raised a powerful argument in favor of continuing the conflict.

Reminiscences taught the nation the name of Harriet Jacobs, and she used that notoriety to lecture publically against slavery. Nursing for the United States Colored Troops and volunteering in contraband refugee camps in Washington, DC, filled the remainder of her time. Once Harriet's daughter, Louisa, finished school, the two women created a school for former slaves in Alexandria, Virginia. Jacobs dedicated the remainder of her life to empowering those who had endured slavery's horrors. After Lee's surrender, she returned briefly to Edenton, North Carolina, to bring relief aid to those suffering in the area. Her footsteps echoed once more across the wooden floors of her grandmother's house, but this time she came and went as a free woman. Louisa continued her mother's work and helped organize the National Association of Colored Women. Harriet's indefatigable spirit and tireless commitment to fight for right is captured in her own words: "My master had power and law on his side; I had a determined will. There is might in each."[19]

RACHEL MOORE BROWNFIELD

Many miles south of Harriet Jacobs, Rachel Ann Moore was born to an enslaved woman who bore at least nine children fathered by several different white men. The condition of slavery followed the mother, so Rachel and her siblings remained part of a shadowed society of children born to enslaved women and their masters. Rachel's father was a merchant known for his justice and integrity, which may have motivated him to have more involvement in his daughter's life than was often the case. Though he never officially acknowledged Rachel as his child, John Moore financially assisted her several times throughout her life, and they seem to have had a relatively close relationship.

At the age of fourteen, Rachel gave birth to her first child, which was followed quickly by two more; all three were fathered by a local white farmer. The births thrust Moore into adulthood, and she hired herself out to be able to provide for her children. In 1850, Rachel's master moved to Savannah, Georgia, taking his slaves with him. Rachel found the move advantageous, and she soon became integrated into Savannah's vibrant black subculture.

Rachel met and married Charles Brownfield in Savannah, with whom she went on to have twelve additional children. In this more forward-thinking city, Rachel proved herself a shrewd investor and apt businesswoman by selling milk, washing laundry, and taking in boarders. Rachel not only made ends meet, but scrupulously set aside all the profits of her business ventures. Within a few years, she opened a lavish boardinghouse on Bryan Street, where tenants and short-term visitors appreciated her mahogany dining table and sixteen elegant bedrooms.

By 1860, Rachel had amassed a small fortune and was ready to try for an even greater prize — her own freedom. If she succeeded, she would be forced to leave the state or take limited employment, so in some ways slavery actually allowed her more opportunities than she would have had as a free black in pre-war Georgia. But Rachel was determined to be free and to see her children free as well. Brownfield entered into a contractual agreement with her owner, Young J. Anderson, to pay $1,900 for herself and her children. Records show that Rachel made regular payments from her own earnings in gold, silver, and bank bills. Her efforts were augmented by her oldest daughters, who hired themselves out to contribute to the effort.

Charles, Rachel's husband, was forced into service for the Confederate army aboard the ironclad C.S.S. *Savannah*. As inflation of Confederate currency soared, panic beset the streets of Savannah. The population was starving. In the bread riots of 1864, a group of armed women broke into storehouses to steal food to feed their emaciated families.

With her boardinghouse and income savings, Rachel was spared the worst of the suffering. Knowing she was far luckier than most, she was determined to aid the Union cause, despite the well-known risks. Brownfield carried food and supplies to Union soldiers languishing in the nearby military prison. On one occasion, guards confiscated her supplies, and on another, a Confederate sympathizer violently knocked the basket from her hands. Rather than stopping her efforts, however, Rachel instead agreed to help with something far more dangerous. Union loyalists in Savannah had created an underground network to help prisoners of war escape camps where as many as twenty-eight percent would die from starvation and rampant diseases.[20] Like the Underground Railroad, this network used a series of safe houses to aid the soldiers escaping to the North. In spite of great personal risk, Rachel offered the use of her boardinghouse as a stop on this underground network. Famished prisoners escaping from Savannah's death camps found refuge in Rachel's home for weeks, and sometimes months, until they grew strong enough to continue onward.

Rumors and whispered secrets about Rachel's clandestine activities soon flew about town. More than once, authorities searched the premises, but they did not find hidden prisoners. One of Rachel's boarders, a washerwoman, did, however, come across a soldier in hiding. Shocked, she said, "If they had caught those people, there would have been a rope around [Rachel's] neck."[21] The family's landlord raised the rent in hopes Rachel would stop her activities, but she continued harboring fugitives even as the war intensified.

On September 24, 1864, Rachel paid the final installment of $550 to Young J. Anderson to purchase her freedom. Anderson had watched his own wealth disappear to Confederate inflation and knew full well that contracts with slaves were not legally binding. Though Rachel had met the terms of the contract and paid her debt in full, Anderson demanded an additional $1,800. When she refused, he withdrew her entire savings from the bank.[22] Sherman's soldiers descended upon Savannah before Anderson could sell Rachel; troops entered the town, bringing utter chaos, along with emancipation, on one of their last stops before reaching the sea. Angry citizens looted Savannah warehouses, and Rachel was injured by an escaped cart during the uproar.

Though she was thrilled by the army's arrival, Rachel was less enchanted when the troops decided to set up camp directly across from her boardinghouse. The commanding officers requested use of her home as a headquarters, limiting the entire family to the use of one room. For two weeks, the Brownfield family fed and housed the soldiers, while the army wore out the property, leaving it in ruins. Captain McIntosh promised to reimburse Rachel for damages, but paid nothing right away.[23]

With the war over at last, Rachel opened a new account at a freedman's bank and began saving money once more. A year later, the Brownfields bought twenty acres outside of Savannah, where the family farmed, and Rachel took in sewing and laundry. Rachel brought suit against her former master to regain the funds he had stolen, but the suit languished in the courts. She also sought reimbursement from the Southern Claims Commission for the damages inflicted by the Union army. Though Brownfield documented $1,659 in damages, she was paid only $253.70. Disappointed by the insufficient settlement, Rachel used it to purchase additional rental property. By her death at age fifty-one, she was able to leave her children with their educations, the deed to three properties, and more than $1,000 in cash — in addition to a legacy of tackling immensely difficult work in the face of overwhelming odds.[24]

■ ■ ■ ■

The irony that a nation founded on the principles of freedom would continue to justify the institution of slavery long after much of the rest of the world had abolished it was not lost on many great voices of the age. Frederick Douglass asked what the Fourth of July could possibly mean to those enslaved within America's borders,[25] and Susie King Taylor wrote, "In this 'land of the free' we are burned, tortured, and denied a fair trial, murdered for any imaginary wrong. . . . They say, 'One flag, one nation, one country indivisible.' Is this true? . . . It is hollow mockery."[26] The voices of Rachel Brownfield and Harriet Jacobs, culled from the stories of millions, represent a sliver of an American experience that went vastly undocumented by those who lived it.

Deep in the wilds of Louisiana, the Whitney Plantation is the only historic plantation home dedicated to telling the story of enslaved individuals. Powerful sculpture, memorials, and original cabins and artifacts preserve slave experience. As I wandered through the memorials being raised in those acres, I marveled at the forces that have sought to bury and erase the brutal reality of this history.

But the suffering of so many cannot be silenced.

Remaining slave narratives are a testament to humanity, which insists on finding a way to speak out and survive. Whether in a closeted garret, an underground network, or in relentless persistence, human beings *will* survive, will strive toward freedom, will foster their ability to learn and progress, in spite of impossible odds. The voices that remain from slavery stand as a reminder of where this nation has been, an understanding of where we are today, and a plea to continue fighting oppression today and into the future. As Ellen Vaden, survivor of slavery in Arkansas, once said: "Times been changing ever since I come in this world. It is the people cause the times to change."[27]

Further Reading

Born in Slavery: Slave Narratives from the Federal Writers' Project, 1936–1938. Available online from the Library of Congress at https://www.loc.gov/collections/slave-narratives-from-the-federal-writers-project-1936-to-1938/about-this-collection/.

David T. Dixon. "The Wealthiest Slave in Savannah, Rachel Brownfield and the

True Price of Freedom." In *Georgia Backroads,* Summer 2014.

Rhiannon Giddens. *Freedom Highway,* Nonesuch Records, 2017. (A musical interpretation of firsthand slave accounts.)

Harriet Jacobs. *Harriet Jacobs: Incidents in the Life of a Slave Girl.* New York: Dover, 2001.

Andrew Ward. *The Slaves' War: The Civil War in the Words of Former Slaves.* New York: Houghton Mifflin, 2008.

Jean Fagan Yellin. *Harriet Jacobs: A Life.* New York: Basic Civitas Books, 2004.

Notes

Epigraph: Booker T. Washington, *Up from Slavery: An Autobiography* (New York: Doubleday, Page, and Co, 1907), 21. Washington was nine years old when the Emancipation Proclamation was read.

1. *Born in Slavery: Slave Narratives from the Federal Writers' Project, 1936-1938;* retrieved from Library of Congress, https://www.loc.gov/collections/slave-narratives-from-the-federal-writers-project-1936-to-1938/about-this-collection/. Accessed January 15, 2018.

2. Andrew Ward, *The Slaves' War: The Civil War in the Words of Former Slaves* (New

York: Houghton Mifflin, 2008), 7.

3. *Federal Writers' Project: Slave Narrative Project, Vol. 9, Mississippi, Allen-Young.* 1936. Manuscript/Mixed Material. Retrieved from the Library of Congress, https://www.loc.gov/resource/mesn.090/?sp=17. Accessed January 16, 2018.

4. *FWP: Slave Narrative, Vol 9.* Retrieved from the Library of Congress, https://www.loc.gov/resource/mesn.090/?sp=19. Accessed January 16, 2018.

5. Harriet Jacobs, *Harriet Jacobs: Incidents in the Life of a Slave Girl* (New York, Dover, 2001) 17.

6. Jacobs, *Incidents in the Life of a Slave Girl,* 18.

7. Jacobs, *Incidents in the Life of a Slave Girl,* 26.

8. Jacobs, *Incidents in the Life of a Slave Girl,* 18.

9. Jacobs, *Incidents in the Life of a Slave Girl,* 48.

10. See Jacobs, *Incidents in the Life of a Slave Girl,* 48–50.

11. Jacobs, *Incidents in the Life of a Slave Girl,* 52.

12. Jacobs, *Incidents in the Life of a Slave Girl,* 92.

13. Jacobs, *Incidents in the Life of a Slave*

Girl, 131.

14. Jacobs, *Incidents in the Life of a Slave Girl,* 142.

15. Jacobs, *Incidents in the Life of a Slave Girl,* 149.

16. Jacobs, *Incidents in the Life of a Slave Girl,* 29.

17. Jacobs, *Incidents in the Life of a Slave Girl,* 40.

18. Jacobs, *Incidents in the Life of a Slave Girl,* 46.

19. Jacobs, *Incidents in the Life of a Slave Girl,* 73.

20. The prisoner of war camps in Georgia had some of the highest fatalities in the nation. Though numbers for the Savannah camps specifically are difficult to separate from others, the notorious Andersonville prison in nearby Atlanta documented twenty-eight percent fatalities. See *Andersonville: Prisoner of War Camp, Teaching with Historic Places Lesson Plan.* Retrieved from the National Park Service, https://www.nps.gov/nr/twhp/wwwlps/lessons/11andersonville/11facts1.htm. Accessed January 16, 2018.

21. In David T. Dixon, "The Wealthiest Slave in Savannah, Rachel Brownfield and the True Price of Freedom." In *Georgia*

Backroads (Summer 2014): 9.

22. Dixon, "The Wealthiest Slave in Savannah," 9.

23. Dixon, "The Wealthiest Slave in Savannah," 10.

24. Dixon, "The Wealthiest Slave in Savannah," 10–11.

25. Frederick Douglass, "What to the Slave is the Fourth of July?" July 5, 1852, retrieved from TeachingAmericanHistory.org. http://teachingamericanhistory.org/library/document/what-to-the-slave-is-the-fourth-of-july/. Accessed January 16, 2018.

26. Susie King Taylor, *Reminiscences of My Life in Camp* (Boston: Susie King Taylor, 1902), 61–62.

27. *FWP: Slave Narrative, Vol. 9.* Retrieved from the Library of Congress, https://www.loc.gov/resource/mesn.027/?sp=7. Accessed January 16, 2018.

CHAPTER 9
MARY ANN SHADD CARY
RECRUITER, NEWSPAPER EDITOR, AND ABOLITIONIST

"We do not know her equal."
— Frederick Douglass,
speaking of Mary Ann Shadd Cary

Mary Ann Shadd's childhood home served as a stop on the Underground Railroad, and she came from a long line of free African Americans who owned successful small businesses: a popular boot and shoe store, a tea shop, and a prospering farm. With the benefit of both education and intellectually engaged parents on her side, Mary Ann found the more prevalent social attitudes about her race and gender deeply vexing. She was destined to become an important and vocal advocate for change.

From the time Mary Ann was ten years old, the family lived in West Chester, Pennsylvania, on the outskirts of Philadelphia, where they enjoyed a number of privileges and opportunities few other black families of the era could claim. Mary Ann was the oldest of thirteen children, and she was educated by Quakers, one of the few religions that believed in education for girls. Shadd's father worked for the abolitionist newspaper *The Liberator,* and it was in his newspaper that Mary Ann first heard about the racial tolerance of Canada. After completing her schooling with honors, Mary

Ann taught children in all-black schools in Delaware, New Jersey, and Pennsylvania for nearly twelve years.

The Fugitive Slave Act of 1850 caused great upheaval in Shadd's family and her broader community. The law, which required Northern states to return fugitive slaves to their Southern masters, ostensibly did not affect free blacks such as the Shadd family; but in reality *all* African Americans were placed in jeopardy, as slave catchers frequently pulled free men and women off the streets, stripped them of identification, and sold them south. Frederick Douglass called the law "The Bloodhound Bill" and claimed it would "place law in direct antagonism with some of the noblest and strongest feelings of human nature."[1] Since blacks could not serve on juries or testify in their own defense in court, the law created an extremely dangerous climate for anyone of African descent, particularly those who had escaped the horrors of slavery.

Outraged by this new legislation, Mary Ann decided to emigrate to Canada, and she convinced her younger brother to join her. Her parents soon followed. In Canada, people of color were able to vote, hold property, and serve on juries, and Mary Ann maintained that in Canada West "the common ground on which all honest and respectable [people] meet, is that of innate hatred of American Slavery."[2] Mary Ann believed that race is socially constructed and that racial differences amount to nothing more than biological differences in complexion to which humans assign interpretation and significance. This concept, to which most sociologists today ascribe, was decades ahead of her time in the 1800s.[3] Hoping that thriving communities in the far North could provide a solution to the racial divides of the United States, Shadd advised organizations working with former slaves, "Do not let the question be asked what shall we do with them? Send them along."[4]

To Shadd, the solution to helping African Americans achieve greater economic independence always came back to education. When she arrived in Canada West, Shadd started a racially integrated school that primarily educated children of former slaves. She dedicated much of her life's work to this cause.

Shadd was never afraid to voice her opinion, even when it got her into trouble. Soon after her arrival, she found herself at odds with Henry Bibb and his wife, Mary, who didn't share Shadd's opinions about the best way to help and educate the newly arriving refugees. Bibb had escaped from slavery himself and created a nonprofit group that claimed to raise money to better the lives of former slaves. In reality, Bibb bought the land and sold it to refugees at a high profit; he also allegedly misused funds and donations. This corruption, masquerading as a philanthropic venture, enraged Mary Ann, and she dared to publicly criticize Bibb, which eventually cost her her teaching position.

Craving a wider audience for her thoughts, in 1853, Mary Ann launched a newspaper to spread the sentiments of universal rights. *The Provincial Freeman* became the first newspaper in North America to be published by an African American woman, and it soon developed a reputation as a bold and fearless voice for freedom. In one issue Mary Ann proclaimed, "We are an abolitionist — we do not want the slave to remain in his chains a second. . . . We go further, we want that the colored man should live in America — should 'plant his tree' deep in the soil . . . he must have his rights."[5] To support the paper, Mary Ann traveled extensively, giving lectures and public speeches on the topics of women's rights and the abolition of slavery. The paper circulated widely in Canada as well as in northern cities of the United States.

In 1856, Mary Ann married Thomas F. Cary, a barber who supported the work of *the Provincial Freeman.* Thomas brought three children to the marriage, and Mary Ann gave birth to her first child a few years later. She continued publishing her newspaper, but the demands of family and finances eventually proved too difficult, and she had to stop publication after six years. Though she frequently told her husband to rest more and cut down on his smoking habit, his health remained fragile, and she was four months pregnant with their second child when he passed away at the age of thirty-five. After five years of marriage, Mary Ann found herself a widow with five children to support. The personal chaos of Shadd's life reflected the political strife of North America, and less than a month after her husband's death, the Southern states seceded. To support herself and her children, Mary Ann moved closer to family and opened an integrated school with her sister.[6]

South of the Canadian border, a debate raged over whether African Americans should be permitted to fight in the war. Mary Ann watched the discussion, never dreaming how much the strife would soon impact her own life. The United States government's early stance was that the conflict was "a white man's war."[7] Those in power feared the uneasy truce with the border states would be compromised if African American men were allowed to enlist, particularly as many of those wanting to enlist were legally bound to be returned by the Fugitive Slave Act. As the war stretched from months into years, public support for the war began to falter and belief in the preservation of "The Union" was simply not enough motivation for Northern armies to continue facing such a determined foe. Black leaders such as Frederick Douglass believed that reason must be a call for the end of slavery. He encouraged African Americans to see the war as one that would lead to new opportunity, and he pled with Lincoln to permit them to fight.

Lincoln had exhausted both his funds and his supply of willing soldiers, and he grew increasingly convinced of the need to do as Douglass suggested. Though some black leaders remained unconvinced soldiers should risk their lives for a country that held "no promised future in store,"[8] by 1862 congressional approval led the way for African Americans to aid in war efforts, first as laborers building fortifications and then gradually in military service. The Emancipation Proclamation of 1863 flung the doors open wide for the creation of black regiments; within six months, more than thirty had been organized. Centuries of racist attitudes led whites to wonder whether African Americans were fit for battle, but early service put that fear to rest. General James Blunt said of the men under his command, "I never saw such fighting as was done by the Negro regiment."[9]

Prominent abolitionist and doctor Martin Delany became a driving force behind the effort to recruit black soldiers for the war effort. He personally knew of Mary Ann Shadd Cary's talent for public speaking and believed she would be perfect for the job. He wrote to Cary, imploring her to join his recruiting efforts. Recognizing the opportunity, Mary Ann decided to temporarily leave her school duties and children with her family and return to the United States. Earning $15 for every former slave and $5 for every freed man she recruited, the job required Mary Ann to travel widely across the Midwestern states, speak in public forums, write recruiting tracts, set up recruiting stations, and draw upon her numerous contacts in the abolitionist movement — in short, the position was a perfect match for her interests and aptitudes.[10]

Though the number of recruits Mary Ann enlisted is unknown, she was by all contemporary accounts a highly successful recruiter. Lieutenant Colonel Benjamin S. Pardee wrote, requesting her assistance, "I have heard from them a most excellent report concerning you."[11] The allure of equality, distant and enticing, provided one of the main methods of persuasion to join the Union's forces. One recruiting tract, like those Cary routinely wrote, rather ironically promised black soldiers, "show yourselves worthy soldiers, and the petty prejudices that weak and wicked men have endeavored to excite against you will be forever swallowed up in the gratitude of a nation that will own and applaud your heroic deeds."[12]

Working across the Midwest, Mary Ann canvassed Ohio, Pennsylvania, Michigan, Wisconsin, Illinois, and Indiana. Many of Mary Ann's recruits found their way into the Connecticut 29th Colored Troops, which laid siege to the cities of Petersburg and Richmond and were the first infantry unit to enter Richmond after it fell.[13] Soldiers enlisted by Cary contributed with outstanding service records to the Union's ability to continue the fight. An estimated 180,000 African American soldiers served in 163 units in the Union army, participating in every major campaign from 1864 to 1865; 40,000 of those who served would lose their lives in the effort; 200 would earn "Butler Medals," medals of honor created by Benjamin Butler; and twenty-five would earn Congressional Medals of Honor.[14] In the final months of the war, Mary Ann returned to her children with great financial stability, knowing she had contributed directly to the conflict's outcome.

From her Northern vantage point, Mary Ann warily watched the changes of Reconstruction even as her disillusionment increased over racial prejudice in Canada. When the 13th Amendment abolished slavery forever, Cary decided to move her children back to the United States. The family settled briefly in Detroit and then in Washington, DC, where Mary Ann became a principal of Lincoln Mission School, one of Washington's sixty black public schools.[15]

In her forties, Cary decided she would be able to make the greatest impact for the causes in which she believed — women's suffrage and racial equality — by entering the field of law. She became the first African American woman to gain admission to law school at Howard University in 1869, continuing to work as a school principal by day and studying law by night. Mary Ann graduated at the age of sixty and practiced law to some extent. Her greatest contribution in her final years, however, were her efforts to carve a place for black women in the national women's suffrage movement. Cary continued to be a loud and outspoken advocate for change for the remainder of her life. She lived out her final years with her children and passed away in 1893. Frederick Douglass, at times a critic and at times a friend, praised Mary Ann's "unceasing industry . . . unconquerable zeal and commendable ability," concluding, "We do not know her equal."[16]

Further Reading

Moira Ferguson. *Nine Black Women: An Anthology of Nineteenth-Century Writers from the United States, Canada, Bermuda, and the Caribbean.* New York: Routledge, 1998.

Carla L. Peterson. *"Doers of the Word": African-American Women Speakers and Writers in the North (1830–1880).* New York: Oxford University Press, 1995.

Jane Rhodes. *Mary Ann Shadd Cary: The Black Press and Protest in the Nineteenth Century.* Bloomington, IN: Indiana University Press, 1998.

Notes

Epigraph: In Jane Rhodes, *Mary Ann Shadd Cary: The Black Press and Protest in the Nineteenth Century* (Bloomington, IN: Indiana University Press, 1998), xi.

1. In Rhodes, *Mary Ann Shadd Cary,* 28.
2. Mary A. Shadd, *A Plea for Emigration, or, Notes of Canada West* (Detroit: George W. Pattison, 1852), 36.
3. Franz Boas (1858–1942), a German-born anthropologist and professor of anthropology at Columbia University, established the idea of cultural relativism, working in the 1910s to 1940s to debunk the idea that Western civilization was superior to other societies. Nazis frequently burned his books. It is largely due to Boas's influence that social scientists began to see that race itself is a social construct.
4. In *Nine Black Women: An Anthology of Nineteenth-Century Writers from the United States, Canada, Bermuda, and Caribbean,* ed. Moira Ferguson (New York: Routledge, 1998), 234.
5. In *Nine Black Women,* 218.
6. In Rhodes, *Mary Ann Shadd Cary,* 85.
7. In New York City, a group of black men began drilling. The police ordered them to stop with these words. Hondon B. Hargrove, *Black Union Soldiers in the War*

(Jefferson, NC: McFarland & Co., 1988), 3.

8. In Rhodes, *Mary Ann Shadd Cary,* 137.

9. In George Washington Williams, *A History of the Negro Troops in the War of the Rebellion, 1861–1865* (New York: Harper & Brothers, 1888), 322.

10. Rhodes, *Mary Ann Shadd Cary,* 153–55.

11. Rhodes, *Mary Ann Shadd Cary,* 157.

12. Rhodes, *Mary Ann Shadd Cary,* 160.

13. Moorland-Spingarn Research Center, Howard University, Washington, D.C., Mary Ann Shadd Cary Papers, Certificates and Statements, 3.

14. This number includes both soldiers and sailors. See Elsie Freeman, Wynell Burroughs Schamel, and Jean West, "The Fight for Equal Rights: A Recruiting Poster for Black Soldiers in the Civil War," in *Social Education* 56, 2 (February 1992): 118–20.

15. Rhodes, *Mary Ann Shadd Cary,* 173–75.

16. In Rhodes, *Mary Ann Shadd Cary,* xi.

CHAPTER 10
ARMS TO SAVE
NURSES, MEDICS, AND
BATTLEFIELD RELIEF

Clara Barton

"No soldier has eaten harder 'tack' or slept on barer ground, or under more malarious damps than I have within these four years."
— Clara Barton,
Civil War nurse

For centuries of time, the practice of home care based on natural remedies has been part of the wisdom tradition of women. The knowledge of herbs to cure a baby's colic and a poultice to ease headaches was passed down as part of midwifery and childcare, from mother to daughter. Within the walls of the home, women have long been the guardians of life and death, caring for the young, infirm, and aged, with only the very wealthy relying on routine access to physicians. Although women could claim extensive experience treating ill family members, Victorian-era gender norms reserved the medical profession grounded in scientific study for males alone. As armies began assembling along newly drawn borders in 1861, the vast majority of nurses were male, while women were viewed as being "utterly and decidedly unfit for such service."[1]

A typical army nurse in the first year of the conflict was a convalescing male soldier[2] with no formal medical training, who served on active duty in a makeshift hospital unit. But as casualties mounted to an overwhelming level, women leveraged nursing shortages to carve new inroads into the field of professional medicine. Shortly after the war's outbreak, Dr. Elizabeth Blackwell, the first woman to graduate from an American medical school, spearheaded the Women's Central Association for Relief (WCAR) to prepare female nurses for wartime service. She held preliminary meetings with interested women at the New York Infirmary for Women and Children, a hospital she founded in 1857. But just as Blackwell's program started gaining traction, the United States government granted Dorothea Dix, who had worked in mental health facilities but had no formal medical training, exclusive permission to recruit female army nurses. Civic leaders working in conjunction with the War Department[3] set up the United States Sanitary Commission (USSC) under the direction of a clergyman, rather than a doctor, and this commission absorbed the remainder of Dr. Blackwell's efforts. Dr. Blackwell and her sister, who was also a medical professional, were not invited to participate. Frustrated by the sudden upheaval, Blackwell wrote to a friend, "The Doctors would not permit us to come forward . . . and they refused to have anything to do with the nurse education plan if 'the Miss Blackwells were going to engineer the matter.' "[4] The military medical establishment was not ready to relinquish power to a female physician just yet.

The Sanitary Commission's choice of Dix, with no training, over Dr. Blackwell, a medical school graduate, may seem baffling; but the solution to the riddle can be found in the fact that Dr. Blackwell was seeking to establish herself as a medical professional, while Dix offered her services on a completely voluntary basis. In an era that viewed working women with skepticism, Dix's efforts were regarded as superior since they were offered from "purely" altruistic motives.[5] Many Civil War-era sources distinguished between lower-class women working "for pay" and upper-class women who gave "purely" from a desire to serve humanity. The paltry pay of forty cents per day plus rations could scarcely be seen as enticement to endure such exhaustive hours and dangerous conditions, but few writers of the day could conceive that a woman might be attracted to the profession for noble reasons *and* be in a position where they needed income to support themselves. In reality, male and female medics in the field often claimed patriotism and altruism as main motivators for their work. Anna Holstein, who nursed in field hospitals for the Army of the Potomac, said, "As the soldiers went out from among us, there came the yearning wish to lessen somewhat the hardships. . . . With all loyal women of the land, I worked zealously in their behalf; worked, because there was irresistible impulse *to do, to act.* Anything but idleness, when our armies were preparing for combat, and we knew not who should be the first to fall."[6]

Thus, Dorothea Dix, who had a reputation for being a bit of a drill sergeant, went to work gathering recruits, while Dr. Blackwell departed for a more appreciative England after the war. The US Sanitary Commission successfully contributed to war financing, raising a staggering fifty million dollars in supplies and funding, mostly through Sanitary Fairs organized and coordinated by volunteers. At the close of one of the largest sanitary fairs held at the Patent Office in Washington, DC, in March 1864, Abraham Lincoln said, "In this extraordinary war, extraordinary developments have manifest themselves . . . and among these manifestations nothing has been more remarkable than these fairs for the relief of suffering soldiers and their families. And the chief agents of these fairs are the women of America . . . if all that has been said by orators and poets since the creation of the world in praise of women were applied to the women of America, it would not do them justice for their conduct during this war."[7]

To participate in the nurse training program, Dix requested women aged thirty-five or older, of "matronly" form, with "habits of neatness, order, sobriety, and industry," and routinely rejected candidates for being "too pretty."[8] Broader Victorian society shared Dix's fear of young, attractive nurses working in a hospital of lonely men far away from their families. The nature of the hospital environment meant unmarried women might be exposed to morally "compromising" situations — including undesirable romantic admirers and accidental lessons in male anatomy. Young and alone for the first time in her life, Cornelia Hancock of Pennsylvania wrote home to assure her family that her "virtue" was safe.[9]

Beyond the question of morality lay the issue of a woman's ability to do the work of nursing itself. Many believed females could not withstand the grueling conditions of the battlefront, where medical staff worked long, physically demanding hours under a sweltering sun, often without adequate food and shelter, while enduring a constant barrage of gruesome images and exposure to virulent diseases. Sophronia Bucklin described the raw conditions of army hospitals: "In the cold dreary weeks . . . we endured the cold without sufficient bedding . . . and with no provision made for fires. On bitter mornings we rose shivering, broke the ice in our pails, and washed our numb hands and faces, then went out into the raw air . . . thence to the wards."[10] Certainly, for many men and women, the wartime environment proved overwhelming, but protests over frail female dispositions would surely have entertained enslaved and lower-class women, whose regular lives required plenty of physical labor. Though some women found themselves unable to adjust, many more endured and thrived under the difficult circumstances.

In addition to the challenging work itself, female nurses also had to contend with hostility from those who felt war was no place for them. Women who held positions of authority were double targets, but none were immune. When Amanda Stearns became a ward master in Armory Square Hospital, the surgeon in charge greeted her with a "little nod" and a "Humph!" A second ward master intervened, making sure Stearns received the respect she deserved, but not every nurse found such a defendant.[11] Sophronia Bucklin, working in Virginia, wondered if surgeons planned "by systematic course of ill-treatment toward women nurses, to drive them from the service."[12] Doctors informed Mary Livermore that Catholic nuns made ideal nurses because they were "properly subordinate."[13] Certainly, hospitals with negative work environments witnessed much higher turnover rates among their female staff. Some women were even told directly that by participating in wartime service, they would grow coarse and unrefined, leaving them unfit to be mothers and wives in the future. One of thousands of medics who rejected these notions, Sarah Palmer insisted she would "[stand] firm against the tide of popular opinion" and against "the loud echoed cry, 'it is no place for woman.' " Palmer continued, "It was well that no one held a bond over me strong enough to restrain me from performing my plain duty."[14]

Over the course of four years of conflict, the persistence of female nurses began to pay off. Rejected by Dix for being "too pretty," Cornelia Hancock sneaked back to another area of service where the casualties were so overwhelming it didn't matter. She was put to work.[15] As the scale of the disaster overwhelmed all resources, people increasingly overlooked concerns about the propriety of female nurses for recognition that the war would require sacrifices from the entire nation. Nurses viewed their efforts in hospitals as equivalent with a man's service in the army. Author Louisa May Alcott, who served as an army nurse before contracting typhoid, wrote a fictional account based on her service: "I tore home through the December slush as if the rebels were after me, and like many another recruit, burst in upon my family with the announcement — 'I've enlisted!' "[16]

As casualties increased, some women were drawn to nursing to assuage their own grief. By being able to help other suffering soldiers, women felt more connected to loved ones who had died far away and, all too often, lay in unmarked graves. Julia S. Wheelock of Michigan traveled to Virginia to care for her wounded brother but found he had died shortly before her arrival. Grieving his loss, Julia wrote, "I resolved to remain and endeavor, God being my helper, to do for others as I fain would have done for my dear brother."[17]

The situation provided many opportunities for women eager to think beyond the traditional confines of gender roles. Clara Barton, who recognized the ground shifting underneath her, said, "I have an almost complete disregard of precedent, and a faith in the possibility of something better. It irritates me to be told how things have always been done. I defy the tyranny of precedent."[18] Eventually more than 20,000 women from both North and South would take up paid nursing posts during the conflict.[19]

Beyond the number of official army medics, thousands more volunteered temporarily when casualties inundated their own communities. Many opened their homes to act as makeshift hospitals, laying out wounded men "on verandas, in halls, in drawing-rooms of stately mansions."[20] Louisa Triplett Harrison of Richmond, Virginia, said: "In our house, as in many in Richmond, one large room was devoted to the sick and wounded soldiers. The cots were arranged as in a hospital, and filled again as soon as emptied."[21] As the wounded sought shelter and relief, civilians were confronted by the cost of war in images they would never forget. Cornelia Hancock, a volunteer from New Jersey, said that in an army hospital, "I saw for the first time what war meant. Hundreds of desperately wounded men were stretched out on boards laid across . . . pews as closely as they could be packed together. . . . I seemed to stand breast-high in a sea of anguish."[22] Constance Cary spent hours searching a battlefield for a wounded cousin and wrote: "The impression of that day was ineffaceable. It left me permanently convinced that nothing is worth war."[23]

Other women became overnight relief workers when raging battles literally arrived at their own front doors. The principal of an all-girls boarding school near Gettysburg, Pennsylvania, Carrie Sheads hoped to take her students on a field trip to visit the Union military camps in early July 1863, but before she got the chance, the sound of close-range gunfire awoke the entire school one morning. The school building was hit more than sixty times during the battle but remained standing.[24] Trapped inside as the battle raged around them for three days, Sheads and her students helped bring wounded soldiers inside, then worked as impromptu nurses attending to the suffering men. Along with many barns and churches in the small town of Gettysburg, the school became an overnight hospital ward to deal with staggering casualties that approached 50,000.[25] The school building still stands in Gettysburg to this day, with a mortar shell permanently lodged in one wall.

THE WORK AT HAND

The lack of consistency in nurse training and certification led to a great deal of ambiguity in the work women might be assigned. Lower-class white and enslaved or free black nurses were routinely assigned the most physically strenuous responsibilities, such as laundering soiled linens, rinsing bedpans, cooking, and general housekeeping; some historians estimate that in many places up to fifty percent of female hospital personnel were African American.[26] Nurses like Susie King Taylor and Harriet Jacobs cared for soldiers from the Colored Troops, who often went untreated by white medical personnel. Nurses with more experience or training were responsible for administering medication and dressing wounds. Sophronia Bucklin of New York offered this insight into daily routines: "Beds were to be made, hands and faces stripped of the hideous mask of blood and grime, matted hair to be combed out over the bronzed brows, and gaping wounds to be sponged with soft water, till cleansed of the gore and filth preparatory to the dressing."[27]

Levy Pember, tasked with feeding 600 soldiers, found rats to be a constant problem — they ate their way through much needed provisions and even nibbled bandages directly off patients' limbs.[28] Diseases rather than bullets claimed the lives of two-thirds of soldiers. When typhoid, cholera, small-pox, and scarlet fever ran rampant through hospitals, nurses also risked illness or death from exposure.

Working on battlefields carried the added danger of injury from stray bullets. Juliet Ann Opie Hopkins, who operated three hospitals for Alabama troops, was shot twice in the left hip while removing soldiers from the field during the Battle of Seven Pines.[29] Annie Etheridge joined the army with her husband as a laundress, then stayed on after he deserted, serving as a cook and nurse as well. Etheridge was among the first to provide relief and food to the wounded after a battle. Even after being shot in the hand by a stray bullet, she remained at her post, much to the gratitude of the soldiers she served.[30]

Some nurses grew accustomed to the intensity of field service, where many came to thrive. Kate Cumming, who nursed in

Tennessee, wrote, "The men are lying all over the house, on their blankets, just as they were brought from the battlefield. They are in the hall, on the gallery, and crowded into very small rooms. The foul air from this mass of human beings at first made me giddy and sick, but I soon got over it. We have to walk, and when we give the men any thing, kneel in blood and water; but we think nothing of it at all."[31]

Middle- and upper-class white women, usually serving as volunteers, administered food to patients, comforted them, and transcribed letters to loved ones. Frequently they took down a patient's last words and sent descriptions of a soldier's final moments along with a lock of hair or other memento to comfort grieving families. These volunteer nurses typically had more flexibility with their time than their paid counterparts; some sat beside shell-shocked soldiers grappling with the throes of PTSD. Louisa May Alcott described a boy from New Jersey who relived the battle of Fredericksburg again and again, pulling at her arm to move her away from the path of a shell falling only in his mind. "He lay cheering his comrades on," she wrote, "hurrying them back, then counting them as they fell around him."[32]

ELLEN ORBISON HARRIS

Shortly after the declaration of war, Philadelphian women met and formed a Ladies' Aid Society to give relief to those affected by the fighting. Ellen Orbison Harris — called Mrs. John Harris by her contemporaries — served as secretary of the Aid Society but soon longed to be more directly involved. She began following the army from place to place, offering relief on every major battlefield in Virginia, Maryland, Pennsylvania, and Tennessee. It was not uncommon for Harris to work until, exhausted, she could stand no more. Then she lay down, not far from those she served, "with the sick, wounded, and dying all around . . . the last sounds falling upon my ear being groans from the operating room."[33]

Though Ellen had no official medical training, she was married to a doctor and learned the basics of nursing at his side. Many accounts praise her for her tenderness in helping those closest to death — holding their hands in their last moments and sending words of comfort to wives and mothers. Harris worked on board ships that removed the wounded from battlefields; she wrote: "When I left the boat, at eleven o'clock at night, I was obliged to wash all my skirts, being drabbled in the mingled blood of Federal and Confederate soldiers, which covered many portions of the floor. I was obliged to kneel between them to wash their faces. This is war."[34]

One of the first to arrive at Gettysburg before the guns ceased firing, Harris brought much needed chloroform to ease suffering. She traveled as near as possible to the scene of the front, treating soldiers even as they streamed away from the battle. On July 9, 1863, five days after the guns fell silent at Gettysburg, Harris wrote: "I am full of work and sorrow. The appearance of things here beggars all description. Our dead lie unburied, and our wounded neglected. Numbers have been drowned by the sudden rising of the waters in the creek bottoms, and thousands of them are still naked and starving. God pity us!"[35]

MOTHER BICKERDYKE

Though the vast majority of female nurses served without broader recognition, a few achieved notoriety. Mary Ann Bickerdyke of Ohio became known as Mother Bickerdyke and worked in tent hospitals close to the front, the grittiest of all medical war environments. Bickerdyke also served on a hospital steamer that made trips between battlefields and hospitals, rescuing men who had been left behind. She earned the admiration of the nation when she insisted on leaving the boat at night to walk the length of the muddy, icy field and ensure that no soldier was left behind. Less than impressed by military bureaucracy, Mother Bickerdyke gained a reputation for simply going around it and carrying on with her job. She once told a doctor attempting to challenge her methods: "It's of no use for you to try to tie me up with your red tape. There's too much to be done to stop for that."[36]

Bickerdyke despised corruption and didn't mind challenging it, no matter how high ranking the perpetrator might be. At one point, she realized food and liquor intended for the wounded were being pilfered by surgeons and ward masters, so she confronted the chief surgeon on the issue. He ordered her to resign her post. In a classic Bickerdyke response, she refused to abdicate and took measures into her own hands by spiking stewed peaches with ipecac syrup instead. Bickerdyke easily identified the culprits the next day; as they writhed and vomited, she told them next time she would use rat poison. If anyone attempted to pull rank on her, she was known to reply: "I have received my authority from the Lord God

Mary Ann Bickerdyke

Almighty; have you anything that ranks higher than that?"[37] Her no-nonsense approach appeared to pay off; when a surgeon complained to General Ulysses S. Grant about Bickerdyke's manner, Grant allegedly responded: "My God man, Mother Bickerdyke outranks everybody, even Lincoln. If you have run amok of her, I advise you to get out quickly before she has you under arrest."[38]

PHOEBE PEMBER

Phoebe Pember of Charleston, South Carolina, lost her husband in the first year of the war and decided to nurse Confederate soldiers in his memory. Pember eventually became chief matron of Chimborazo Hospital, the world's largest military hospital at the time, which treated 76,000 patients between 1862 and 1865.[39] An incredibly efficient organizer, Pember was widely respected for her integrity and will of steel. One night, just as she was finally about to leave the hospital for the evening, wagonloads of wounded men from a nearby battlefield arrived at her door. The surgeon in charge informed the ambulance drivers the men had to be taken somewhere else, but Pember couldn't stand the thought of the soldiers "being driven from one full hospital to another" and begged the surgeon to allow her to care for them. Pushing aside her own exhaustion, Phoebe tended to these new arrivals long past midnight, "armed with lint, bandages, castile soap, and a basin of warm water."[40]

Pember washed and dressed the wounds of one man who had been injured in both arms. "I hope that I have not hurt you much," she said when she finished. He replied, " 'Sure they be the most illegant

[sic] pair of hands that ever touched me, and the lightest. . . . And I am all right now.' "[41] When a doctor told Pember there was no hope for another wounded soldier, Phoebe treated the man for five days and nights, providing food and drink, sitting by his side and reading to him until the end drew near. Finally the man said, "Tell [my mother] I died in what I consider the defense of civil rights and liberties. I may be wrong. God alone knows. Say how kindly I was nursed, and that I had all I needed. I cannot thank you, for I have no breath, but we will meet up there."[42] He pointed toward heaven and closed his eyes for the last time.

Pember remained by her sick and wounded even as the city of Richmond fell around them. After the Union army took over, Pember was the last to leave, refusing to go until every remaining Confederate soldier had been healed, buried, or transferred home. In her memoir published after the war, Phoebe addressed the criticisms of some who claimed a woman would lose her delicacy by working in a hospital environment, asking, "How can this be? . . . In the midst of suffering and death . . . closing the eyes of boys hardly old enough to realize man's sorrows . . . a woman must soar beyond the conventional modesty considered correct under different circumstances. If the ordeal does not chasten and purify her nature, if the contemplation of suffering and endurance does not make her wiser and better . . . then, indeed a hospital has been no fit place for her!"[43]

SALLY TOMPKINS

When wounded men from the First Battle of Bull Run flooded the city of Richmond, Virginia, Sally Tompkins opened a private military hospital at her own expense and operated it for the duration of the war. Placing extra emphasis on hygiene, Tompkins's establishment — Robertson Hospital — earned a reputation for excellent care and held the highest rate of survival of any civil war hospital, North or South. Of 1,333 patients treated by Tompkins during the four years of war, only 73 perished, a mortality rate of 5.5 percent, compared with the staggering 41.2 percent of soldier fatalities at nearby facilities.[44] At one point, the Confederate government planned to consolidate all army hospitals, which meant Sally's hospital would be discontinued, but Tompkins gained an audience with President Jefferson Davis and presented her institution's statistical success. Impressed, Davis not only allowed her hospital to continue, but he named Sally a commissioned officer so the facility could be absorbed into the military. Captain Sally Tompkins became the only woman, North or South, to receive an official army commission; she also received several marriage proposals from her patients, but turned them down to focus on her work. Tompkins continued treating patients for several months after the war had ended and was heralded as a hero by her community. Diarist Mary Chesnut volunteered as a nurse in Robertson Hospital and recorded, "Our Florence Nightingale is Sally Tompkins."[45]

CLARA BARTON

The woman whose name is practically synonymous with Civil War nursing needs little introduction; Clara Barton had an incredible ability to witness a need and set about at once to meet it. Shortly after the fall of Fort Sumter, the former schoolteacher and patent office employee learned that wounded soldiers from a Massachusetts unit had been transported to Washington, DC, though no army hospitals would be able to receive them. Clara departed at once, arriving in time to meet the transport at the station and arrange temporary housing for the soldiers. To gather and organize supplies, Barton visited dozens of local businesses and relief groups. Clara refused to work within the government system as she found the official processes far too tedious. Within a few months, Barton's personal supply stores filled three warehouses, and the army began notifying her before a battle took place. To those who felt women did not belong near the conflict, Barton said: "If you chance to feel that the positions I occupied were rough and unseemly for a woman — I can only reply that they were rough and unseemly for men."[46]

As the war progressed, Barton increasingly chose to serve at the frontlines, often arriving on the scene with her supply carriage before the fighting had even concluded. She was one of the first on the scene at Antietam, Maryland, the site of the single bloodiest day in American military history, where more than 22,000 men fell in the space of just twelve hours. Covered in blood and grime, Clara moved across the field, a solitary female figure in that vast wilderness of pain — removing visible bullets with her knife, and wrapping wounds with cornhusks when she ran out of bandages. As she held one wounded man, Barton felt a tug at her sleeve; she glanced down to find a bullet had passed through her clothes and killed the man she held in her arms. Laying the body down, Barton decided she would never sew up the hole in her sleeve. As night fell, Clara built a fire and prepared caldrons of stew to spoon into the mouths of the hungry and fallen. Days later, Barton collapsed from lack of sleep and the beginnings of typhoid fever. When she finally chanced to look in a mirror, she found her face was the "color of gunpowder, deep blue."[47]

During the Battle of Fredericksburg, Barton worked at Lacy House, a plantation home turned Union army headquarters and hospital. Clara assisted wounded soldiers from both sides and refused to leave her post even when shells hit the house itself. In her journal she recorded the names of the men who died and the location of their burials. From the eastern entrance to Lacy House, Barton watched in horror as a shell exploded on the grounds outside, severing a man's artery. Comrades dragged him inside, and Barton applied her handkerchief as a tourniquet. Each time she passed him after that, he whispered, "You saved my life."[48] Dr. James Dunn, a surgeon who often worked by Barton's side, once said, "In my feeble estimation, General McClellan, with all his laurels, sinks into insignificance beside the true heroine of the age, the angel of the battlefield."[49] Dunn's nickname for the beloved nurse stuck. As the war stretched on and some wondered how long Barton would continue working, she replied, "I don't know how long it has been since my ear has been free from the roll of a drum. Tis the music I sleep by and I love it. . . . I shall remain here while anyone remains, and do whatever comes to my hand. I may be compelled to face danger, but never fear it, and while our soldiers can stand and fight, I can stand and feed and nurse them."[50] After the war, Barton would go on to establish the American Red Cross and serve as its first president for twenty-three years.

MOVING FORWARD

Women who served in Civil War hospitals felt a sense of pride and satisfaction in their accomplishments, as many worked outside their homes and traveled for the first time in their lives. Occasionally these new employees needed to remind their families that times were swiftly changing. When Emily Parsons's parents wrote to tell her she should abandon her position and return home, she replied, "I am in the army just as Chauncey [her brother] is, and I must be held to work just as he is."[51]

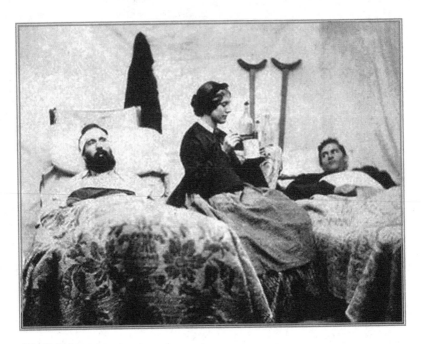

Civil War nurse

During her years of service, Sarah Palmer found that in spite of what she had been told, war "*was* a place for woman." She continued, "All of man's boasted ingenuity had been expended to devise terrible engines with which to kill and maim God's own image and if war was right, it was right for women to go with brothers, and husbands, and sons."[52] Even when their families did not understand, women found satisfaction in the gratitude of soldiers who, hungry for home and family, cherished their interaction with kind nurses. Hannah Ropes wrote to her daughter, "I miss you and mother very much, but I can't go back unless you need me more than the soldiers do."[53]

By the end of the war, Clara Barton believed that "Woman was at least fifty years in advance of the normal position which continued peace would have assigned her."[54] A door had opened, and through it, many women glimpsed a world they might never have seen otherwise. In a letter to her sister, Amanda Stearns confided, "This life is one of constant interest and excitement, like a journey through foreign lands."[55] Indeed, for women stepping beyond the boundaries of home and community for the first time in their lives, wartime service *was* a journey through a foreign land. Working aboard a Union hospital ship, Katharine Wormeley dashed off a letter to a friend as she waited for another load of wounded soldiers to arrive. "Goodbye!" she penned. *"This is life."*[56]

Further Reading

Louisa May Alcott. *Civil War Hospital Sketches.* Dover Publications, 2006.

M. R. Cordell. *Courageous Women of the Civil War: Soldiers, Spies, Medics, and*

More. Chicago: Chicago Review Press, 2016.

Judith E. Harper. *Women During the Civil War: An Encyclopedia.* New York: Routledge, 2004.

Elizabeth Brown Pryor. *Clara Barton: Professional Angel.* Philadelphia: University of Pennsylvania Press, 1988.

Jane E. Schultz. *Women at the Front: Hospital Workers in Civil War America.* Chapel Hill: University of North Carolina Press, 2004.

Nina Silber. *Daughters of the Union: Northern Women Fight the Civil War.* Cambridge: Harvard University Press, 2005.

Notes

Epigraph: In Nina Silber, *Daughters of the Union: Northern Women Fight the Civil War* (Cambridge: Harvard University Press, 2005), 201.

1. Judith E. Harper, *Women During the Civil War: An Encyclopedia* (New York: Routledge, 2004), 285.

2. It is estimated that 75 percent of ranking personnel in Union and Confederate hospital were male. See Harper, *Women During the Civil War,* 316.

3. See http://archives.nypl.org/mss/3101.

4. Nancy Kline, *Elizabeth Blackwell: A*

Doctor's Triumph (Berkeley, CA: Conari Press, 1997), 163.

5. For a discussion of the politics involved in this decision, see Jane E. Schultz, *Women at the Front: Hospital Workers in Civil War America* (Chapel Hill, NC: University of North Carolina Press, 2004).

6. In Elizabeth D. Leonard, *Yankee Women: Gender Battles in the Civil War* (New York: W. W. Norton, 1994), 4.

7. J.G. Holland, *Holland's Life of Abraham Lincoln* (Lincoln, NE: University of Nebraska Press, 1998), 464.

8. Silber, *Daughters of the Union,* 198.

9. Leonard, *Yankee Women,* 15.

10. In Leonard, *Yankee Women,* 13.

11. Leonard, *Yankee Women,* 30.

12. In Leonard, *Yankee Women,* 33.

13. Silber, *Daughters of the Union,* 212.

14. Leonard, *Yankee Women,* 13–14.

15. M. R. Cordell, *Courageous Women of the Civil War: Soldiers, Spies, Medics, and More* (Chicago: Chicago Review Press, 2016), 130.

16. Louisa May Alcott, in *The Civil War Era: An Anthology of Sources,* ed. Lyde Cullen Sizer and Jim Cullen (Malden, MA: Blackwell Publishing, 2005), 294.

17. In Leonard, *Yankee Women,* 9.

18. Clara Barton, Missing Soldiers Office Museum, Washington, DC.

19. Harper, *Women During the Civil War,* 285.

20. Sara Agnes Pryor, *Reminiscences of Peace and War* (New York: Macmillan, 1904), 171.

21. Louisa Triplett Harrison, in Thomas Cooper De Leon, *Belles, Beaux, and Brains of the 60's* (New York: G.W. Dillingham Co, 1907), 127.

22. In Ina Chang, *A Separate Battle: Women and the Civil War* (New York: Puffin Books, 1996), 39.

23. Mrs. Burton Harrison [Constance Cary], *Recollections, Grave and Gay* (New York: Charles Scribners Sons, 1911), 83.

24. Today, Sheads's school still stands in Gettysburg, with a 10-pound shell embedded in the building's mortar. See https://www.gettysburgdaily.com/gettysburgs-carrie-sheads-house-artillery-shell/.

25. Frank Moore, *Women of the War: Their Heroism and Self-Sacrifice* (Hartford, CT: S. S. Scranton & Co., 1866), 238–44.

26. Jane E. Schultz, *Women at the Front: Hospital Workers in Civil War America* (Chapel Hill, NC: University of North Carolina Press, 2004). See also Drew Gil-

pin Faust, *Mothers of Invention: Women of the Slaveholding South in the American Civil War* (Chapel Hill, NC: University of North Carolina Press, 1996), 92.

27. In Leonard, *Yankee Women,* 19.

28. Harper, *Women During the Civil War,* 302.

29. Glenna R. Schroeder-Lein, *Encyclopedia of Civil War Medicine* (New York: Routledge, 2008), 137–39.

30. Cordell, *Courageous Women of the Civil War,* 165.

31. Kate Cumming, in *Women in History: A Social, Political, and Cultural Encyclopedia and Document Collection: Precolonial North America to the Early Republic,* ed. Peg A. Lamphier and Rosanne Welch (Santa Barbara, CA: ABC-CLIO, 2017), 239.

32. In Chang, *A Separate Battle,* 34.

33. In L. P. Brockett and Mary C. Vaughan, *Woman's Work in the Civil War: A Record of Heroism, Patriotism, and Patience* (Philadelphia: Zeigler, McCurdy & Co., 1867), 153.

34. In Moore, *Women of the War,* 185.

35. In Moore, *Women of the War,* 201.

36. Chang, *A Separate Battle,* 41.

37. Chang, *A Separate Battle,* 41–42.

38. Mary Elizabeth Massey, *Women in the*

Civil War (Lincoln: University of Nebraska Press, 1966), 49.

39. Harper, *Women During the Civil War,* 301.

40. Pheobe Yates Pember, *A Southern Woman's Story: Life in Confederate Richmond* (New York: G. W. Carelton & Co., 1879), 57.

41. Pember, *A Southern Woman's Story,* 57–58.

42. Pember, *A Southern Woman's Story,* 60.

43. Pember, *A Southern Woman's Story,* 191–92.

44. Harper, *Women During the Civil War,* 374.

45. Bonnie Tsui, *She Went to the Field: Women Soldiers of the Civil War* (Guilford, CT: Globe Pequot Press, 2006).

46. In William Eleazor Barton, *The Life of Clara Barton, Founder of the American Red Cross, Volume 1* (Boston: Houghton Mifflin Company, 1922), 173.

47. Elizabeth Brown Pryor, *Clara Barton: Professional Angel* (Philadelphia: University of Pennsylvania Press, 1987), 98–102.

48. Stephen B. Oates, *A Woman of Valor: Clara Barton and the Civil War* (New York: Simon and Schuster, 1994).

49. "Clara Barton at Antietam," National

Park Service; see https://www.nps.gov/anti/learn/historyculture/clarabarton.htm. Accessed February 16, 2018.

50. In Elizabeth Brown Pryor, *Clara Barton: Professional Angel* (Philadelphia: University of Pennsylvania Press, 1987), 79.

51. In Silber, *Daughters of the Union,* 201.

52. In Leonard, *Yankee Women,* 40.

53. In Leonard, *Yankee Women,* 46.

54. Richard Nelson Current, *The Essentials of American History to 1877* (New York: Knopf, 1985), 150.

55. In Leonard, *Yankee Women,* 47.

56. In Leonard, *Yankee Women,* 46.

CHAPTER 11
DR. MARY WALKER
CIVIL WAR SURGEON AND ACTIVIST

> "Why has she been muzzled so callously and so persistently? . . . We receive the impression of an unkind and intolerant conspiracy against one of the most gifted and willing teachers of the age."
> — The Washington Post,
> *speaking of Dr. Mary Walker*

Wielding sentiments plucked from future decades, Dr. Mary Walker's voice echoes with a resonance both eerie and remarkable, a harbinger of a future time she would never live to see. Public opinion has rarely been kind to such time travelers, unmoored and drifting through centuries, and it's unsurprising that Mary was regarded by her contemporaries as crazy, baffling, dangerous, or a combination of all three. In spite of inevitable conflict with those less ready for change than she, Dr. Mary Edwards Walker accomplished what would have been impressive in any era; but in Victorian times, her achievements set her apart as both strange and inspiring.

A strong, opinionated, intelligent woman, Dr. Walker created a stir wherever she went. In an age that imposed severe separation between genders, Dr. Walker advised men to be more involved at home and women to lend their voices to public discourse. In a period that considered upper-class women too fragile for work, Dr. Walker dared suggest that labor is necessary to every human being, whether married, divorced, single, rich, or poor.[1] In a place where abolitionists were called extremists, Dr. Walker advocated for universal suffrage regardless of race, gender, or economic status. And in a time when women wore corsets, hoop skirts, and layers of stifling fabrics, Mary refused to participate in what she termed "dressical slavery."[2]

In one of the more generous contemporary reactions to Mary's persona, B. M. Reese in Annapolis acknowledged that Mary was "a powerfull [sic] writer and a deep thinker . . . there is truth in all you assert — but who cares to hear truth from that little nondescript Dr. Mary Walker. . . . of course you have a right to dress as you please, but it would please me and many others to see you doff them funny looking coat & breeches."[3] Mary ignored Reese's advice regarding her clothing preferences and dressed as she pleased, advocating "reform dress" — a practical, calf-length skirt worn over trousers. Even today, when it's difficult to imagine so much animosity evoked by a few inches of fabric, accounts of Dr. Walker's life are still plagued by an obsession with her appearance. It's unfortunate that something as trivial as clothing would distract from Mary's far more important accomplishments.

Mary Walker was raised in a home and a community steeped in radical ideas. Her parents, Vesta and Alvah Walker, were freethinkers, nearly as far ahead of their time as their daughter was destined to be. The couple established a farm in the Oswego area of New York State, a hotbed of progressive ideas. Their home became a stop on the Underground Railroad, and at a very young age, Mary listened to eye-witness accounts of slavery. The Grimké sisters and Frederick Douglass passed through the area on lecture tours, while the writings of Lydia Maria Child circulated through the community, igniting the intellect of Mary and her siblings.

The Walkers enjoyed a highly egalitarian marriage, and Alvah frequently cleaned the house, while Vesta and her daughters did their share of work in the fields, dressed for labor. This arrangement, which was a dramatic departure from other homes of the day, seemed entirely natural to Mary. Encouraged by her parents to explore different religious sects, Mary was drawn to Spiritualism, one of the few groups of the day that advocated women speaking in public.

Believing that girls deserved an education, the Walkers encouraged their youngest daughter's interest in her father's medical library; Mary read everything she could find on the subjects of anatomy and hygiene.[4] From a very young age, she was fascinated by the practice of medicine and solicited local doctors — unsuccessfully — for the chance to observe a surgery. It was a dramatic shock when Walker left behind the bastion of free thinking from her youth and realized the broader country was decades behind Central New York in its attitudes. Fortunately, progressive stances were not all she adopted from her parents' attitudes — from them she also retained a fierce determination to find her own way. She said, "I have felt that I must do what I believed to be right regardless of consequences. . . . I could not do otherwise."[5] It was a sentiment that would not go untested.

The medical world of Walker's day predated the discovery of germ theory, and the cause behind the spread of infectious disease remained unknown. The use of leeches, bloodletting, and administering large doses of potent drugs were all still common medical practices. At odds with these invasive techniques, some medical schools advocated homeopathic approaches. Syracuse Medical College was one of these, and Mary chose to apply to their "eclectic" program, which encouraged the use of natural patient treatment, an attitude which fit Mary's thinking about the world. Syracuse was also one of the few medical schools to admit women, and Mary entered six years after Elizabeth Blackwell made history by receiving her medical degree. Mary studied obstetrics, anatomy, surgery, pathology, disease treatment, pharmacology, and pediatrics, and interned with practicing physicians between terms. One of Mary's professors recalled her as a "faithful and diligent student" who made "rapid and meritorious progress."[6] She graduated in 1855, earning the right to practice medicine and surgery. Mary spoke at the commencement ceremony, where she addressed the challenges facing female physicians and advised her graduating classmates that the most important trait to learn as a physician or as a human being was liberty of thought.[7]

Shortly after graduation, in November of 1855, Walker married fellow medical student Albert Miller. Albert was a similarly progressive medical student, and Mary believed she was entering into a marriage of equals, one she hoped would be reminiscent of the enduring love her parents shared. Walker wore a reform-style wedding dress, retained her last name, and rewrote the traditional wedding vows to omit the word *obey* and fashion a ceremony where "*two* intelligent beings" promised "to love and cherish each other as long as both shall live.' "[8] Medical journals reported on the nuptials of these two promising physicians who set up their practice with a sign that read: "Miller and Walker, Physicians." Initially, Mary planned to treat only women and children, but as her reputation within the community grew, she occasionally attended to male patients as well.

Walker also began a writing career, contributing regularly to publications addressing the health benefits of the dress reform movement[9] and delivering public lectures on the same topic. Just when Dr. Walker seemed capable of almost anything, in the summer of 1859 she began missing deadlines and skipping important conventions, and in the spring of 1860 her medical practice was abruptly relocated.

During the intervening months, Mary had discovered that her husband had engaged in multiple extramarital affairs. When she confronted him about it, Albert not only admitted to the infidelity but suggested that she might do likewise. Devastated, Mary ordered him to leave the house; a short time later, Mary's brother-in-law found her weeping hysterically. Plagued with the difficulty and expense of moving her practice while grappling with intense emotional distress, Walker began divorce proceedings, which would take years to finalize. Eventually the courts would establish that Albert had fathered an illegitimate child, seduced at least one female patient, and used occupational travels to engage in multiple affairs. Mary started over again as a childless, divorced, educated professional who insisted on wearing trousers under her dresses. Any one of these aspects of her life might have led to social ostracism in Victorian society — the combination of all these elements together unleashed decades of mischaracterization and hostility.

Dr. Walker contended that corsets compressed female organs, impeded movement, and made women more likely to become light-headed. Long skirts also collected dirt and filth from the streets, contributing to illness, she liked to point out. Though society acknowledged the necessity of wearing pants or "bloomers" to engage in menial labor, nineteenth-century culture had no place for women who wore the costume outside of a wheat field. Other members of the National Women's Suffrage Association, who temporarily adopted the style, later abandoned it as too extreme, and labeled Mary crazy for her persistence. From Walker's earliest adoption of the outfit, people felt licensed to verbally and physically assault her. On one occasion, a farmer watched her walk home and gathered a group of local boys to chase after her, yelling obscenities and throwing stones and eggs.[10] This type of treatment was not uncommon; Mary frequently had objects thrown at her in the street, including a brick thrown by a twelve-year-old boy in Washington.[11] In fact, Mary was actually arrested for her attire on multiple occasions; in Baltimore in 1873, a police officer locked her in her hotel room for wearing "male attire." In New York City in 1878, another officer demanded to know if Mary was a man or a woman.[12] Though these type of incidents caused Walker pain, she refused to back down from dressing as she chose. She confided, "Many times I have gone to my room and wept after being publicly derided. No one knows, or will ever know, what it has cost me to live up to my principles . . . but I have done it, and am not sorry for it."[13]

Most early female doctors faced challenges building successful practices once they finished medical school, and Dr. Walker was no exception, particularly once she struck out on her own. When the Civil War broke out, Mary hoped the country might be willing to set aside concerns over gender and employ a talented female physician. After closing her private practice, Walker lent her services to the Union army, believing "the God of justice would not allow the war to end without its developing into a war of liberation."[14] Shortly after the battle of Bull Run, Walker departed for the nation's capital to seek an appointment as surgeon from the Secretary of War.

Secretary Simon Cameron, however, was appalled by Walker's dress as well as her gender and emphatically denied her an appointment. Undeterred, Walker visited a number of makeshift hospitals set up to treat the wounded, hoping medical personnel dealing with casualties on the ground would be less judgmental. In the US Patent Office, Mary met Dr. J. N. Green, who ran the overnight hospital. Overwhelmed and understaffed, Green was in no position to turn Dr. Walker away. He wrote to the Surgeon General requesting permission to hire Mary as an assistant surgeon, but his request was denied. Frustrated by the relentless bureaucracy, Mary offered to volunteer as assistant surgeon without pay. A sympathetic Green offered her part of his own salary (which Mary declined) and gratefully provided her with the workload of a commissioned surgeon.

Soon Dr. Walker oversaw hundreds of patients, worked long nights and slept at intervals during the day in an alcove of the Patent Office hospital. She wrote to her family, eager about the work before her and the opportunity to see the effects of war firsthand. Smallpox ravaged the soldier population, and Dr. Walker established a ward for men suffering with the dreaded disease. In rare moments of free time, Mary explored the Patent Office, interested in each new invention. Word of this female surgeon in her quirky dress began to spread, and soldiers and their families came to love and appreciate her service.

After months of faithful work, Walker asked Dr. Green to write again, requesting her appointment as assistant surgeon. Green obliged and wrote that Mary had "rendered me valuable assistance . . . and I commend her as an intelligent and judicious physician."[15] Once more, his request was denied. The *New York Tribune* reported: "She can amputate a limb with the skill of an old surgeon, and administer medicine equally as well. Strange to say that, although she has frequently applied for a permanent position in the medical corps, she has never been formally assigned to any particular duty. . . . We will add that the lady referred to is exceedingly popular among the soldiers in the hospitals, and is undoubtedly doing much good."[16] Though the army didn't mind making use of Dr. Walker's services, they were clearly not ready to recognize and compensate her for her work.

Like all Civil War surgeons, Dr. Walker confronted the controversial issue of limb amputation. In Northern hospitals, the procedure was typically done with anesthetic, but infection rates remained high, partly because surgeons, unaware of germ theory, didn't bother washing their surgical instruments between amputations. As an advocate for less invasive treatments, Dr. Walker felt that the rate of amputation was simply too high. Frequently when another doctor ordered an amputation, Mary stepped in to do her own examination. If she deemed the surgery avoidable, she discreetly advised the soldier that amputation was his own choice and that he could fight to retain his limb. Many soldiers wrote to her at the war's conclusion to thank her for this intervention.

Mary developed a reputation for having a kind and compassionate heart, and many sought her out when they needed assistance. One evening, two distraught women begged Mary to help their son and husband, Lieutenant Wren, who had been seriously injured near the battlefield of Bull Run. Afraid he would die in the rough conditions near the front lines, the women implored Mary to go to the field, claim Wren, and bring him back so they could care for him. Mary explained that she didn't have a pass that would allow her access to the front but promised to do what she could. At first light the next morning, Mary departed, taking a train as far as she could, then borrowing a horse to carry her over the roads marred by battle. Somehow, Walker managed to persuade the guards to let her through to the front lines, located Wren, and accompanied him by train and streetcar back to Washington. "I need not express the delight felt by all parties upon the lieutenant's arrival home,"[17] she noted.

Another time, a note addressed to "Lady Dr. Walker, the soldier's true friend,"[18] arrived from prisoners who claimed to have been unlawfully incarcerated for desertion.

Dropping all other engagements, Dr. Walker traveled to meet the group, who pled with her to intervene on their behalf. Mary spent six hours taking down dictation as each soldier told his story, then she submitted the transcript to the War Department with a letter requesting the prisoners' release if they agreed to help defend the city. Her petition was approved, though officers later reneged on their promise and reincarcerated some of the men. Walker responded with an additional twenty-five letters to commanders, admonishing them to honor their original agreement. There was little Mary would not do to right an injustice.

In 1862, Dr. Walker traveled to war hospitals, providing medical service wherever it would be accepted. In Warrenton, Virginia, an overwhelmed officer led her into an abandoned house filled with ill and wounded soldiers, saying, "If there is anything you can do for these men, for God's sake do something."[19] Lacking even the most basic supplies, Walker paid a local woman for a basin and set about tearing up her own nightdress to use as rags. After doing all she could to ease their suffering, Mary insisted the men be transferred to Washington and volunteered to accompany them. General Burnside signed the permission for Mary to accompany the men, though when they arrived at the train station, the engineer looked around in confusion for someone in charge. When Walker asked why the train did not depart, he replied that he didn't have the authority. "I have the authority," Mary replied, showing her letter from Burnside.[20] The train soon pulled out for Washington.

Following the Union's devastating defeat at Fredericksburg, Walker traveled to help the nearly 13,000 casualties.[21] Working at Lacy House, a plantation home that had been turned into Union army headquarters and hospital, Mary met Clara Barton and the poet Walt Whitman, who was volunteering as a nurse.

During the Battle of Chickamauga, Dr. Walker cared for sixty patients, assisted with surgery, and oversaw the work of assistant surgeons. Military personnel tried once more to obtain a commission for Walker, but once again their requests were denied. For her labors day and night, Dr. Walker received rations to eat and a tent to sleep in. Walker designed and made herself a uniform, including a sash that identified her as a surgeon. The *New York Tribune* acknowledged, "Since the commencement of the war . . . [Dr. Walker] has been constantly seen in the various hospitals of the Capital, performing with great skill surgical operations, prescribing for the sick, or soothing them with smiling words."[22] As Mary's fame grew, she gave lectures about her service and was invited to meet President Lincoln. Though these recognitions were satisfying, they hardly compensated for the repeated denial of formal employment.

Mary returned to Washington, DC, and marveled at the chaos of the capital at war. Hundreds of women searched through dozens of hospitals in search of their injured loved ones. Many of these women traveled unchaperoned, which meant "respectable" establishments denied them lodging. As these women sought shelter with acquaintances or even on the city's streets, Mary determined to help. She wrote to the mayor, requesting support and supplies, gave speeches to raise funds, and located a housing space, offering her own home as backup when needed. Dr. Walker commissioned a driver and carriage and often accompanied the women as her schedule permitted. To continue these efforts, she organized "The Women's Relief Association"[23] and served as its first president until others were trained to take over the work.

As the war entered its third year, Dr.

Walker wrote bold letters to the Secretary of War, members of Congress, and Lincoln himself, asking for a paid position. Eventually, Mary was asked to report to a medical board for evaluation of her skills. The invitation initially seemed like a positive development, but when Dr. Walker presented herself before the board, she quickly realized the panel of physicians opposed her appointment due to her gender, dress, and orientation toward homeopathic approaches. One member of the panel wrote that the group doubted whether Mary had pursued the study of medicine at all and claimed her knowledge was "not greater than most housewives possess."[24] Mary, for her part, was furious about the procedure, claiming the physicians did not actually ask her about medical practices and procedures. She lamented: "The examination was intended to be a farce, & more than half the time was consumed in questions regarding subjects that were exclusively feminine & had no sort of relation to the diseases and wounds of soldiers."[25]

Some six months prior to the medical board's review, Mary had met General George H. Thomas at the Chattanooga battlefield hospital after the Battle of Chickamauga. General Thomas had observed Mary's medical expertise directly, watching her take charge of several wards and oversee the work of the assistant surgeons. In the intervening time, General Thomas was named Commander of the Cumberland Army, and he used his authority to overrule the board's insulting assessment and assign her a position as a contract surgeon. Still, there was no commission. But, after years without compensation, at last she would be paid, a salary of $80 per month, the only woman to be so contracted during the war. Stationed in northern Georgia, Mary's commanding officer Colonel Dan McCook immediately demonstrated his confidence in Mary's abilities. McCook even allowed Mary to review the troops in his absence, an honor typically reserved for officers. Thriving in this environment, Dr. Walker cared for soldiers and ill patients in the surrounding community too.

Mary traveled the region widely, caring for the sick and engaging in espionage activities for the Federal government as well. Much of Walker's work as a spy remains unknown, but in 1865 a judge revealed that Mary "gained information that led General Sherman to so modify his strategic operations as to . . . obtain success where defeat before seemed inevitable."[26] Dr. Walker often traveled through enemy territory alone on her excursions to help the wounded though she knew it was dangerous. On April 10, 1864, Mary's string of good luck met an abrupt end when she was taken captive at gunpoint by Confederate soldiers. Several days later, they transferred her as a prisoner of war to Castle Thunder Prison in Richmond, Virginia, a penitentiary nicknamed the "Southern Bastille." A crowd turned out to marvel at the oddity of her arrival, and Confederate Captain Benedict J. Semmes wrote his wife: "[We] were all amused and disgusted . . . at the sight of a thing that nothing but the debased and depraved Yankee nation could produce. [A woman] was dressed in the full uniform of a Federal surgeon . . . she would be more at home in a lunatic asylum."[27]

During the months she spent in prison, Mary contracted chronic bronchitis, dropped to an unhealthy weight, and sustained eyesight damage due to the gas-burning lamps. Fleas, bedbugs, and rats scampered through her room; she subsisted on moldy bread and rice filled with maggots. Walker wrote letters to her parents downplaying the conditions and encouraging them not to worry. Somehow Mary managed to retain a fan decorated with a United States flag during her incarceration, and several prisoners recorded the sight of a woman encouraging them with the make-shift banner as they marched to their cells. After four long months, Dr. Walker was exchanged for a six-foot-tall Confederate major[28] and returned home to a hero's welcome. President Lincoln requested a meeting with Mary to ask about prison conditions and thank her for her service.

Dr. Walker was soon back at work, despite her poor eyesight, treating soldiers and assisting wherever she was permitted to serve. Secretary of War Edwin Stanton paid her $432.36 for the work she had done as an assistant surgeon — the first time she received pay for her war services. The compensation, however, accompanied another denial for commission.[29] For six months Mary served as surgeon over a female military prison, a role she found difficult due to memories of her own recent incarceration. In the final days of the war, Mary received a brief reassignment before unceremoniously being informed her services were "no longer required in this department."[30]

Dr. Walker celebrated the war's conclusion by returning to Richmond, where she walked through Castle Thunder, this time as a visitor rather than a prisoner. She was invited to read the Declaration of Independence while wearing her surgeon's uniform on the steps of Richmond's capitol building in an unification ceremony. Though injuries sustained during her imprisonment continued to plague her, Walker still sought for a surgeon's commission. President Andrew Johnson was in favor of it, but military officials, in their longstanding commitment to bureaucracy, insisted it was unheard of to honor a woman in such a way and could set an "inconvenient precedent" going forward. In spite of the denial, General Joseph Holt acknowledged Dr. Walker's "sacrifices, her fearless energy under circumstances of peril, her endurance of hardship and imprisonment at the hands of the enemy and especially her active patriotism." These qualities, he said, set her apart as "isolated" in the "history of the rebellion."[31]

Although he was unable to grant the commission Mary wanted so badly, President Johnson did not want to let her "valuable service" go unrecognized. On November 11, 1865, he ordered the Congressional Medal of Honor to be awarded to Dr. Mary Walker. To this day, she is the only woman to have ever received this honor, and the medal became one of her most cherished possessions; she pinned it to her lapel daily until her death.

With the war behind the country, Walker discovered that many nurses had been paid very little or nothing at all for working exhaustive hours under excruciating circumstances. In 1872, Mary collected the nurses' experiences and petitioned Congress on their behalf. Benjamin Butler presented her request to the House of Representatives, and, thanks to Walker's efforts, the bill passed, granting women who served for ninety days or more as nurses during the war pensions of $20 per month.[32] Ironically, her attempts to secure a pension for herself were far less successful. As she was neither a nurse nor a commissioned surgeon, she was singularly overlooked in the legislation. Even as Walker struggled with disabilities from her imprisonment, more than twenty-five bills related to her pension were submitted to the House or Senate over thirty years. Finally, in 1874, she was granted a pension of $8.50 per month, less than half of what most nurses were paid.[33]

In 1890, still maintaining this discrepancy was unfair, Walker again petitioned Congress for an increase in her pension. Incredibly, she was told her request was denied in part because she did not "dress like other women."[34] Her sardonic response to the verdict was published in newspapers of the time: "Be it enacted, That the Constitution of the United States be amended so as to read: That a National costumer for the women of the United States be selected from some foreign court whose special duties shall be to devise costumes for every woman in the United States . . . that shall seem appropriate to him."[35] Her public criticism had little effect beyond releasing her own frustrations, but in 1898, after thirty years of effort, her pension was at last raised to $20 per month.[36]

Dr. Walker refused to allow the repeated denials to consume her life; her thirst for knowledge about the world was exhaustive. In the decades after the war, she obtained a patent on a system to teach orthography and studied law extensively. Though she did not take the bar, people often sought her advice on legal issues. She was present at the proceedings for several high-profile legal cases, including the trial of Lincoln's assassins, and she believed there were many important connections between law and medicine. Walker maintained a presence in the public sphere by lecturing on many topics, and her successes with disease treatment were published in homeopathic medical journals of the time. In 1890, she ran for Congress and for the Senate in 1892.[37] She raised her voice in favor of prison reform and transgendered individuals and fought against the United States annexation of the Hawaiian Islands. Mary spoke out against the death penalty and about atrocities the United States had committed against Filipinos in the 1890s.

It's not surprising that Dr. Walker, a dedicated feminist, became involved in the fight for women's suffrage. In 1873, Mary presented to the House Judiciary a petition for suffrage signed by 35,000 women, and in 1915, she marched in New York City with 30,000 women from 20 countries in the largest march for women's suffrage in world history.[38] Mary authored a number of pamphlets advocating women's suffrage.

In 1878, Dr. Walker published her second book, *Unmasked, or the Science of Immorality,* which dealt with double standards in marriage and how to eliminate them. In the volume, she dared write openly about sexuality and menstruation, claiming, "Knowledge must ever be the basic principle upon which the purest morals are founded."[39] Shocking her readership, Walker also spoke out about domestic abuse, affirming that "No woman's body can be abused without suffering of soul, and vice versa."[40] Mary wrote about her experience treating sexually transmitted diseases that were rampant during the Civil War, and she argued that women's sexual desire was at times just as strong as men's, but they were less sexually promiscuous due to consequences they could not escape. If women were capable of controlling themselves sexually, she claimed, men were too.[41] Dr. Walker discussed rape and advised her readers to attack back if rape was attempted, claiming that rape could exist within marriage (a controversial stance at the time). She advised that many problems would be solved by "woman always having supreme control of her person."[42] These radical notions elicited wide criticism of her book, and some police departments even threatened to suppress sales, deeming it "broad vulgarity."[43]

Never one to be muzzled by controversy, Mary changed her style of clothes again in the year *Unmasked* was published, choosing an even more radical overcoat with straight pants underneath and cutting her hair short in a more masculine style. While she claimed she did not wear male clothing, the move was a deliberate affront to her critics.

In 1917, during the throes of World War I, the army changed the rules for receiving a Medal of Honor. Recipients were now required to have "actual combat with an enemy . . . above and beyond the call of duty." In a rather appalling turn of events, the government rescinded 911 Medals of Honor, asking recipients, Walker among them, to return the accolade. Burning with indignation over this slight, Dr. Walker replied with a strongly worded statement of protest and refused to return her medal.[44]

As decades passed, society finally began to catch up with some of Mary's outlandish ideas. Dress reform became more widespread, and people began calling trousers for women "Mary Walkers."[45] With the enactment of suffrage for African American men, universal suffrage seemed like less of an impossibility with every passing year. On February 27, 1898, *The Washington Post* wrote of Dr. Walker: "Why has she been muzzled so callously and so persistently? . . . We receive the impression of an unkind and intolerant conspiracy against one of the most gifted and willing teachers of the age."[46]

Mary continued writing well into her eighties, finally succumbing to chronic bronchitis in 1919. Eighteen months after

Mary's death, the nineteenth amendment was ratified, and United States women at last had the right to cast their ballots. During World War II, a Liberty ship called the SS *Mary Walker* took to the seas. In 1977, an army board reinstated Mary's Medal of Honor and praised her "distinguished gallantry, self-sacrifice, patriotism, dedication, and unflinching loyalty to her country despite the apparent discrimination because of her sex."[47]

Mary died believing the world would eventually reconcile itself to the ideals she championed throughout her life. In her mind, it was simply a matter of time, as truth was irrefutable. In 1897 she lamented, "I have got to die before people know who I am and what I have done. It is a shame that people who lead reforms in this world are not appreciated until after they are dead; then the world pays its tributes by piling rocks over the grave of the reformer. I would be thankful if people would treat me decently now instead of erecting great piles of stone over me after I am dead. But, then, that's human nature."[48]

Perhaps one of the greatest tributes to Mary Walker's life would come decades later from fellow physician Dr. Bertha Van Hoosen, who said, "Dr. Mary's life should stand out to remind us that when people do not think as we do, do not dress as we do, and do not live as we do, that they are more than likely to be a half century ahead of their time, and that we should have for them not ridicule but reverence."[49] It is a tribute Mary would be proud of.

Further Reading

Stephanie Fitzgerald. *Mary Walker: Civil War Surgeon and Feminist.* North Mankato, MN: Compass Point Books, 2009.

Judith E. Harper. *Women During the War: An Encyclopedia.* New York: Routledge, 2007.

Sharon M. Harris. *Dr. Mary Walker: An American Radical, 1832–1919.* Piscataway, N. J.: Rutgers University Press, 2009.

Jane Hollenbeck Conner. *Sinners, Saints, and Soldiers in Civil War Stafford.* Stafford, VA: Parker Publishing, 2009.

Elizabeth D. Leonard. *Yankee Women: Gender Battles in the Civil War.* New York: W. W. Norton, 1994.

Joanne Mattern. *Life Stories of 100 American Heroes.* New York: KidsBooks, 2001.

Notes

Epigraph: In Sharon M. Harris, *Dr. Mary Walker: An American Radical, 1832–1919* (Piscataway, N. J.: Rutgers University Press, 2009), 216.

1. Harris, *Dr. Mary Walker: An American Radical,* 132.

2. Harris, *Dr. Mary Walker: An American Radical,* 149.

3. In Harris, *Dr. Mary Walker: An American Radical,* 146.

4. In order to find cures for health problems that plagued the family, Mary's father, Alvah Walker, had done extensive reading in the medical sciences.

5. Stephanie Fitzgerald, *Mary Walker: Civil War Surgeon and Feminist* (North Mankato, MN: Compass Point Books, 2009), 33.

6. In Judith E. Harper, *Women During the Civil War: An Encyclopedia* (New York: Routledge, 2007), 446.

7. See https://oswegocountytoday.com/hundreds-turn-out-to-pay-tribute-to-dr-mary-e-walker/.

8. In Harris, *Dr. Mary Walker: An American Radical,* 15.

9. The Dress Reform movement of the late Victorian era sought to free women of the

bustles, corsets, crinolines, and other restrictive clothing of the time in exchange for more comfortable clothing that was easy to move and work in.

10. In Harris, *Dr. Mary Walker: An American Radical,* 9.

11. In Harris, *Dr. Mary Walker: An American Radical,* 178.

12. In Harris, *Dr. Mary Walker: An American Radical,* 164.

13. In Harris, *Dr. Mary Walker: An American Radical,* 186.

14. In Harris, *Dr. Mary Walker: An American Radical,* 32.

15. In Harris, *Dr. Mary Walker: An American Radical,* 33.

16. In Harris, *Dr. Mary Walker: An American Radical,* 42–43.

17. In Harris, *Dr. Mary Walker: An American Radical,* 36.

18. In Harris, *Dr. Mary Walker: An American Radical,* 37.

19. In Harris, *Dr. Mary Walker: An American Radical,* 40.

20. Elizabeth D. Leonard, *Yankee Women: Gender Battles in the Civil War* (New York: W. W. Norton, 1994), 121.

21. *The War of the Rebellion: A Compilation of the Official Records of the Union and*

Confederate Armies, Series 1, Vol. 21, U.S. War Dept., 129; see http://ebooks.library .cornell.edu/cgi/t/text/pageviewer-idx?c =moawar&cc=moawar&idno=waro0031 &node=waro0031%3A1&view=image& seq=145&size=100.

22. In Harris, *Dr. Mary Walker: An American Radical,* 45.

23. In Harris, *Dr. Mary Walker: An American Radical,* 47–49.

24. In Harris, *Dr. Mary Walker: An American Radical,* 51.

25. In Harris, *Dr. Mary Walker: An American Radical,* 51.

26. In Harris, *Dr. Mary Walker: An American Radical,* 58.

27. Carol Mattingly, *Appropriate[ing] Dress: Women's Rhetorical Style in Nineteenth Century America* (Carbondale, IL: Southern Illinois University Press, 2002), 85.

28. Jane Hollenbeck Conner, *Sinners, Saints, and Soldiers in Civil War Stafford* (Stafford, VA: Parker Publishing, 2009), 80.

29. Conner, *Sinners, Saints, and Soldiers in Civil War Stafford,* 81.

30. In Harris, *Dr. Mary Walker: An American Radical,* 68–69.

31. In Harris, *Dr. Mary Walker: An American*

Radical, 73.

32. Harris, *Dr. Mary Walker: An American Radical,* 138–39.

33. Harris, *Dr. Mary Walker: An American Radical,* 187.

34. Harris, *Dr. Mary Walker: An American Radical,* 187.

35. In Harris, *Dr. Mary Walker: An American Radical,* 188.

36. Harris, *Dr. Mary Walker: An American Radical,* 219.

37. Harris, *Dr. Mary Walker: An American Radical,* 172.

38. Harris, *Dr. Mary Walker: An American Radical,* 250.

39. In Harris, *Dr. Mary Walker: An American Radical,* 157.

40. In Harris, *Dr. Mary Walker: An American Radical,* 158.

41. Harris, *Dr. Mary Walker: An American Radical,* 159.

42. Harris, *Dr. Mary Walker: An American Radical,* 159.

43. Harris, *Dr. Mary Walker: An American Radical,* 162.

44. Harris, *Dr. Mary Walker: An American Radical,* 251.

45. Harris, *Dr. Mary Walker: An American Radical,* 217.

46. In Harris, *Dr. Mary Walker: An American Radical,* 216.
47. In *It's My Country Too: Women's Military Stories from the American Revolution to Afghanistan,* ed. Tracy Crow and Jerri Bell (Lincoln, NE: Potomac Books, 2017), 41–42.
48. George R. DeMass, *Town of Oswego* (Mount Pleasant: Arcadia Publishing, 2014), 123.
49. In Harris, *Dr. Mary Walker: An American Radical,* 252.

CHAPTER 12
FIRST NATIONS IN A
DIVIDED NATION

Chipeta

> "The story of [Native] women . . . is not
> one of declining status and lost culture,
> but one of persistence and change,
> conservatism and adaptation,
> tragedy and survival."
> — Professor Theda Perdue

Pioneer children often searched the base of monstrous anthills formed from mud to find smooth, colorful orbs — Indian beads that had been dropped and later collected by the insects. Frontier settlers would gather and string the decorations together with little understanding that they gathered pieces of nations threatened by their very passage. Searching for accounts of Native American women during the Civil War years is much the same. You can gather fragments and snatches — a name here, a photo there. The residual stories about women are usually brief, and tribal members are understandably hesitant to trust those stories with audiences outside their own communities. But the remaining fragments can be woven — like bird feathers, yucca, agave, and bear grass have been woven into blankets by Pueblo women for thousands of years — to create an image of native women during the Civil War.

The splintering of the United States

placed the first nations to inhabit this continent in a very difficult position. Disgusted by the continued breaking of treaties, many Native nations were understandably reluctant to defend a government that had forcibly removed them from their homelands and continued to deny them citizenship or voting rights. When Fort Sumter fell, the federal government withdrew officials from posts in Indian Territory, effectively abandoning tribes who had exchanged their lands in return for supplies and protection. Confederate troops moved into many of these territories, confiscating deserted outposts and seeking to form new alliances.

Some few tribes, like the Creek, Cherokee, and Choctaw, identified more with the Confederacy ideologically, as they owned slaves themselves. The Confederacy also promised tribes representation in their Congress, a benefit the federal government still denied all people of color. Some tribal leaders argued it was a grave mistake to aid the rebels, fearing their inevitable defeat would create far greater problems for native nations. The debate split many tribes, as a portion of the population aligned with the Confederacy, while other members joined the Union army's Indian Home Guard.

More than 28,000 Native Americans would eventually serve both the Union and Confederate armies — most aligning with the United States.[1] Tribes that sent soldiers to fight for the Union hoped their military contributions would motivate the government to honor treaties they had made.

WOMEN WARRIORS AND THEIR VETERANS

Though many pioneer journals comment derisively on the subservient role of Native women, ironically, in many indigenous cultures, women held far more rights and privileges than their white counterparts. The Hopi tribe, for instance, has a long tradition of female superiority, drawing their power from Mother Earth, tracing their genealogy through matrilineal lines, with women leaders holding most of the economic and political power. The Cherokee people also practiced matrilineal genealogy, and believed women derived their power from their sacred roles as givers and sustainers of life.[2] Sacred stories of warrior women have been passed down by many tribes. In the Pend d'Oreilles and Flathead tribes of Montana, women routinely took an active role in warfare. *Kuilix,* or "Red One," is a woman who led a group of warriors into battle against the Blackfeet in 1832. *Lozen* was a female warrior, medicine woman, and spiritual leader of the Chihenne Chiricahua Apache. She participated in warrior ceremonies, and said she could sense the location of her enemies by stretching out her arms and praying to the Apache Creator of Life. Though there are no recorded accounts of Native American women disguising themselves to serve in the Civil War, it is very likely some did.

For every Native man who left to serve in the Civil War, mothers, daughters, sisters, and wives bore much of the impact created by the departure. Women made significant sacrifices as they allowed their main breadwinners to go and struggled to survive on limited resources. Some Native soldiers served in the United States Colored Troops alongside African Americans,[3] while others served in integrated Confederate units; several saw action with the infamous Company K of the 1st Michigan Sharpshooters, part of the Army of the Potomac. Natives served both North and South as highly valuable scouts, since they tended to be astutely familiar with the land and ways to traverse it. Ely Parker, a Tonawanda chief, drafted the surrender documents signed by Grant and Lee at Appomattox. Cherokee general Stand Watie was the last Confederate general to surrender in the war, more than two months after the signing at Appomattox.[4]

The infamous Andersonville prison in Georgia housed a number of native prisoners of war, including Joseph Gibson, who had grown up on Odawa lands in Michigan, the son of a devoted mother. The chief of Joseph's tribe encouraged parents to send their children to school because he regretted not being able to read the English words of a treaty he had signed on behalf of his people. When Joseph was ten years old, he broke his leg. To make sure he didn't miss a day, his mother carried him to school and home daily on her back until his leg healed. Before leaving to join the 1st Michigan Sharpshooters, Joseph wrote a note to the owner of the general store asking him to please give his mother whatever food she might need in his absence. She was understandably devastated when Joseph succumbed to disease in Andersonville.[5]

By the end of the war, one out of three Cherokee women was widowed and one in four children had been orphaned.[6] Hannah Hicks's husband fought for the Union in a company comprised of several native tribes. He was killed in 1862 when his unit attacked a group of Confederates aligned with Tonakawa Indians. Left alone to care for four children and an infant, Hannah tried her best to survive on her own, even as the Confederate army passed through her neighborhood, regularly confiscating food and supplies. Hicks recorded: "How gladly I would have given up everything if they only would have spared my husband."[7]

Electa Quinney was a Mohican woman raised in New York who was removed with her people to the Kaukauna area of Wisconsin in 1827. An advocate for education and literacy, Quinney opened the first free school in Wisconsin, teaching both Mohican and white children who would not otherwise have been able to afford an education. Her son, Daniel Adams, enlisted for the Union, fighting in the cavalry unit in Wisconsin Company A. He wrote frequently to Electa, to ask advice: "I don't think that the Hospital Doctors know any to[o] much. There are a great many of our boys getting sick. . . . Do you know what would be good for them[?]"[8] Quinney responded, sharing her extensive knowledge of herbal remedies and medicines with her son. Daniel was killed in battle in 1863. Though he was buried in a national cemetery, it took Electa nineteen years to successfully receive his military pension of $8 a month.[9]

HANGING CLOUD

Hanging Cloud (*Aazhawigiizhigokwe* in Ojibwe, meaning "Goes Across the Sky Woman") was the daughter of a chief. She served as an integral member of the war council, performing war dances and ceremonies and taking part in her tribe's battles and hunting rituals. When Hanging Cloud's village was ambushed by a nearby tribe, she assisted in the defense and killed her own cousin (part of the attacking force) during the battle. Hanging Cloud married three times and had five children. Her sister *Waabikwe* ("the gray-haired") married a man who departed to serve the Union army during the Civil War. While he was away, Waabikwe and Hanging Cloud received mistaken news that he had fallen during battle. Lacking further information, Waabikwe remarried after a period of mourning. But shortly after the end of the war, her original husband appeared unscathed. His arrival in the village must have made for an awkward homecoming.

SALLIE PEACHEATER MANUS

The Confederate army very nearly shot Union-aligned Cherokee Sallie Peacheater Manus when they passed through her lands in Oklahoma. Fortunately for Manus, a member of the war party recognized Sallie and persuaded the others to spare her life. A few weeks later, another compassionate soldier warned Manus his unit planned to raid her house the next morning. For Sallie, times were far too difficult to see her money gobbled up by marauding soldiers. At daybreak, Sallie donned all the clothing she could wear, pinned her last $50 to her apron, and bridled her pony. As she led her mount out to the yard, she watched the posse approaching from a distance. Manus looked deep into the animal's eyes and spoke to him quite seriously. "Pony Babe, you got to make your best run of your dear life. Our enemy is after us." She mounted as the soldiers' whoops rang out behind her, but the pony carried Sallie safely to a friend's home. She hid the pony and the money, which they used to survive. Manus said of that last $50, "sure enough we got by with it."[10]

SALLIE WATIE

Sallie Watie was also familiar with the problem of shifting army territory. Sallie's story is much better preserved than most, due to the fact that she and her husband played prominent roles in the Cherokee nation. Sallie married Stand Watie in 1842 as his fourth wife and gave birth to five children. When the Civil War broke out, the Cherokee tribe swiftly divided along lines of residual conflict from the 1830s, when they were removed from their ancestral lands.[11] Chief John Ross led those who sided with the Union, while Stand Watie emerged as leader of the Confederate Cherokee faction. Sallie spent the war years defending her lands against raids by Yankee soldiers, providing for her children, and equipping the army with food and clothing.

Prior to the conflict, the Waties, as with much of the Cherokee nation, were quite prosperous. Sallie's husband owned a general store in Millwood, Oklahoma, and also practiced law. They lived in a comfortable two-story cabin home. However, six major battles were fought on or near Cherokee land,[12] and suddenly Sallie found herself living in a war zone. Each time territory shifted between the armies, the other side retaliated, raiding farms for supplies and terrorizing local populations. In 1862, Sallie's new home was burned to the ground by Federal troops. Suddenly impoverished and homeless, survival at the most basic level became a challenge. As the wife of the chief, Sallie was also often expected to help other soldiers' families.

Soon after their home was destroyed, Sallie and her children fled the area. They joined a camp along the Red River in Texas, where refugees battled constant illness, unsanitary conditions, and a lack of food and medicine. Dismayed by local reactions to the displaced people, Sallie wrote, "I use to think that every one had some sort of a soul but one half of them has only gizards and some only craws."[13]

On June 25, 1863, Cherokee leaders agreed to free the remainder of their nation's 4,000 slaves, roughly half of whom were female.[14] These freedmen and women became members of the Cherokee nation and were given land allotments with the tribe. The same year, people grew tired of the strain of thousands of Cherokee refugees living on their border and demanded the refugees return to their own lands. Colonel William Phillips escorted the refugees home, and freedwoman Emily Walker acted as Phillips's interpreter and guide.[15]

As she faced deprivation and poverty, Sallie believed the conflict caused far worse things than physical deprivation. She recorded: "This war will ruin a great many good people[;] they will not only lose all their property but a great many will lose their character which is more value than all their property."[16] Sallie wrote regularly to her husband and son serving in the Confederate army, reminding them to live by their values, even during warfare. She reminded her husband to be merciful to his enemies, saying, "I believe you have always done what you thought best for your people and I want to die with that last belief."[17] At one point during the conflict, Stand Watie succeeded in capturing his enemy, John Ross, and chose to spare his life in respect to his wife's request.

Sallie decided she would not allow instability to threaten her children's education. Even when she had no idea where she would be living, she reassured her husband that it would be near a school. Throughout those difficult years, Sallie did everything necessary in order to survive. When inflation rendered Confederate money nearly worthless, Sallie began bartering and dealing in tobacco. When she was in one place long enough, Sallie planted crops to augment food supplies. Constant spinning and weaving to provide clothing for family and soldiers occupied much of her time. When Stand's army ran short on supplies, he sent requests to find needed items. Sallie assisted many in the community when they were ill, and she developed a reputation as a skilled nurse. In June 1864, Sallie wrote to her husband from a Texas camp, "I would like to live a short time in peace just to see how it would be. I would like to feel free once in life again and feel no dread of war."[18]

Devastation to farms, crops, and businesses meant the Cherokee Nation's means of support were largely destroyed by the conflict. Twenty-five to fifty percent of the male population was dead, and the US government was not sure which faction of the tribe to recognize. Due to poverty and continued tensions, it took years for the remaining Cherokee war refugees to return to their homes.[19] Tragically, Sallie, in her later years, buried her husband and each one of her five children, who all preceded their mother in death. Sallie's legacy is one of incredible compassion and endurance.

LANDS TO THE WEST

Part of Abraham Lincoln's Republican party platform was "Free Speech, Free Soil, and Free Men."[20] While "Free Men" indicated Lincoln's progressive views regarding slavery, his actions toward the Native Americans were far less tolerant. The promised "free soil" depended on large tracts of uninhabited land to the West for the taking; unfortunately, this idea was nothing more than a fantasy. These same lands were already inhabited by native people whose lifestyles depended on their ability to travel with the seasons, reliant on the same water and grazing pasture which the new settlers also needed. With many men fighting in the Civil War or in wars to retain their lands, native women were forced to provide for their children alone, through battles, forced relocations, and massacres. Surviving accounts from these events contain heartrending and sobering tales from the 500 nations that once inhabited North America.

BEAR RIVER MASSACRE

One of the worst massacres of Native Americans that occurred during the period of the Civil War is one few people have heard of. The Northwestern Shoshone traveled seasonally between present-day northern Utah and southern Idaho, following the cycles of game and food. The tribe spent each winter camped in Cache Valley, a sacred space they called "The House of the Great Spirit." The nearby Mormon settlements were friendly with the Shoshone, and Brigham Young encouraged his people to befriend the tribe, but a constant stream of visitors to the Shoshone settlements reduced the game and pasturelands to the breaking point. The discovery of gold on Grasshopper Creek in Montana in 1862 attracted even more settlers, as the road to reach the diggings wound directly through Shoshone lands. By winter, the tribe was starving.[21]

Less than a month after the Emancipation Proclamation, the Shoshone gathered near Bear River to hold a ritual called a Warm Dance to herald the end of winter and beginning of spring. As tribal members came together, a few minor incidents of cattle theft and fighting were blamed on the Shoshone, though other tribes were actually at fault. Colonel Patrick Connor led a group of Union volunteers from California — men anxious to take part in Civil War battles and spend their time shooting Confederates rather than protecting overland mail routes and tangling with Indians. Determined to chastise the Shoshone for their alleged actions, Colonel Connor rounded up his company of enlisted soldiers and descended on the peaceful winter settlement.[22]

Two nights before the army's arrival on January 29, 1863, an older member of the tribe, Tin Dup, tossed and turned in his sleep, unable to shake off dreams of soldiers descending on the unprotected camp. In the morning, Tin Dup spoke of what he had seen, and some families chose to move their teepees away from the settlement as a precaution. Soldiers approached the following dawn.[23] Chief Sagwitch went to meet them, hoping to negotiate peace. Instead, the soldiers proceeded to shoot, kill, rape, and maim men, women, and children. Mothers dove into the icy river water with their babies on their backs. Some were shot as they swam. One woman, Anzee Chee, was shot in the shoulder and breast; she escaped by diving into the semi-frozen river and seeking shelter under an overhanging bank. From this hiding spot, she watched the soldiers continue their work of death.[24]

An elderly woman, Que he gup, sought shelter inside a small grass teepee crowded with other terrified members of the tribe, when her twelve-year-old grandson found her. In an urgent voice, she suggested they go outside and pretend to be dead because she feared the soldiers would set the teepee on fire at any moment. Together they lay among the fallen until the soldiers departed.[25] The army burned almost all the teepees, except for one they riddled with bullet holes, where Chief Sagwitch found the body of his wife stretched out beside his infant daughter. Though the soldiers claimed they killed 200 Shoshone at the Bear River Massacre, James Hill, a Mormon missionary who visited the day after the massacre placed the number at 368.[26] The Bear River Massacre is the worst massacre of natives in US history, though it is often overlooked, partly because the attention of the nation was focused on the Civil War fighting in the East. Not surprisingly, the rate of retaliatory attacks increased after this event. In the aftermath of the violence at Bear River, half of the remaining northwestern Shoshone were transferred to the Fort Hall Reservation; the other half integrated themselves into nearby Mormon communities. Patrick Connor was promoted to Brigadier-General and was never held accountable for his actions toward the Shoshone people.

SAND CREEK MASSACRE

As General Thomas Sherman marched through Georgia to the sea in 1864, the tragedy of Sand Creek Massacre unfolded in the West, where hordes of settlers streaming into Colorado territory for the gold rush had pushed resources to a breaking point. To ease tenuous relations, territorial governor John Evans invited peaceful tribes to set their camps at Sand Creek. There the tribes were offered both provisions and protection; 600 nonviolent Cheyenne, led by chiefs Black Kettle and White Antelope, joined 652 Arapahoe. The camp was comprised mainly of women, children, and the elderly who were not away at war.[27]

Colonel John M. Chivington, commander of Union troops for Colorado territory, already felt frustrated about missing out on the Civil War action in the East. In addition, he did not agree with sentiments of peace with the natives. In late November 1864 Chivington decided to deal with the "Indian problem" himself by assembling a unit of seven hundred men to attack the tribes camped at Sand Creek. When soldiers serving under Chivington realized he intended to attack natives who were under the express promise of protection by the US army, two officers completely refused to order their men to fire; these units stood by as silent witnesses to the events that followed. The remainder of Chivington's men descended upon the camp in the morning hours of November 28, 1864. Even as the army approached, Chief Black Kettle assured his people not to be frightened, that the camp was not in danger. Black Kettle came out to meet the approaching men, waving both a US flag and a white flag of surrender.

In a matter of minutes, the bewildered leader realized that Chivington's men truly intended to kill all men, women, and children in their path. Not content with killing alone, they mutilated the bodies and collected body parts for souvenirs. In horror, Black Kettle ran to his wife, Medicine Woman Later, and attempted to lead her to shelter in shallow mud pits along the riverbanks. The soldiers found their hiding place, however, and shot Medicine Woman Later nine times. Reeling with shock, Black Kettle left his wife behind, believing her to be dead.

Chief White Antelope, who had previously traveled to Washington, DC, to negotiate for his tribe, refused to fight the approaching army. After begging them to stop, he simply crossed his arms over his chest before being gunned down. White Antelope sang the Cheyenne death song as he lay dying: "Nothing lives long, only the earth and the mountains."[28]

A group of thirty or forty women gathered

in a crevice, seeking shelter from the gunfire exploding around them. They sent out a little girl, around the age of six, holding a white flag on a stick, to plead for mercy. She had taken only a few steps before she was shot and killed.[29]

One soldier broke into the teepee of a woman and her twenty-four-year-old daughter. He shot the older woman and then attempted to rape the young Cheyenne, named Mochi. The terrified young woman snatched up her father's rifle and shot the soldier dead. Mochi later became a famous Cheyenne warrior who fought in many other battles and raids for more than eleven years at the side of her husband. Mochi is the only Native American female ever taken as a prisoner of war by the US army. She was known to kill settlers with an ax to the head — in the same manner her family was killed at Sand Creek.[30]

After nightfall, Chief Black Kettle crawled back to his wife's body and miraculously found her still alive. He lifted Medicine Woman Later to his back and carried her to shelter; the next day he carried her over miles of frozen prairie to find medical assistance in another Cheyenne encampment.

Colonel Chivington returned to Denver with a collection of fetuses, genitalia, 100 scalps, and two young native girls and one young boy whom he exhibited like trophies. Chivington was initially welcomed as a hero; but public response turned to horror when the details of the Sand Creek Massacre became known. Condemned by three investigatory committees, one judge called the incident a "cowardly and cold-blooded slaughter."[31] In a rare moment of contrition, the US government admitted fault and paid indemnities directly to the families affected by the massacre, which benefited some survivors. Though Chivington had argued in favor of the massacre by claiming the aggression would force the Cheyenne to quit fighting, the violence made the road to peace far more difficult because the attack killed off many of the native groups most interested in resolution and because survivors understandably no longer trusted the government to honor their promises. The massacre left Mochi and other warriors more determined to fight than ever before.[32] Chivington was forced to resign from the army, but he never expressed remorse for his decision. The event was highly influential in shaping public opinion and paving the way for more tolerant government policies.

THE NAVAJO LONG WALK

To this day, members of the Navajo Nation refer to the 1860s as "The Fearing Time." Traditional Navajo homeland ranged from modern-day Arizona through New Mexico, where the tribe practiced farming and raised livestock. The Nation relinquished a third of its lands in return for promised protection and grazing rights, but as settlers continued moving into the area, the army confiscated prime grazing land and slaughtered Navajo livestock. The Nation retaliated by attacking Fort Defiance, which led to escalating violence on both sides. Eventually, Kit Carson led efforts to completely destroy the Navajos, ruining irrigated fields, burning houses, poisoning wells, chopping down orchards, and killing livestock. Anyone who resisted was killed, though some escaped to the hills. The rest of the Nation was forced to relocate between 1863 and 1866, enduring a series of forced marches to Bosque Redondo, Fort Sumner in New Mexico, called *Hweeldi* or "the place of suffering" in Navajo. Thousands of Navajo who embarked on this 300-mile journey were not given supplies or any information about where they were going. More than 200 people died along the route from hunger and exposure.[33]

This story of a pregnant woman on the Long Walk has been handed down through the years by oral storytellers of the Navajo Nation:

"It was said that those ancestors were on the Long Walk with their daughter, who was pregnant and about to give birth. Somewhere . . . south of Albuquerque, the daughter got tired and weak and couldn't keep up with the others or go further because of her condition. So my ancestors asked the Army to hold up for a while and to let the woman give birth. But the soldiers wouldn't do it. They forced my people to move on, saying that they were getting behind the others. The soldier told the parents that they had to leave their daughter behind. 'Your daughter is not going to survive, anyway; sooner or later she is going to die,' they said in their own language. 'Go ahead,' the daughter said to her parents, 'things might come out all right with me.' But the poor thing was mistaken, my grandparents used to say. Not long after they had moved on, they heard a gunshot from where they had been a short time ago. . . . A soldier came riding up from the direction of the sound. He must have shot her to death. That's the way the story goes."[34]

Once the Navajo arrived at the Bosque

Redondo Reservation, they faced an unbearable situation as nine thousand people were crammed into a space intended for no more than 5,000. Water and food supplies were scarce, and nothing could be grown on the land. Diseases such as smallpox swept through the community, leading to the deaths of an additional 2,000 Navajo within two years — roughly a quarter of the population.[35] Women and children were enslaved by local settlers in return for the promise of something to eat.

Through this anguishing time, the Navajo people continued to adapt, incorporating new methods of preparing clothing, food, and weaving into their traditional practices. Navajo fry bread was first created during this time as a way to endure on scarce food supplies. Suffering from an inadequate supply of clothing and blankets, and without access to their sheep flocks, the Navajo asked the government for yarn. The government responded by sending machine-spun yarn from Germantown, Pennsylvania, dyed in colors the Navajo had never worked with before. The combination of new yarn colors and the influence of local Spanish artistry created a burst of creativity, transforming weaving practices and traditional Navajo blouse styles.[36] These incredible Navajo women found ways to survive and even artistically flourish under the harshest of circumstances.

In the spring of 1868, Navajo leaders traveled to Washington and successfully persuaded the government to return them to their native lands. Major General William Sherman, along with three other appointed peacekeepers, visited the Nation, hoping to persuade the Navajo to settle in Oklahoma instead, but leader Barboncito tried to explain the connection to their home lands. Barboncito told Sherman of the enslavement of Navajo women and children and asked for his help to end the atrocity. Sherman acknowledged he knew little of the Navajo people or their struggles, but he had just finished fighting a war to end slavery in the United States. He promised to aid them in their return. When 7,000 Navajo journeyed home to a portion of their native lands in the summer of 1868, many wept at the sight of *Tsoodzil,* Mount Taylor, one of their four sacred mountains. Today, the Navajo Nation includes 300,000 people living on more than 17 million acres.[37] Their artistic tradition continues as strong as ever before.

MARY SCHWANDT AND MAGGIE GOOD THUNDER

The Dakota Sioux of Minnesota also watched arriving settlers encroach on land and resources as the Civil War to the East disrupted deliveries of food, money, and supplies guaranteed by treaty. By 1862, the tribe was starving, and the situation deteriorated into the Dakota War, or Sioux Uprising of 1862. Bands of Dakota warriors launched attacks on white settlers and immigrants in retaliation for the government's broken promises.

Mary Schwandt, a German immigrant, was fourteen years old and working for the Reynolds family when word came that a Dakota band had attacked the nearby town of Ulm. Mary, the Reynoldses, and a group of neighboring families were overtaken by a band of Dakota as they attempted to flee. The Natives opened fire, killing the entire Reynolds family and many others in the company. They captured Mary and took her to the Dakota settlement where she recognized cattle and items stolen from her own home and realized that her family had likely been among those attacked.

Schwandt said, "when I realized my utterly wretched, helpless and hopeless situation, . . . I became as one paralyzed, and could hardly speak."[38]

A few days after her arrival in the Dakota camp, Mary was traded for a pony to an older Dakota woman. The woman's daughter, Snana "Maggie" Good Thunder, had lost a child of her own just a week earlier. The older Dakota woman gave Mary to Maggie, who later wrote, "The reason why I wished to keep this girl was to have her in place of the one I lost. I loved her and pitied her, and she was dear to me just the same as my own daughter."[39] Bound together by bonds of grief, Mary and Maggie immediately formed a close relationship.

Mary began calling Maggie "Mother" and later wrote: "Maggie could not have treated me more tenderly if I had been her daughter. Often and often she preserved me from danger, and sometimes, I think, she saved my life."[40]

Eventually, Mary was rescued and carried to a nearby white settlement, where she reunited with her brother, the only surviving member of her family. Decades passed away, and when Mary was in her forties, a newspaper reporter asked her to recount her story. She said, "Wherever you are, Maggie, I want you to know that the little captive German girl you so often befriended and shielded from harm loves you still for your kindness and care."[41]

In a remarkable turn of fate, Mary's plea was read by a friend of Maggie's who passed on the message. In 1894, after thirty-two years, Maggie and Mary were reunited. Maggie said of the visit, "It was just as if I went to visit my own child."[42] Their affectionate and grateful reunion stretched far beyond the borders of culture and conflict.

The Civil War was a brutal time to be a Native American woman. By the end of the war, the counts of the dead among the Cherokees, Creeks, and Seminoles amounted to twenty-five percent of these entire populations.[43] In the aftermath of the conflict, the attention of a reunited nation would turn once more to settlement of the West, leading to more violence with Native nations. Tribes that aligned with the Confederacy were punished with further treaty violation and land confiscation during Reconstruction, an era that continued to decimate Native populations.

Far too rarely did the United States honor the sacrifice of tribes who had fought on their behalf. The Delaware tribe that fought for the Union was removed after the war and forced to assimilate into the Cherokee nation.[44] An 1866 Cherokee Delegation

Maggie and Mary

pled: "The graves of eight hundred Cherokee warriors, fallen by our side in your
service, testify that we have done our duty.
Now, . . . all we ask is that the Government
do its duty to us. . . . We entreat you to
regard sacredly your past treaties with us."[45]

In spite of agreements that went dishon-
ored and unfulfilled, the Native women and
cultures of this continent could not be
destroyed or fully assimilated. To this day
they remain, with much to teach our mod-

ern nation about how to live sustainably and peacefully upon this land. Though much of the fabric that once held these stories in place has been lost to the intervening years, the pieces that remain are still unspeakably beautiful. As one Native historian has said: "Our histories, even at their darkest moments, were not about what we lost or what was done to us, but what we saved. We drew on the powers of place not as resources, but understood and respected as relatives. We remain rich in relatives."[46]

Further Reading

Annie Heloise Abel. *The American Indian in the Civil War, 1862–1865.* Lincoln, NE: University of Nebraska Press, 1992.

American Indians and the Civil War: Official National Park Service Handbook. Fort Washington, PA: Eastern National, 2013.

Notes

Epigraph: Theda Perdue, *Cherokee Woman: Gender and Culture Change, 1700–1835* (Lincoln, NE: University of Nebraska Press, 1998), 195. Though Perdue was speaking of Cherokee women specifically, her sentiment applies equally to Native women as a whole, and particularly to the period of the Civil War.

1. In Annie Heloise Abel, *The American Indian in the Civil War, 1862–1865* (Lincoln, NE: University of Nebraska Press, 1992), 109.

2. According to Carolyn Ross Johnston, American missionaries and the federal government were concerned by the level of power held by Cherokee women and used programs to attempt to curtail it. See Johnston, *Cherokee Women in Crisis: Trail of Tears, Civil War, and Allotment, 1838–1907* (Tuscaloosa AL: University of Alabama Press, 2003). See also Fay A. Yarbrough, "Whiteness and Racialization in Appalachia," *Journal of Appalachian Studies,* Vol. 10, No. 1/2 (Spring/Fall 2004): 208–10.

3. Well into the twentieth century, the term "colored" was applied to Native Americans as well as African Americans. For more on this, see Sean P. Harvey, "Ideas of Race in Early America," Oxford University Press, April 2016; http://american history.oxfordre.com/view/10.10936./ acrefore/9780199329175.001.0001/ acrefore-9780199329175-e-262.

4. Robert Marshall Utley, *The Indian Fron-*

tier, 1846–1890 (Albuquerque: University of New Mexico Press, 1984), 75.

5. *American Indians and the Civil War: Official National Park Service Handbok* (Fort Washington, PA: Eastern National, 2013), 58–59.

6. *American Indians and the Civil War,* 186.

7. In Theda Perdue, "The Civil War in Indian Territory," *The Journal of Southern History,* Vol. 78, no. 1 (Feb. 2012): 97.

8. *American Indians and the Civil War,* 78.

9. *American Indians and the Civil War,* 78.

10. In *American Indians and the Civil War,* 109.

11. Linda W. Reese, "Cherokee Freedwomen in Indian Territory, 1863–1890," *Western Historical Quarterly,* Vol. 33, No. 3 (Autumn 2002): 279.

12. Reese, "Cherokee Freedwomen in Indian Territory," 279.

13. James W. Parins, "Sallie Watie and Southern Cherokee Women in the Civil War and After," *Native South,* Vol. 2 (2009): 58.

14. Reese, "Cherokee Freedwomen in Indian Territory," 276.

15. Reese, "Cherokee Freedwomen in Indian Territory," 283.

16. Reese, "Cherokee Freedwomen in Indian Territory," 58–59.

17. Reese, "Cherokee Freedwomen in Indian Territory," 59.

18. Reese, "Cherokee Freedwomen in Indian Territory," 56.

19. Clarissa W. Confer, *The Cherokee Nation in the Civil War* (Norman, OK: University of Oklahoma Press, 2007).

20. John C. Fremont, the first Republican party candidate for president, ran on this platform in 1856. It continued to be the slogan of the Republican party, used by Lincoln in his 1860 campaign. See Henry W. Box, ed. *In Memoriam, Abraham Lincoln* (Buffalo, NY: Printing House of Matthews & Warren, 1865), 50.

21. Kass Fleisher, *The Bear River Massacre and the Making of History* (Albany, NY: SUNY Press, 2004), 10.

22. William D. Edmo, *History and Culture of the Boise Shoshone and Bannock Indians* (Pittsburgh: Dorrance Publishing, 2010), 183.

23. Edmo, *History and Culture,* 175–76.

24. Brigham D. Madsen, *The Shoshoni Frontier and the Bear River Massacre* (Salt Lake City: University of Utah Press, 1985), 234.

25. Madsen, *The Shoshoni Frontier,* 235.

26. *Bear River Massacre Site,* Idaho, Na-

tional Park Service, 1996, 6.

27. See *American Indians and the Civil War.*

28. Dee Alexander Brown, *Bury My Heart at Wounded Knee: An Indian History of the American West* (New York: Picador, 2007), 106.

29. Eyewitness testimony taken from Robert Bent. See Wm. J. Allinson, ed., *Friends' Review: A Religious, Literary, and Miscellaneous Journal* (Philadelphia: Merrihew and Sons, 1868), 244.

30. Chris Enss and Howard Kazanjian, *Mochi's War: The Tragedy of Sand Creek* (New York: TwoDot, 2015), 43.

31. *United States Congressional Record: Proceedings and Debates of the 109th Congress,* 14359.

32. Enss and Kazanjian, *Mochi's War,* 48.

33. Jennifer Denetdale, *The Long Walk: The Forced Navajo Exile* (Langhorne, PA: Chelsea House, 2007), 51.

34. Ruth Roessel, ed., *Navajo Stories of the Long Walk Period* (Tsaile, AZ: Navajo Community College Press, 1973), 31.

35. Matthew J. Barbour and Donald E. Tatum, "Research Notes: Archaeology in the Place of Suffering," *El Palacio,* vol. 118, no. 3 (Fall 2013): 66.

36. Sky Kalfus, "Weaving Cultures," in *Dis-*

tillations Magazine, Science History Institute; online at https://www.sciencehistory.org/distillations/magazine/weaving-cultures.

37. *American Indians and the Civil War,* 179.

38. Mary Schwandt, "The Story of Mary Schwandt," in *Minnesota Historical Society Collections, Vol. 6,* 469; online at https://archive.org/details/storyofmaryschwa00schwrich. Accessed February 17, 2018.

39. Snana Maggie Good Thunder, "Narration of a Friendly Sioux: By Snana the Rescuer of Mary Schwandt," in *Minnesota Historical Society Collections, Volume 9* (St. Paul, MN: Pioneer Press Company, 1901), 429.

40. Schwandt, "The Story of Mary Schwandt," 470–71.

41. Schwandt, "The Story of Mary Schwandt," 471.

42. Good Thunder, "Narration of a Friendly Sioux," 430.

43. *American Indians and the Civil War,* 102.

44. Brice Obermeyer, *Delaware Tribe in a Cherokee Nation* (Lincoln, NE: University of Nebraska Press, 2009), 120.

45. In Patrick N. Minges, *Slavery in the Cherokee Nation: The Keetoowah Society and the Defining of a People, 1855–1867*

(New York: Routledge, 2003), 159.

46. Daniel Wildcat, professor, Haskell Indian Nations University, Yuchi member of the Muscogee Nation, in *American Indians and the Civil War,* 207.

CHAPTER 13
LOVE IN THE TIME
OF DYSENTERY

Sarah and William McEntire

"Put a creature you don't care for in the least, in a situation that commands sympathy, and nine out of ten girls will fall desperately in love."
— Sarah Morgan Dawson

Even with disease and destruction reigning over the nation, people still fell in love. Attending bazaars, balls, and parties to support war fundraising efforts now seemed like a patriotic duty, so, in some ways, finding romance was easier than ever before. Men and women also enjoyed more socially acceptable familiarity than they had prior to the conflict, and rushing to the altar seemed less foolhardy when there might not be another opportunity later. Soon, many popular etiquette journals counseled readers on how to hold tasteful wartime weddings.

As the Civil War stretched from months into unanticipated years, casualties mounted and the numbers of eligible single men dwindled, particularly in the South. Marrying quickly over a furlough seemed preferable — for some women — to facing the likely prospect of never marrying at all. Once the weddings were over and done, however, continued conflict usually meant years of loneliness and separation. For some, the rupture of years apart, combined with the trauma and pain of warfare, was simply too much to endure. Other couples found themselves pulled apart by split familial allegiances that pitted not only brother against brother but also husband against wife. But for the most ardent of lovers, neither long separations nor a split nation could threaten their devotion. Passion, denial, death, and distance — the Civil War era held all the essential ingredients for the most heart-wrenching of love stories.

BETTIE SMITH AND JOHN COKER

While combat separated some couples, it introduced others, like Bettie Smith and Second Lieutenant John Coker, who served in the Union army near Wartrace, Tennessee. During a long march with his unit, Coker fell ill and became dangerously separated from his comrades deep within enemy territory. Having few other options, John sought assistance at a nearby farm, where the Smith family took the Yankee soldier in, and young Bettie Smith nursed him back to health. The two were immediately attracted to each other despite holding allegiances to opposite sides of the conflict.

The convalescing soldier was still lingering at the Smith house when the Confederate cavalry galloped onto the property a few weeks later. Rushing Coker out the back door even as the soldiers approached the front, Bettie lowered John down a well, where he stayed hidden while she informed the Confederates that, no, she had certainly not seen any Yankees in the area. Once the Confederate soldiers cleared out, Bettie fetched John from the well and helped him rejoin his unit. The two exchanged letters for six months until Coker was discharged from the army and returned to Tennessee to marry the Southern woman who had saved his life. [1]

ANTONIA FORD AND JOSEPH C. WILLARD

The infamous Confederate spy Antonia Ford and Union Major Joseph C. Willard were another couple separated by their respective loyalties. When the Union forces occupied Fairfax, Virginia, they set up headquarters in the Ford family home. Antonia charmed and conversed with the men, then passed valuable bits of intelligence along to her family friend J.E.B. Stuart. Her information proved so valuable in the First Battle of Manassas that Stuart commissioned Ford to be an honorary member of his staff. US Major Joseph C. Willard, stationed in Fairfax, found himself immediately drawn to the elegant Antonia. Meanwhile, her espionage acts finally caught up with her, and Ford was arrested. Willard was assigned to escort Antonia to the notoriously dismal Old Capitol Prison in Washington, DC, but he couldn't stand the thought of her being there and lobbied for her release. After finally convincing Antonia to take the oath of allegiance to the US government — a common thing forced on former Confederates — Willard resigned from his post in the army. The couple married seven months later and went on to have three children.[2] When a relative criticized Antonia for marrying a Northerner, she teasingly responded: "I knew I could not revenge myself on the whole nation, but felt very capable of tormenting one Yankee to death, so I took the Major."[3]

KADY AND ROBERT BROWNELL

Kady Brownell was a newlywed of one month when her husband decided to enlist; she refused to be separated from him in spite of his protests. Kady accompanied Robert to the enlistment agent, who adamantly refused to grant her entrance to the army. But her determination proved stronger than the military's, and she applied directly to the governor instead. Brownell was so persuasive that the governor accepted her into the First Rhode Island Infantry as a color guard and "daughter of the regiment."[4]

Kady designed her own army uniform to match her husband's in color and design and then practiced with a rifle and a saber until she could handle both with facility. Color guards were among the first to be targeted and fired upon, but she accepted the dangerous job and performed it with valor. During the Battle of Bull Run, Brownell maintained her position with the

Kady Brownell

flag through hours of fighting; as billowing smoke and enemy fire threatened to separate the soldiers, she held the colors high so the company could hold ranks. When Kady and Robert were honorably discharged after three months of service, they reenlisted with the Rhode Island Fifth, where Kady's actions during battle saved the regiment, and the men in the company began referring to her as the Heroine of New Bern.[5] Robert was shot in the thigh during this conflict, and Brownell accompanied him to military hospitals in Rhode Island and New York to aid in his recovery. Eventually, they were honorably discharged from the service; the couple lived together to old age and died eight months apart.[6]

SARAH AND WILLIAM MCENTIRE

Sarah McEntire of Virginia had been married several years and already had a number of children when her husband, William, left to fight with the Confederate forces. Unable to stand the thought of separation, Sarah entrusted her little ones to her stepmother's care and traveled to Richmond, where she volunteered with the army hospital, distributing "coffee, donuts, and plugs of tobacco" to the soldiers.[7]

As night began to fall, however, Sarah

would pull on trousers and a spare Confederate uniform and make her way to her husband's encampment. William placed his tent at the outskirts of the camp and marked it so that Sarah could steal inside and spend the night in his arms. Just as pink streaks of dawn began to touch the sky, Sarah would creep away shortly before the morning bugle sounded. With this clever conspiracy, the couple refused to be separated, and lessened the impact of war on their love.

ELLEN AND WILLIAM CRAFT

Born on a cotton plantation near Macomb, Georgia, Ellen witnessed her mother being routinely sexually assaulted by her white master. Ellen served as a lady's maid and protected her younger half-sister from attempted rape and floggings, often taking punishments in her sister's stead. Ellen met and fell in love with William Craft, a man who was no stranger to the horrors of slavery himself, as his parents and siblings had been auctioned off to pay his master's gambling debts.

Ellen and William "jumped the broomstick" together, the only wedding ceremony available to most slaves. The Crafts were both determined to raise their future children in freedom. William hired out for carpentry work and was able to save a bit of money, while Ellen used her skills as a seamstress to make herself the outfit of a wealthy gentleman planter. Ellen bandaged her arm and passed herself off as a wounded slave owner traveling to receive medical treatment. William, meanwhile, masqueraded as her faithful servant. Because she had been denied literacy, Ellen had an ally write her alleged name — William Johnson — on the inside of her sling should she be called upon to print her name.

The disguised couple departed during the Christmas holidays, traveling first to Philadelphia and then on to Boston. Concerned by the increasing racial tensions in the United States, the Crafts departed for England, where they waited out the war. After the Confederacy's surrender, the couple returned to Georgia so Ellen could rescue her mother from the plantation. The couple had several children, born, as they had intended, into freedom. Ellen raised her children and fought for women's suffrage; she and her husband remained devoted to each other until the end of their lives.[8]

RACHEL BOWMAN AND SAMUEL CORMANY

The diaries of Rachel and Samuel Cormany of Pennsylvania offer a rare snapshot of the impact of the war on a young, working-class couple, drawing in clear strokes the range of emotions the war evoked. Both of their detailed journals survived the conflict, so the two accounts can be placed side by side. When Rachel Bowman enrolled at Otterbein University in Westerville, Ohio, her family took in boarders to help cover her tuition. Samuel Cormany, who took up lodging with Rachel's family, found himself smitten from their first meeting. He confessed in his journal: "I actually admit I entertain what I suppose is called love, but being . . . my superior in College Education, I dare scarcely hope for actual return, were I to declare my feelings, and desires."[9]

Samuel must have not been very clear about his growing regard, because Rachel felt uncertain about his intentions: "Some thing makes me half think that he loves me. But I am older than he, if it were the other way something might grow out of our regard for each other."[10] Samuel finally cleared things up by proposing, and Rachel accepted, marrying him in a simple ceremony at home on November 25, 1860. Rachel wrote, "I am happy & yet my heart is almost full to bursting."[11]

The couple began their life together in Samuel's native Canada, postponing their return to the United States in the hopes that the tense political situation there would be resolved. In a rather unusual choice for the times, Samuel stayed by Rachel's side throughout her first labor and childbirth, writing, "I took it in my arms & kissed it. and then I held it to its Mother — who smiled upon it, and named it Mary Brittania."[12]

When news of secession reached the Cormanys, Samuel felt he must take up arms in support of America. "I really inwardly feel that I want to go and do my part — as a Man — as a Volunteer . . . and Darling is likeminded — That is, she is loyal and true — and wants to see the South subdued — and however hard it would be to be alone here amongst strangers."[13] The couple returned to Chambersburg, Pennsylvania, where Rachel and her daughter stayed with Samuel's parents. Rachel urged Samuel to go fight but confessed, "It went hard to see him go. For he is more than life to me. . . . at times still I am overcome, tears relieve me very much."[14]

After Samuel's departure, the two lived

for moments when Samuel could return home on leave. A few times the army passed close enough to Chambersburg that Samuel was able to stop and see his family. On October 14, 1862, Samuel wrote, "I took my Pet by Surprise. . . . Oh! It seemed so sweet again to meet and pour out our very souls to each other."[15]

In July of 1863, as the fighting drew closer to Chambersburg, Rachel watched with increasing nervousness as gray-clad soldiers passed outside her windows. She did not know that twenty-five miles away Samuel was witnessing the horrors of Gettysburg. "Dead men, horses, smashed artillery, were strewn in utter confusion. . . . Their bodies so bloated . . . that they were utterly unrecognizable. . . . The scene simply beggars description."[16] After the battle at Gettysburg, Samuel's unit pursued the enemy toward the Potomac River, and Samuel was among the first soldiers to reenter Chambersburg, where he found Rachel watching the scene from the window with her baby in her arms.

In spite of their hopes the conflict would soon draw to a close, the war dragged on. In utter loneliness Rachel wrote, "What will woman not do or endure for the man she loves."[17] In late February 1865, Samuel received a month's leave; but parting once more at the end of it was almost more than Rachel could bear. Samuel, too, suffered the impact of such a long separation. After receiving a letter from Samuel, Rachel wrote, "He has been tempted so severely & seems so depressed in spirits. I fell on my knees & tried to pray to the Lord in his behalf."[18] It appears that Samuel had given in to the same temptations of many soldiers around him — drinking alcohol and enjoying the women who followed the army, though he didn't confide the details to Rachel at the time.

Samuel's unit pursued General Robert E. Lee and witnessed the surrender at Appomattox. Though he was one of the first to receive word the war would soon be over, Samuel was one of the last discharged, since he was sent to Lynchburg, Virginia, as part of a peacekeeping force. His letters evidenced his increasing boredom and frustration. Finally, on August 21, 1865, Samuel returned home to Rachel. "Joy to the world," she wrote. "My little world at least. I am no more a war widdow — My Precious is home safe."[19] Equally overcome by emotion, Samuel recorded, "O what a joy to press my Darlings to my bosom and know that now we can plan to be together . . .

and live with and for each other."[20]

A few days after his return, Samuel chose to be entirely honest with his wife about his actions during the conflict. He spoke openly of "the very worst features of my shortcomings and lapses," and Rachel called the revelation "the saddest week of my life." But she noted, "He seems almost heartbroken over his missteps & I feel that it needs an effort to save him from despair."[21] The couple decided to start over together, departing by prairie schooner to Kansas, where Rachel opened a school and Samuel took up preaching at a frontier mission. The couple eventually had two more children.

Rachel and Samuel were buried beside each other in Johnstown, Pennsylvania, to part no more.

ARABELLA AND FRANCIS BARLOW

Of course, not all wartime love stories can have happy endings. Francis and Arabella Barlow married on April 20, 1861, the day before he departed to serve the Union army.[22] Arabella was a brilliant and witty socialite of New York City; Francis was a Harvard-graduated lawyer ten years her junior. Francis served with valor in some of the most intense battles of the war, including those in the Shenandoah Valley and the

Peninsula campaign. A year after her husband enlisted, Arabella followed him into the army as a nurse, arriving on the battlefield of Antietam just in time to see him carried off, shot in the groin. She cared for him as he convalesced, and ten months later he returned to the field.

Francis fought in the campaign at Gettysburg, while Arabella nursed fallen soldiers nearby, and they visited each other during lulls in the fighting. When a Confederate attack penetrated the lines, Francis was shot in the back while attempting to defend Cemetery Hill. In the aftermath of the battle, a Confederate officer recognized Barlow and moved him into the shade. Francis informed the officer that his wife worked as a nurse nearby and pled with him to send Arabella word of his injury. Believing Barlow would soon be dead, the officer complied, and promised to grant Arabella permission to pass through the Confederate lines.

Arabella braved rifle fire as she rode through Gettysburg bearing a white flag to search among the fallen for her husband. At the battlefield, she informed the commanding officer, "My husband is wounded and left within the enemy's lines, I must go to him."[23] Believing Francis to be mortally wounded, the Confederates left the Barlows in Gettysburg when they retreated. In spite of the doctors' predictions, Arabella nursed Francis back to health, and eventually they both returned to the field.

Some time later while serving near the battle of Fredericksburg, Francis grew alarmed by his wife's condition, as she showed signs of typhus, a common disease at the front. Arabella collapsed while working at a hospital and was soon admitted as a patient herself. Believing she was on the mend, Francis returned to his post, but while leading an attack at Deep Bottom on July 28, 1864, he received word that Arabella had died.[24] Stricken by grief, Francis found himself unable to continue fighting. He left to bury his wife, fully aware of the irony that she had saved his life twice from the ravages of war, but it was she who finally fell as a casualty.

LUCY WOOD AND WADDY BUTLER

Love stories in all ages have inspired beautifully written letters and journals, and some haunting correspondence remains from the Civil War. The following innocuous note marked the beginning of courtship for Lucy Wood and Waddy Butler: "Miss Lucy," Waddy wrote, "will you give me the great pleasure of permitting me to accompany you to church this evening at half past eight?"[25] Lucy Wood met Waddy Butler when he was a student at the University of Virginia, and his first shy note began their romance. By October, Waddy's correspondence had grown far more intimate: "Many people have married with less, have lived contented, and died happy. You and I may and can do likewise. Let us get married, go to some place where we know no one, live quietly and economically, and strive to be contented. If we do this, I think as much happiness as usually falls to the lot of mortals will be ours."[26]

The couple wed on July 3, 1861, at home with relatives and friends. Lucy said the event was "as much importance to me as the wonderful affairs of state are to the rest of the world." For the ceremony, she wore "a plain muslin skirt" and "dressed as simply as possible," claiming she would not have wanted to wear anything expensive "at such a time as this."[27] Ten days after the wedding, Waddy enlisted with the Second Florida Regiment.

Though Lucy claimed to "have no political opinion, and have a peculiar dislike to all females who discuss such matters," she refused to entirely support secession, since she feared the South would attempt to reopen the slave trade, an idea which she deemed "extremely revolting." But once war became a reality, Butler fully rallied behind the Confederate cause, "let the dangers be what they may."[28]

Those dangers soon became reality as casualties lists circulated month after month, cutting the community of Richmond to its core. "We live from day to day," Lucy wrote, "knowing not what a day or an hour may bring forth, waiting to hear perhaps that he who is nearest us has fallen by the hand of disease or in the battlefield. How fast is every house becoming the house of mourning."[29] To support war efforts, Lucy spent long hours preparing food, nursing soldiers, and endlessly sewing uniforms. In 1862, Waddy received sick leave, and Lucy gladly nursed him back to health. Of the time he was by her side, she wrote: "We forgot the war and the trouble thereof for a short time in our own happiness at home."[30]

But all too soon he returned to the front lines, and on May 7, 1863, Lucy wrote: "I am very anxious to hear from Mr. Butler. I received a letter written by him a week or more ago, and he was then very confident of a victory."[31] She could not know that her beloved husband had fallen two days previously in the Battle of Chancellorsville. She would not receive word of his passing until July 3, while the Battle of Gettysburg captured the attention of the nation. When word of Waddy's death reached her in early summer, on the evening of her wedding anniversary, she sat down and wrote: "Just two years since tonight I was a bride. A few kind friends stood around me . . . and yet, though many had already rushed to arms, we were too happy to take warning. Since that night, four of the little company have been taken to their final resting place . . . and rivers of blood have been poured forth, and I, I am left alone without hope save in the grave which God be thanked must come someday."[32] This heartbreaking account is the last entry in Lucy's journal. After becoming a Confederate war widow, she essentially disappeared from public life, taking up residence with her family, and never remarrying. Butler stayed close to her three brothers and their families, and lived out the remainder of her seventy-nine years in the same Virginia county.

ANNA MORRISON AND THOMAS "STONEWALL" JACKSON

Heartbreak also inspired the writings of Mary Anna Morrison Jackson. Though

Mary Anna swore she would never marry a Democrat, a soldier, or a widower, she married all three when she wed Confederate general Thomas "Stonewall" Jackson in 1857. The couple married at home, and their first child died in infancy a year later. Mary Anna moved in with relatives during the war and gave birth to their second child, daughter Julia, in 1862, just before Jackson fought in the Battle of Fredericksburg. He saw and held his daughter for the first time in April 1863. Around the same time, he wrote to his wife, "Pray for a realization of all our beautiful dream, sitting beside our own hearthstone in our own home. . . . May God in his mercy spare my life and make it worthy of you. *Your soldier.*"

Alas, their prayers were not answered as they hoped, and only a few months later, this beloved general tragically fell to accidental fire from his own men. Surgeons removed Jackson's arm in an attempt to save his life, but the wound became infected, and Mary Anna traveled to be by his side in his final moments. He said goodbye to their child and passed from life, holding on to Mary Anna's hand. His last words to her were "Let us pass over the river and rest under the shade of the trees."[33]

Several years later, in 1891, Mary Anna

undertook to publish her husband's biography, choosing to include many personal details from their life together, as well as letters exchanged during the war. She said in the preface, "For many years after the death of my husband the shadow over my life was so deep, and all that concerned him was so sacred, that I could not consent to lift the veil to the public gaze. But time softens, if it does not heal, the bitterest sorrow. . . . In forcing my mind and pen to do their task, I found some 'surcease of sorrow.' "[34] Mary Anna never remarried and wore mourning clothes for the remainder of her life.

SARAH SHUMWAY AND SULLIVAN BALLOU

Sullivan Ballou, a successful Rhode Island attorney who fought for the Union army, had the distinction of writing what is perhaps one of the most hauntingly beautiful love letters ever written. Sarah Shumway and Sullivan Ballou had been married for six years when Abraham Lincoln called for volunteers to join the Union army. Wanting to show his great admiration for the president, Ballou left a thriving law practice and political career to enlist in the service. He bade goodbye to his wife and two young sons, to whom he wrote regularly. A week before the First Battle of Bull Run, one night he found himself plagued by premonitions and unable to sleep. Sullivan had been raised himself by a widowed mother,[35] and this background surely influenced his thoughts of what his potential death would mean to Sarah. He picked up his pen and wrote:

"Sarah, my love for you is deathless. It seems to bind me with mighty cables, that nothing but Omnipotence can break; and yet, my love of country comes over me like a strong wind, and bears me irresistibly on with all those chains, to the battlefield. The memories of all the blissful moments I have spent with you come crowding over me, and I feel most deeply grateful to God and you, that I have enjoyed them so long. And how hard it is for me to give them up, and burn to ashes the hopes of future years, when, God willing, we might still have lived and loved together, and seen our boys grow up to honorable manhood around us.

"I know I have but few claims upon Divine Providence, but something whispers to me, perhaps it is the wafted prayer of my little Edgar, that I shall return to my loved ones unharmed. If I do not, my dear Sarah, never forget how much I love you, nor that, when my last breath escapes me on the battle-field, it will whisper your name.

"Forgive my many faults, and the many pains I have caused you. How thoughtless, how foolish I have oftentimes been! How gladly would I wash out with my tears, every little spot upon your happiness, and struggle with all the misfortune of this world, to shield you and my children from harm. But I cannot, I must watch you from the spirit land and hover near you, while you buffet the storms with your precious little freight, and wait with sad patience till we meet to part no more.

"But, O Sarah, if the dead can come back to this earth, and flit unseen around those they loved, I shall always be near you in the garish day, and the darkest night amidst your happiest scenes and gloomiest hours always, always, and, if the soft breeze fans your cheek, it shall be my breath; or the cool air cools your throbbing temples, it shall be my spirit passing by.

"Sarah, do not mourn me dear; think I am gone, and wait for me, for we shall meet again.

"As for my little boys, they will grow as I have done, and never know a father's love and care. Little Willie is too young to remember me long, and my blue-eyed Edgar will keep my frolics with him among the dimmest memories of his childhood. Sarah, I have unlimited confidence in your maternal care, and your development of their characters. Tell my two mothers, I call God's blessing upon them. O Sarah, I wait for you there! Come to me, and lead thither my children."[36]

Major Ballou was struck by a cannonball that simultaneously shattered his leg and killed his horse during the Battle of Bull Run; he died several days later in a field hospital from the amputation wound. Sullivan's body was eventually buried in Swan Point Cemetery, Providence, Rhode Island. He never mailed this letter, but it reached Sarah with the rest of his personal effects a few months after his death. Though Sarah was only twenty-four years old when her husband died, she never remarried. She supported her two sons, aged two and four at the time of their father's death, with their father's military pension and by teaching piano lessons.[37] When Sarah passed away at the age of eighty, she was buried beside Sullivan. Legend has it that a copy of the letter was buried with her.

The war changed people — romantically as well as in almost every other way. It brought couples together, introducing some who wouldn't have met otherwise, drove distance between others, and left thousands to grieve by the side of a headstone. More than 200,000 women became widows from the conflict; and in the South particularly, few homes were untouched by loss.[38] The "cost" of a conflict is typically measured in military casualties and in dollars of destruction; quantifying the emotional impact on families and relationships is far more difficult to do. There is no question, however, that the Civil War left a deep and profound impact on the emotional health of the nation. For survivors, the intensity of the war years threw the enjoyment of domestic life into sharp relief, and many who endured years of separation vowed they would never again take for granted everyday moments spent by the side of the people they loved most in this world.

Further Reading

Kristen Brill, ed. *The Diary of a Civil War Bride: Lucy Wood Butler of Virginia.* Baton Rouge, LA: LSU Press, 2017.

M. R. Cordell. *Courageous Women of the Civil War: Soldiers, Spies, Medics, and*

More. Chicago: Chicago Review Press, 2017.

Rachel Bowman Cormany. *The Cormany Diaries: A Northern Family in the Civil War,* ed. James C. Mohr and Richard E. Winslow. Pittsburgh: University of Pittsburgh Press, 1982.

Elizabeth D. Leonard. *All the Daring of the Soldier: Women of the Civil War Armies.* New York: Penguin Books, 1999.

H. Donald Winkler. *Stealing Secrets: How a Few Daring Women Deceived Generals, Impacted Battles, and Altered the Course of the Civil War.* Naperville, IL: Cumberland House, 2010.

Notes

Epigraph: Sarah Morgan Dawson, *A Confederate Girl's Diary* (London: William Heinemann, 1913), 403.

1. H. Donald Winkler, *Stealing Secrets: How a Few Daring Women Deceived Generals, Impacted Battles, and Altered the Course of the Civil War* (Naperville, IL: Cumberland House, 2010), xiii.

2. Larry G. Eggleston, *Women in the Civil War: Extraordinary Stories of Soldiers, Spies, Nurses, Doctors, Cursaders, and Others* (Jefferson, NC: McFarland & Com-

pany, 2003), 97–101.

3. In David Williams, *A People's History of the Civil War: Struggles for the Meaning of Freedom* (New York: The New Press, 2005), 140.

4. M. R. Cordell, *Courageous Women of the Civil War: Soldiers, Spies, Medics, and More* (Chicago: Chicago Review Press, 2017), 155.

5. Cordell, *Courageous Women of the Civil War,* 160.

6. Cordell, *Courageous Women of the Civil War,* 153–62.

7. From Norma Timm family history. See also Beatrice Pritchett Budvarson, *Lest We Forget: The Pritchetts' History* (Murray, UT: Roylance Publishing, 1989).

8. For more information on Ellen Craft, see Ann Chirhart and Betty Wood, eds., *Georgia Women: Their Lives and Times, Volume 1* (Athens, GA: University of Georgia Press, 2009), 83–99.

9. Rachel Bowman Cormany, *The Cormany Diaries: A Northern Family in the Civil War,* ed. James C. Mohr and Richard E. Winslow (Pittsburgh: University of Pittsburgh Press, 1982), 28.

10. Cormany, *Cormany Diaries,* 29.

11. Cormany, *Cormany Diaries,* 123.

12. Cormany, *Cormany Diaries,* 192.

13. Cormany, *Cormany Diaries,* 229.

14. Cormany, *Cormany Diaries,* 253.

15. Cormany, *Cormany Diaries,* 241.

16. Cormany, *Cormany Diaries,* 326.

17. Cormany, *Cormany Diaries,* 378.

18. Cormany, *Cormany Diaries,* 550.

19. Cormany, *Cormany Diaries,* 582.

20. Cormany, *Cormany Diaries,* 579.

21. Cormany, *Cormany Diaries,* 582.

22. Christian G. Samito, ed., *Fear Was Not in Him: The Civil War Letters of Major General Francis C. Barlow, USA* (New York: Fordham University Press, 2004), xx.

23. Samito, *Fear Was Not in Him,* 159–61.

24. Samito, *Fear Was Not in Him,* xxxix.

25. Virginia Historical Society, Richmond, VA, Lomax Family Papers, Mss1L8378a, Lucy Wood Butler and Waddy B. Butler, 22 May 1859–3 July 1863, section 27, 1.

26. Virginia Historical Society, 14.

27. Virginia Historical Society, 14.

28. Virginia Historical Society, 20.

29. Lucy Wood Butler, *The Diary of a Civil War Bride: Lucy Wood Butler of Virginia,* ed. Kristen Brill (Baton Rouge, LA: LSU Press, 2017), 98.

30. Butler, *Diary of a Civil War Bride,* 137.

31. Butler, *Diary of a Civil War Bride,* 177.

32. Butler, *Diary of a Civil War Bride,* 178. The word "company" in her journal entry refers to the friends who attended her

wedding — four of whom were now dead.

33. Mary Anna Jackson, *Life and Letters of General Thomas J. Jackson* (New York: Harper, 1892), 471.

34. Jackson, *Life and Letters of General Thomas J. Jackson,* preface.

35. Sullivan Ballou Papers, 1858–1873, MSS 277, Rhode Island Historical Society.

36. Sullivan Ballou Papers.

37. Wiley Sword, *Courage under Fire: Profiles in Bravery from the Battlefields of the Civil War* (New York: St. Martin's Press, 2011).

38. It is difficult to estimate the number of widows created by the Civil War. J. David Hacker estimates 200,000, based on the assumption that 28 percent of the 750,000 men who died were married at the time of their deaths. The toll was far heavier in the South, which sustained slightly fewer losses than the North but had drawn troops from a population half the size. Very few, if any, able-bodied men in the South between the ages of 15 and 60 were not in service. See "A Census-Based Count of the Civil War Dead," *Civil War History,* 57(4), December 2011: 307–48.

CHAPTER 14
PATHWAYS TO PEACE

Harriet Tubman

"The time has come when we can do justice to those who were once in arms against us. . . . Hostile armies now fall into line in the great procession to that realm of silence in which all enmities are buried."
— Henry M. Field, in the introduction to Mary Anna Jackson's biography of her husband

Abraham Lincoln kept his second inaugural address short and to the point during the final days of the war, stating that there was little need for an extensive speech to people already more than familiar with his objectives. He spoke of the intense suffering of the nation and the irony that both North and South had prayed for God's assistance in the conflict; he spoke of the scourge of slavery disappearing from the land; and he concluded: "With malice toward none; with charity for all; with firmness in the right, as God gives us to see the right, let us strive on to finish the work we are in; to bind up the nation's wounds; to care for him who shall have borne the battle, and for his widow, and his orphan — to do all which may achieve and cherish a just, and lasting peace, among ourselves, and with all nations."[1]

With these words, Lincoln hoped to establish the tone of the reunification of the nation that would shortly come to pass. Aware more than anyone of the deep divides and animosity on both sides, Lincoln hoped that a compassionate and lasting peace would be possible, for in his own words, "There has been enough bloodshed."[2]

The nation's wounds that Lincoln spoke of could not have been overemphasized. From a financial standpoint, the federal government was flat broke, in spite of the nation's very first income tax that had been levied to raise much needed funds. More than 600,000 soldiers from both sides lay dead, buried in graves marked and unmarked, on land appropriated for battlefields that had once been the site of prosperous farms and settlements. The South, which had been the seventh strongest economy in the world at the outbreak of the war, lay in literal ruins. Thriving towns such as Richmond, Virginia, had been nearly obliterated, and the burned skeletons of shelled buildings mirrored the mourning clothes of its citizens. In addition to the staggering military casualties, more than 50,000 civilians had perished in the conflict. Many displaced and wounded soldiers found themselves unable to travel the long miles that lay between themselves and home. Former slaves had been scattered to the winds — many as refugees released from slavery into an uncertain future. While wealthy white Southerners had watched their resources disappear in the smoke of house fires and inflation, the working class struggled to subsist at the most basic of levels.

General Ulysses S. Grant hushed soldiers that began firing their weapons in celebration of the surrender at Appomattox, saying, "The war is over. The Rebels are our countrymen again."[3] But others who lived through the horrors of the conflict were not as ready to be forgiving.

Confederate soldiers were not permitted burial beside Union soldiers, and today, when you visit many Civil War military graveyards, you find headstones often eerily segregated by race as well. Confederate graves remain common objects of vandalism, despite the fact that in a restored nation all who fought are now fallen US veterans. I sensed an echo of this same unease in a gift shop in Fredericksburg, where I purchased postcards with quotations by both Grant and Lee. The man ringing up my purchase teased me about needing to pick a side. "I respect both these men," I said, returning his banter, "and the war is over now, so I don't have to choose."

Five short days after Lee's surrender at Appomattox, John Wilkes Booth sought to vindicate the South by firing the shots that rang through Ford's Theatre and echoed across the nation. In the delusions of his mind, he believed the act would make him a hero, but the country that had already lost so much now reeled from the shock of Lincoln's assassination. As I retraced the events of the conflict through Mississippi, across Louisiana, Georgia, Virginia, and into Ford's Theatre, I could not help wondering how differently events might have played out if Lincoln had lived. In many regards, the hope for a reunification based on forgiveness and compassion died with him in the small bedroom across from the theater; and the events of Reconstruction and post-Reconstruction all too often only reinforced and deepened divides that led to conflict in the first place.

Of course, the nation had experienced horrific events not easily forgotten. Battling the throes of overwhelming grief and PTSD, people coped as best they could, and some were simply unable to put aside the past and face a new reality. Thousands of Confederates chose exile in Mexico, Belize,

Egypt, and Brazil (where they established a colony called Americana that still exists today)[4] rather than face life under the flag they had fought against. Many Confederate widows wore black mourning clothes for the remainder of their lives in perpetual tribute to their loss. Other women who played a significant role in the war's conclusion showed a remarkable capacity to turn away from violence and bitterness, laying the foundation for a reconciliation that, though far from perfect, was possible nonetheless.

VIRGINIA MASON MCLEAN

Virginia Mason McLean had the dubious honor of watching the opening and closing scenes of the Civil War from a firsthand vantage point. Virginia grew up on a 1,200-acre plantation named Yorkshire, near Manassas Junction, Virginia, which she later inherited from her parents.[5] A small stream called Bull Run meandered across the land where she lived until her first marriage. After her first husband passed away, Virginia returned to Yorkshire with her three daughters, Maria, Ocie, and Sarah.[6] In 1853, the wealthy widow married debt-laden Wilmer McLean and had two additional children, Wilmer and Lula, born on the property. The youngest was nearly four when the war broke out.

Fort Sumter fell on April 14, 1861, but no major battles had yet taken place when General Pierre Beauregard met with the McLeans sometime in early summer to discuss the use of Yorkshire as a headquarters for the Confederate army. General Robert E. Lee stationed troops at Manassas Junction in May, since it was a strategic railroad point. The family allowed officers to move into the house on July 17 and convert the barn into a hospital. It seems most likely the family stayed in the vicinity with neighbors for a short time before removing to a safer area. On July 18, as servants prepared the noonday meal for the general and his staff, a Union cannonball smashed into the Yorkshire's log cabin kitchen and exploded into a skillet of stew. Beauregard's chief signal officer reported that no one was hurt, but the dinner was ruined "by the mud daubing between the logs jarred out as the shell passed through both walls falling into the sliced up meat & dished up vegetables."[7]

Forces continued arriving in the area, but that didn't stop Virginia's second daughter, Ocie Mason, a headstrong teenager and accomplished equestrienne, from taking her daily ride. In the early hours of July 21, she boldly rode out across her mother's land, and came across Union soldiers building a barricade. "Why are you obstructing our roads?" she demanded, before galloping back to inform General Ewell of all she had seen.[8] The battle of Bull Run began in earnest a few short hours later, directly outside Virginia's home.

When fighting subsided a few days later, Yorkshire was used as a hospital, headquarters, and military prison. The situation hadn't long stabilized when the Second Battle of Bull Run overran the plantation again a year later. Like many war refugees, Virginia and her children stayed in several different places with family and friends for the early years of hostilities even as the McLeans sought for a more permanent place to wait out the war, knowing the entire Manassas area would be volatile for quite some time. In the fall of 1862,[9] the family purchased property 150 miles southwest of the Yorkshire plantation in the village of Appomattox Court House. In January 1863, Virginia gave birth to her daughter Nannie, giving the couple even more motivation to find a permanent spot. In the fall of 1863, they moved into a red brick home with a white front porch in Appomattox Court

House, where they hoped to enjoy peace and safety. In an incredibly ironic twist, that home too became an important landmark in Civil War history.

Four years and 600,000 deaths after the initial battle at Bull Run, what remained of Robert E. Lee's army retreated from Petersburg and the fallen Confederate capital through the countryside of Virginia, traveling southwest in a last desperate attempt to join forces with General Joseph Johnston's army in North Carolina. However, Union generals Sheridan and Ord intercepted Lee's troops, cutting off the path of his escape and leaving Lee trapped between Sheridan and Ord on one side and Meade on the other. The position left Lee little alternative beyond surrender. On April 9, 1865, Lee sent a message to Grant stating that he wished to work out terms, and Lee's aide-de-camp, Lieutenant Colonel Charles Marshall, looked for an appropriate building in Appomattox Court House for the auspicious event to take place. Wilmer McLean was the first person Marshall saw when he entered the town, and he sought the local's advice for a suitable signing location. Wilmer first showed the aide an uninhabited structure, which Marshall rejected;

McLean then said, "Maybe my house will do."[10]

We can only imagine Virginia McLean's feelings as she prepared her home on Palm Sunday to welcome two legendary generals as they worked out the terms that would bring an end to Lee's army, signaling the end of the war. McLean had already sacrificed one home to the conflict, and the very event she hosted would soon render the McLean family's wealth — or the portion held in Confederate bills, at any rate — worthless. It can be assumed that food and housing details were prepared and readied by the hands of slaves overseen by Virginia — slaves who would very soon be freed as an inevitable result of the actions that occurred in her parlor.[11]

Forty-six years old and pregnant with her last child, Virginia likely ensured that everything was prepared for the meeting, and then she retreated upstairs with her children, where she may have entertained the little ones so they would not interrupt the proceedings below.[12] Did eight-year-old Lula become upset when she realized she had left her favorite doll, handmade by her mother, on the sofa in the room where the meeting took place? It was too late to retrieve the toy, and Virginia probably quieted the child as best she could as Grant and Lee continued negotiations. Soldiers in the parlor placed Lula's doll on the mantel for the solemn event.

Without immediate means to broadcast news, knowledge of the surrender was limited to persons in the vicinity; even as Grant and Lee formalized the terms of surrender, other armies remained in the field. Indeed, Lee reminded Grant that he did not hold the power to surrender the entire Confederate army, though his Army of Northern Virginia was by far the most important Confederate military force. Certainly the surrender came as no surprise to those in the immediate area. Ellen Bryant lived near the village and described the Confederate soldiers who passed by her home. "They were almost starved, and in ragged and tattered clothes."[13] By the time Lee handed over his army, one regiment recorded that only 72 of their 175 soldiers even had firearms.[14] In keeping with Lincoln's instructions to show mercy, Grant allowed Lee's men to retain their sidearms and horses so they could return to their families and begin the work of spring planting. He also ordered that rations be distributed to the hungry Confederate soldiers.

Grant set up printing presses in Clover

Hill Tavern near the McLean home that worked night and day to print nearly 30,000 parole passes so discharged soldiers would be able to travel through Union lines.[15] The two generals shook hands and Lee returned to his troops to inform them of the agreement, while Grant remained in the McLean home, organizing logistics. Three days later in the official surrender ceremony that lasted six hours, Lee's men relinquished their firearms and battle flags, stacking them in rows along the Richmond-Lynchburg Stage Road. Union soldiers gave a marching salute to the bedraggled troops, their countrymen once more, and tears were shed on both sides as soldiers recognized that the horrific war that had taken such a toll on the nation would soon be drawing to a close.

Virginia and her children returned downstairs to a world quite changed from the one they had departed. Lula's doll was nowhere to be found. The doll had been pilfered by a member of Sheridan's staff, who called her the "silent witness"[16] and tossed the plaything back and forth. The doll was one of many McLean family possessions taken or purchased by those who wanted a piece of the momentous event. Wilmer sold the tables where the terms had been written as well as several of the chairs in the room. Lula's doll appeared to be just one more casualty of the war. But miraculously, in 1992, the doll, made of coarse unbleached cotton with two inked eyes, reappeared, rescued from the attic of the Moore family, descendants of the Union officer who had kept the plaything for more than a century.[17] Lula's doll was at last returned to the Appomattox Court House National Historical Park, where she is still on display today.[18]

In a seeming statistical impossibility, Virginia Mason McLean's two homes played central roles in the beginning and the ending of the Civil War.

THE FREEDMEN (AND WOMEN)

Nearly four million enslaved men, women, and children were freed by the events of the Civil War. Many former slaves had training in specific skills they could now use to gain employment, but others languished in poverty, their families devastated by the institution of slavery and its lingering effects. In response, thousands of northern women, black and white, traveled south after the war to teach freed slaves. These women established "freedmen" schools, recognizing the key to further advancement lay with education.

Large groups of refugees that had followed the Union army remained in temporary circumstances or refugee camps, needing space to build new communities and help to reunite lost family and friends. Many communities established Freedmen settlements, while 15,000 formerly enslaved "Exodusters" claimed free farmland in Kansas. Four thousand former slaves opted to emigrate to Liberia, Africa, while others cast their fortune in the American West, hoping to encounter less racial prejudice in unsettled lands.

Aunt Clara Brown, pioneer and philanthropist, escaped slavery herself and devoted her time and fortune to helping other survivors. Brown succeeded in purchasing her own freedom in 1856 and made her way west with a wagon train to settle in frontier Colorado. Brown established a successful laundry business in the mining town of Central City, and she invested her money in surrounding mines until she became one of the wealthiest African American women in the West. After the Civil War, Clara traveled back to the South, looking for her beloved daughter, Eliza Jane, who had been sold on the auction block at the age of ten. Though she didn't find Eliza at that time, Clara did find hundreds of desperate refugees. She paid to equip a wagon train and accompanied dozens of these men and women to Colorado, where she provided homes and jobs to help them get established in the community. When Clara heard about the plight of the Kansas Exodusters, she journeyed east once more and spent a year volunteering in a refugee camp, providing food, comfort, and counsel to those in need.[19] Dazzled by all that Brown had accomplished, the *Rocky Mountain News* wrote, "We will put 'Aunt Clara' against the world, white or black, for industry, perseverance, energy, and filial love."[20]

Susie King Taylor (see chapter 3) established a school for freed children in Savannah after the war. Harriet Jacobs spent the war years teaching refugees and also fighting to protect their rights against abuses of authority. Jacobs used the fame and financial proceeds from *Incidents in the Life of a Slave Girl* to support this work. At the war's conclusion, she and her daughter fought to establish fair wages and education for slavery survivors.[21]

Fannie Jackson Coppin, who escaped slavery at the age of twelve, ran a night school to educate freed slaves. She graduated from Oberlin College in 1865, and began teaching mathematics, Latin, and Greek at the Institute for Colored Youth in Philadelphia. A few years later, Jackson became the first female African American school principal at the same institution, where she served for thirty-seven years, making vast improvements in the quality of education in Philadelphia. Coppin established homes for working and poor women and wrote newspaper columns to defend the rights of black women.[22]

Retired spy Harriet Tubman also dedicated the remainder of her life to assisting other survivors of the slave system. After the war, Tubman married a Civil War veteran, and they adopted a baby girl. Never properly compensated for her years of espionage, Harriet sold pies, gingerbread, and root beer, wrote a biography, and delivered speeches to supplement her income.[23] When Tubman did finally receive $200 for her spying, she immediately spent it on a washhouse, where she trained freewomen to use this marketable skill. Tubman spoke out regularly on behalf of voting rights for African American women and established the Harriet Tubman Home to shelter former slaves as they aged.[24] In Harriet's seventieth year, a friend wrote of her, "Her home is filled with 'odds and ends' of society and to every one outcast she gives food and shelter."[25]

During the post-war years, sisters Sarah and Angelina Grimké, outspoken advocates of abolition (see chapter 1), learned their late brother Henry had fathered three children with his former slave Nancy Weston. Though most white Southerners ignored African American family branches, the Grimké sisters reached out to their nephews in an uncommon move toward racial unity. Hoping to make some small amends for their family's involvement in slavery, Angelina wrote, "As this name is a very uncommon one it occurred to me that you had been probably the slave of one of my brothers & I feel a great desire to know all about you."[26]

The young men, Francis and Archibald, were eager to learn more about their father, and a warm friendship sprang up between them and the sisters. Soon the nephews were frequent visitors in the Grimké home.[27] The women supported their nephews' education as they attended freedmen's schools and went on to Howard and Harvard Universities. Francis and Archibald entered successful careers in ministry and law, respectively, and both went on to play significant roles in the struggle for civil rights. They were proud of the roles their aunts had played in emancipation, and Archibald named his first daughter Angelina.[28]

In many ways, the promises made to slaves during and after the war were never delivered on. Though the Reconstruction era saw initial surges in political positions held by African Americans, within a few decades northern leaders seemed more concerned with making peace with former Confederate leaders than they were with bringing about rights for the slaves they had freed. Black men could technically vote after 1870 (with the adoption of the Fifteenth Amendment) and black women in 1920 (with the adoption of the Nineteenth Amendment), but the reality was that voter intimidation and fraud erased many of the gains made by constitutional amendments, and the abolishment of slavery lapsed into the era of Jim Crow laws, necessitating a continued fight for civil liberties. All too often the peace brought about between the US and the former Confederacy was a peace brokered between white factions only, and was in many ways purchased at the expense of African American advancement.[29]

NURSES AND CLARA BARTON

Women who had found so much purpose in their wartime medical service had no desire to abruptly stop once the guns fell silent. And indeed, the cessation of violence heralded only the beginning of the healing process for thousands of survivors. Mother Bickerdyke (see chapter 10) tended Union soldiers returning from the horrific Confederate prison in Andersonville, Georgia. She went on to work as an attorney, assisting veterans in establishing land claims and receiving their pensions. Former Civil War nurse Georgeanna Woolsey established some of the first US training schools for nurses.[30]

Clara Barton's work after the war is less well-known, but no less remarkable. Barton surveyed the chaos of Washington, DC, which was a jumble of suffering friends and family attempting to find their wounded and lost loved ones. Clara received letters from around the country from separated soldiers and families, who were pleading for similar help. Realizing the chaos in DC represented only a small fraction of the problem, Barton wrote, "a very large number of our soldiers had disappeared from view without leaving behind them any visible trace or record. Whether they had fallen in battle, were lingering in rebel prisons, or had perished in some other way was only to be conjectured. In the then painfully excited state of the public mind, any information respecting them would have afforded the most grateful relief to their families."[31] Employing her uncanny ability to identify and solve problems, Clara sought the support of Abraham Lincoln and opened the Office of Missing Soldiers in 1865. Working with a handful of employees and volunteers to improve the situation, Clara compiled lists of missing soldiers and then published the lists in newspapers or posted them in public places, requesting anyone with information to contact her.

The discovery of the register from Andersonville Prison in Georgia played a major role in Barton's postwar work. In Andersonville, 30,000 prisoners of war had subsisted in disease-ridden quarters intended to house half that number. A Union prisoner, Dorence Atwater, had recorded the burials during his incarceration there. Barton contacted Atwater, and the two worked together to identify soldier remains. They opened mass graves and reburied 13,000 dead soldiers in marked, individual plots. Then Clara notified the grieving families. Recognizing the peace that would come to

Clara Barton

loved ones when provided with information beyond "missing in action," Barton's work was an incredible mission of empathy and compassion. The US military dedicated Andersonville National Cemetery on August 17, 1865, and invited Clara to raise the flag over the grounds. By the time the Office of Missing Soldiers closed its doors in 1868, it had responded to more than 63,000 letters of inquiry and located more than 22,000 men.[32]

Not content with these accomplishments alone, Barton went on to assist with relief efforts around the world. She organized the American branch of the Red Cross and expanded its mission to include natural disasters as well as war relief. When the United States refused to ratify amendments to the Geneva Convention, Clara lobbied Congress and waged a public opinion campaign. The resulting treaty established humanitarian practices for warfare, including protection for medical professionals. The US Senate ratified the updates in 1882, establishing Barton as a pioneer in the area of humanitarian law and international relief work.

Clara was beloved by all she served. In a fitting tribute to her life, a newspaper in Johnstown, Pennsylvania, said, "We cannot thank Miss Barton in words. Hunt the dictionaries of all the languages and you will not find the signs to express our appreciation of her and her work. Try to describe the sunshine. Try to describe the starlight. Words fail."[33]

MARY ANNA CUSTIS LEE, SELINA GRAY, AND THE BURYING OF THE DEAD

Mary Anna Custis, the great-granddaughter of First Lady Martha Washington,[34] was born and raised at Arlington House, a beautiful 5,000-acre estate built by slave labor on a hill overlooking the nation's capital. She was acquainted with her third cousin — and future spouse — Robert E. Lee from childhood, and they often played together at Arlington. Her husband's biographer, Douglas Freeman, would later write, "She loved wild flowers, and old gardens and evening skies."[35] An avid artist, many of Mary's paintings adorned the walls of the family estate. Custis was well educated, versed in literature, Greek, and Latin, and enjoyed discussing politics. Like her mother, Mary was a masterful gardener; she grew eleven varieties of roses in her flower garden and chose her childhood bedroom for its view over the grounds — the same bedroom she would retain with Robert after they were married.

Robert E. Lee, son of a Revolutionary War general and a distinguished military officer in the United States army in his own right, had no wealth to offer Custis, but when he proposed at Arlington House, she accepted. Mary descended the stairs of Arlington to piano accompaniment and married Robert in a quiet ceremony beneath flowers hung from the arches of the parlor.[36] Six of their seven children were born in the bedroom they shared. Each morning Robert was home, he gathered blossoms for her break-fast plate, and they remained deeply in love throughout their lives. Freeman wrote, "Rarely was a woman more fully a part of her husband's life."[37] A devout Episcopalian, Mary believed slaves would eventually be freed and needed to be ready to support themselves, so she broke state law to teach them to read and write.[38]

Robert had spent thirty-two years serving in the US army and traced his family history to two signers of the Declaration of Independence as well as through 220 years of Virginians back to the original colony at Jamestown. Because the Lees were opposed to secession, the Virginians' legislature's decision on April 4, 1861, to leave the Union left the Lees in a heart-wrenching position, struggling with "irreconcilable loyalties."[39] When the secession was announced, Abraham Lincoln offered Robert a military position, and he spent an agonizing night deliberating. At a time when state identity was at least as important as national identity, Lee found himself unable to take up arms against his own people since "All the Lees had been Americans, but they had been Virginians first."[40] While the rest of the South rejoiced, Lee's daughter later recalled, "Arlington became as still and gloomy as if a death had occurred."[41] In the morning, Lee told Mary he had no real choice, for, as he wrote in a letter a few weeks later, "I have been unable to make up my mind to raise my hand against my native state, my relations, my children & my home."[42] He dispatched his resignation from the US army to his army chief and longtime mentor, Simon Cameron. Months later, Mary wrote, "My husband has wept tears of blood over this terrible war, but as a man of honor and a Virginian, he must follow the destiny of his state."[43]

And so Mary's husband and three sons rode away to take up posts in the Confederate army on April 22, leaving Mary at Arlington House. Given the estate's position so close to the Capitol, the United States government could not allow it to remain in Confederate hands. Mary knew it was only a matter of time before she too would have to leave.

At the urging of her husband, Mary and her daughters said goodbye on May 15 to the home that had been connected to her family for decades. "Were it not that I would not add one feather to his [Robert's] load of care, nothing would induce me to abandon my home,"[44] she confided to a friend.

Knowing she would leave behind irreplaceable family heirlooms, including many that had belonged to George and Martha Washington, Mary entrusted the house keys to longtime family servant Selina Gray. Gray's family had been slaves to the Custis family for generations and were descendants of Mount Vernon staff who had once served the Washingtons. Selina had been born on the Arlington estate, had married her husband in the parlor, and had raised seven children in the slave cabins behind the home.

As expected, Union troops moved in to occupy the mansion a few short weeks after the Lees' departure. Though one person was little match for the overwhelming number of troops eager to defile the home of an enemy officer, Selina Gray bravely attempted to perform her final duty, even after Mary's father's will freed her in 1862. Selina continued at Arlington for the remainder of the war, but with the army occupying the home, Gray knew it was only a matter of time before many of the family treasures were ruined. She sent word to General Irvin McDowell, pleading with him to help preserve the heirlooms of the Washington family, which were in danger of being lost forever. With McDowell's assistance, Gray arranged for many items to be housed in the US Patent Office for the duration of the war.

Pain ruled Mary's life in the form of rheumatoid arthritis, which gradually worsened over the war years, compounded by the stress and difficulties of the conflict. Mary's health declined, and she soon required the use of a wheelchair. Fully aware of Mary Lee's poor health and her position behind Confederate lines, in 1863 the federal government demanded payment of taxes on Arlington.[45] Mary's arthritis would not permit her to travel, so she sent her cousin to make the payment; but the commissioner used a technicality to refuse the fee so the estate could be seized for nonpayment. Approximately 14,000 Union troops stationed at the estate looted family belongings, built latrines, cut down trees and outbuildings, and scrawled graffiti across the walls of the mansion. News of the devastation reached Robert, and he wrote to Mary: "It is better to make up our minds to a general loss. They cannot take away the remembrances of the spot, and the memories of those that to us rendered it sacred. That will remain to us as long as life will last and that we can preserve."[46]

The war years were devastating ones for the Lee family. Mary lost her twenty-three-year-old daughter, Annie, and her two-year-old grandson to typhoid fever in 1862. Weeks later, Mary's daughter-in-law delivered a baby who lived only a few short hours. The Lees' son Rooney was shot in battle in 1863, and Mary nursed him during his convalescence until he was captured and placed in prison. Her daughter-in-law passed away the day after Christmas. Bowed down by immense physical and emotional pain, Mary continued to support her husband and his troops by hand-knitting hundreds of pairs of socks for barefoot soldiers. She remained in Richmond for the major part of the conflict and flatly refused to leave when the city fell to the Federal army. In a merciful miracle, Mary's Richmond house was spared from burning by a sudden shift in the wind.

By 1864, the military cemeteries of Washington had filled to capacity, and Quartermaster General Montgomery C. Meigs suggested using Arlington as a cemetery to punish Lee and ensure he would never be able to return to the estate. Meigs ordered a large number of burials close to the house to render it unlivable, and soon the corpses of dozens of Union officers were laid to rest in Mary's flower gardens, including Meigs's own son. Meigs also helped establish a freedman's village on one portion of the extensive grounds.

When the war finally concluded, Mary petitioned the government for the return of Arlington, but her petition was denied. She never quite got over its loss. "Dear old Arlington," she wrote, "I cannot bear to think of that used as it is now & so little hope of my ever getting there again. I do not think I can die in peace until I have seen it once more."[47] Robert passed away in 1870 without seeing the estate again, but in 1873, Mary made the journey to visit her former home. Because she was unable to leave her carriage, former servants, including Selina Gray, came to greet Mary and bring her a drink of water from the well. "I rode out to my dear old home," Mary wrote of the visit, "but so changed it seemed but a dream of the past — I could not have realised [sic] it was Arlington but for the few old oaks they had spared & the trees planted by the Genl and myself which are raising their tall branches to the Heaven which seems to smile on the desecration around them."[48] Mary passed from life a few months later.

In 1882, the Supreme Court of the United States ruled the house had been "illegally confiscated" and paid the Lees' oldest son $150,000, half the property's estimated value. President McKinley ordered the return of confiscated artifacts to the family. In 1925, restoration work on the mansion began, initially restoring it to the period of the 1830s, *before* the time of the Lees (effectually erasing their time spent in the house). Finally, in 1955, the mansion was renamed Arlington House, the Robert E. Lee Memorial, and the furnishings were reinterpreted to the time of Mary and Robert. Selina Gray's children provided essential details regarding the restoration work of the mansion in the 1920s and 1930s. Today the home broods over 400,000 graves, with a view of the Potomac River and the Capitol beyond. In many ways the story of Arlington itself encapsulates the entire story of the conflict, complete with the initial flush of retribution, followed by a gradual easing of hostility — until the lives of those on all sides can hopefully be viewed with more equity and grace.[49]

VARINA DAVIS AND JULIA GRANT

A resort on the Hudson River witnessed an unlikely friendship that came to symbolize the postwar nation. In 1893, Varina Davis, wife of former Confederate President Jefferson Davis, happened to be vacationing when she heard that Julia Grant, wife of General

Ulysses S. Grant, had taken a room close by. Julia knocked on Varina's door and introduced herself. A few hours later, the two women sat on the outdoor piazza, as passersby marveled at this unlikely pair.

Though Varina may have been the First Lady of the Confederacy and Julia the former First Lady of the United States, the two women soon realized what the passersby did not: in spite of obvious differences, they shared far more in common. Both women had been raised in the South, had married West Point graduates, and had spent challenging years relocating in support of their husbands' military careers. Both were recent widows and were enjoying a period of reemerging identity. While Julia worked on her memoirs, Varina had become a popular journalist and writer for Joseph Pulitzer at *The New York World.* Both women hoped to use their work to reconcile tensions between the formerly divided nation. Varina once closed a letter to Julia "with sympathy of one who has suffered in a like way. I am affectionately your friend."[50] Their ability to look beyond differences and see all that unified them set a remarkable example for the nation to follow.

Varina and Julia often took lunch together, went for long drives, and rented adjoining vacation cottages in the Canadian village of Coburg. They found solace in their similar challenges and in the fact that many saw their friendship as a symbol of the slowly reconciling nation.

When Grant's tomb was dedicated, Julia invited Varina to the ceremony, where the women knelt together in prayer. When asked to write a response to a book that disparaged Grant, Varina responded: "I hope there are people both north and south who are already looking above and through the smoke of battle to take the just measure of

Varina Davis

the statesmen and commanders. . . . In this galaxy I think General Grant will take his place unquestioned."[51]

Varina responded to the news of Julia's passing by falling to her knees in prayer. A public defendant of the Grants for the rest of her life, she said she felt for Julia "a great respect and sincere affection."[52] When Varina passed away in 1906, Julia's son sent an artillery escort to accompany the funeral procession through the streets of New York. Confederate veterans marched side by side with Union soldiers for the event, and Grant's son sent a military band to play "Dixie" and "The Bonnie Blue Flag"[53] in honor of a woman who had suffered through some of the worst days of the war but had chosen to relinquish her grief in favor of peace. When asked about her friendship with Julia, Varina once said, "Northerners and Southerners had more in common than they knew,"[54] a shocking sentiment to many who felt the two halves of the country were worlds apart. Her words are just as applicable today, across every line of conflict.

In some ways, given the deep scars inflicted by four years of war, it's remarkable that reunification of this country was possible under any circumstances. The women in this chapter are notable examples of abilities that are, in some ways, far more difficult than routing and whipping an enemy: they embody the qualities needed to turn from war and instead wage peace.

In spite of real tragedy, profound suffering, and destruction, these remarkable women found a way to make space for forgiveness — not because their enemies necessarily deserved it but because forgiveness is good for a soul — and good for a nation.

Further Reading

Joan E. Cashin. *First Lady of the Confederacy: Varina Davis's Civil War.* Cambridge, MA: Belknap Press, 2006.

Bruce Catton. *A Stillness at Appomattox.* New York: Anchor Books, 1953.

Frank P. Cauble, *Biography of Wilmer McLean, May 3, 1814–June 5, 1882, Appomattox Court House National and Historical Park,* Office of Archeology and Historic Preservation, October 31, 1969, NPS, 38; http://npshistory.com/publications/apco/mclean-bio.pdf.

Mark Perry. *Lift Up Thy Voice: The Sarah and Angelina Grimke Family's Journey from Slaveholders to Civil Rights Leaders.* New

York: Penguin Books, 2001.

Robert M. Poole. *On Hallowed Ground: The Story of Arlington National Cemetery.* New York: Bloomsbury, 2009.

Elizabeth Brown Pryor. *Clara Barton: Professional Angel.* Philadelphia: University of Pennsylvania Press, 1987.

Robert Brent Toplin, ed. *Ken Burns's The Civil War: Historians Respond.* Oxford: Oxford University Press, 1996.

Anne Carter Zimmer. *The Robert E. Lee Family Cooking and Housekeeping Book.* Chapel Hill, NC: University of North Carolina Press, 1997.

Notes

Epigraph: Mary Anna Jackson, *Life and Letters of General Thomas J. Jackson* (New York: Harper, 1892), introduction.

1. Abraham Lincoln, "President Abraham Lincoln's Second Inaugural Address (1865)," retrieved from Our Documents, https://www.ourdocuments.gov/doc.php?flash=true&doc=38. Accessed February 19, 2018.

2. Lincoln said this at his first Cabinet meeting after receiving word of the surrender at Appomattox: "I hear cries here and there, 'Hang this man and hang that

man.' Gentlemen, there has been enough bloodshed in this country; and I want to say to you for myself that, instead of catching anybody and hanging anybody, I wish all those who feel that they might leave their country for their country's good might go away without anybody's catching them." Emanuel Hertz, *Lincoln Talks: A Biography in Anecdote* (New York: Viking, 1939), 367.

3. Ronald C. White, *American Ulysses: A Life of Ulysses S. Grant* (New York: Random House, 2016), 407.

4. "A Slice of the Confederacy in the Interior of Brazil" by Simon Romero, May 8, 2016. *The New York Times.* Accessed online at: https://www.nytimes.com/2016/05/09/world/americas/a-slice-of-the-confederacy-in-the-interior-of-brazil.html.

5. Many sources mistakenly say the war began at Wilmer McLean's house, but this is technically incorrect, as the home belonged exclusively to his wife, Virginia. When they married, they signed a prenuptial agreement that Yorkshire would remain "to her sole and separate use" (Frank P. Cauble, *Biography of Wilmer McLean, May 3, 1814–June 5, 1882, Appomattox Court House National and Historical Park,* Office of Archeology and Historic

Preservation, October 31, 1969, NPS, 38; http://npshistory.com/publications/apco/mclean-bio.pdf).

Prior to her marriage, Virginia owned 330 acres in Fairfax County, 500 acres in Prince William County, and 14 slaves, in addition to the 1,200 acres at Yorkshire.

6. Some sources mistakenly list two daughters from her first marriage, but Sarah Berber Mason was born on June 3, 1848, and died February 5, 1857, at Yorkshire. National Park Service document, 37.

7. In Herbert, *God Know All Your Names,* 244.

8. Don Johnson, *Thirteen Months at Manassas/Bull Run: The Two Battles and the Confederate and Union Occupations* (Jefferson, NC: McFarland, 2013), 55.

9. Patrick A. Schroeder, *Appomattox County* (Chicago: Arcadia Publishing, 2009), 21.

10. National Park Service, 80.

11. The McLeans owned eighteen slaves, according to the 1860 census. Appomattox Court House National Historical Park, Appomattox, Viriginia.

12. Schroeder, *Appomattox County,* 22.

13. National Park Service, 150.

14. National Park Service, 149.

15. Schroeder, *Appomattox County,* 33.

16. *Appomattox Court House* (Washington,

DC: National Park Service, 2003), 73.

17. Robin Friedman, *The Silent Witness* (New York: HMH Books for Young Readers, 2008), author's note.

18. See https://www.nps.gov/apco/silent-witness.htm.

19. See Marianne Monson, *Frontier Grit: The Unlikely True Stories of Daring Pioneer Women* (Salt Lake City: Shadow Mountain, 2016) and Linda Lowery, *One More Valley, One More Hill: The Story of Aunt Clara Brown* (New York: Random House Books for Young Readers, 2002).

20. Linda Lowery, *One More Valley: The Story of Aunt Clara Brown* (New York, Random House, 2002), 169.

21. M. R. Cordell, *Courageous Women of the Civil War: Soldiers, Spies, Medics, and More* (Chicago: Chicago Review Mask, 2016), 119.

22. Fannie's name is spelled "Fanny" in some sources. Karen Janita Carrillo, *African American History Day by Day: A Reference Guide to Events* (Santa Barbara: Greenwood, 2012), 300.

23. In 1895, Tubman finally succeeded in obtaining her husband's pension for his wartime service. Her own service remained largely unrecognized. Milton C.

Sernett, *Harriet Tubman: Myth, Memory, and History* (Duke University Press: London, 2007), 95.

24. Tubman turned her home into the Home for Indigent and Aged Negroes.

25. Her birth year is only approximately known, but this letter was sent April 9, 1894, by Jane Kellogg. See Jean M. Humez, *Harriet Tubman: The Life and the Life Stories* (Madison, WI: University of Wisconsin Press, 2004), 97.

26. Katherine DuPre Lumpkin, *The Emancipation of Angelina Grimke* (Chapel Hill, NC: University of North Carolina Press, 1974), 221.

27. Lumpkin, *The Emancipation of Angelina Grimke,* 226.

28. Faith Berry, *From Bondage to Liberation: Writings by and About Afro-Americans from 1700 to 1918* (New York: Continuum, 2006), 137.

29. For a thorough examination of this topic, see David W. Blight, *Race and Reunion: The Civil War in American Memory* (Cambridge: Harvard University Press, 2002).

30. Judith E. Harper, *Women During the Civil War: An Encyclopedia* (New York: Routledge, 2004), 292.

31. Clara Barton, Report to the 40th Congress, 3rd Session, No. 57, 1869, retrieved from National Park Service; https://www.nps.gov/museum/exhibits/clba/exb/Work/Office_of_correspondence/CLBA46_letterFront.html. Accessed February 19, 2018.

32. "Clara's Story," Clara Barton Missing Soldiers Museum; see http://www.clarabartonmuseum.org/clarasstory/. Accessed February 19, 2018.

33. The editorial responded to Barton's Red Cross Initiative to aid recovery efforts after floods decimated the town. In William Eleazar Barton, *The Life of Clara Barton: Founder of the American Red Cross, Volume 2* (Boston: Houghton Mifflin Company, 1922), 236.

34. She was the step–great-granddaughter of President George Washington.

35. Douglas Southall Freeman, *R. E. Lee: A Biography, Volume 1* (New York: C. Scribner's Son), 108.

36. Elizabeth Brown Pryor, *Reading the Man: A Portrait of Robert E. Lee Through His Private Letters* (New York: Penguin Books, 2008), 83.

37. Freeman, *R. E. Lee,* 108.

38. Freeman is admittedly one of the most avid admirers of Lee's biographers. Ac-

cording to Elizabeth Brown Pryor's more thorough examination of the Lees' attitudes towards slavery, Mary had a fundamentally different and more compassionate approach to slavery than her husband. See Pryor, *Reading the Man,* 140, 143–54.

39. Pryor, *Reading the Man,* 278.

40. Freeman, *R. E. Lee,* 440.

41. In Freeman, *R. E. Lee,* 442.

42. Letter dated April 20, 1861, in Pryor *Reading the Man,* 276.

43. In Freeman, *R. E. Lee,* 442.

44. Douglas Savage, *The Last Years of Robert E. Lee: From Gettysburg to Lexington* (Lanham, MD: Taylor Trade Publishing, 2016), 211.

45. Mary Lee, afflicted as she was with rheumatoid arthritis and behind Confederate lines, was not able to pay the taxes, which an 1863 amendment required be paid in person, mainly to punish those aligning themselves with the Confederacy. The estate was sold at auction and the US government paid $26,800 for the property. Anthony J. Gaughan, *The Last Battle of the Civil War: United States Versus Lee, 1861–1883* (Baton Rogue: Louisiana State University Press, 2011), 28.

46. In Jones, *Personal Reminiscences,* 153.

47. In "Mary Anna Randolph Custis Lee,"

National Park Service; see https://www
.nps.gov/arho/learn/historyculture/mary-
lee.htm. Accessed February 19, 2018.

48. Mary P. Coulling, *The Lee Girls*
(Winston-Salem, NC: Blair, 1987), 91.

49. I want to acknowledge a potential
contradiction inherent in the statement
that people on all sides of the conflict
deserve to be viewed with equity and
grace. The reader could potentially interpret this as advocating a conciliation
toward Confederate principles. One of the
major challenges that faced me while writing this book was a desire to fairly represent the point of views of all sides. Though
it requires a complexity of thinking not
often present in US political discussions,
there has to be a way to acknowledge the
significant personal trauma and loss experienced by white Southerners during the
war without condoning the political aims
of the Confederacy that undoubtedly had
as one of their main objectives the preservation of the slave system, which led to
the subjugation and abuse of millions.
Historian David W. Blight discusses this
dilemma often in his own work, particularly when he explores the desire the nation had at the end of the conflict to find
justice. See David W. Blight, *Race and*

Reunion (Cambridge: Harvard University Press, 2002).

50. Hadley Meares, "How First Ladies on Opposing Sides of the Civil War Forged an Unlikely Friendship," Feb 22, 2016; see https://www.atlasobscura.com/articles/how-first-ladies-on-opposing-sides-of-the-civil-war-forged-an-unlikely-bond.

51. Ishbel Ross, *First Lady of the South: The Life of Mrs. Jefferson Davis* (New York: Harper, 1958), 345.

52. Joan E. Cashin, *First Lady of the Confederacy: Varina Davis's Civil War* (Cambridge: Harvard University Press, 2009), 302.

53. Meares, "How First Ladies on Opposing Sides of the Civil War Forged an Unlikely Friendship."

54. Cashin, *First Lady of the Confederacy,* 282.

AUTHOR'S NOTE

Latin American journalist and novelist Eduardo Galeano once said, "History never really says 'goodbye.' History says, 'See you later.' "[1]

Writing this book has been a little like peering into a mirror hanging on the wall of a carnival funhouse — though the picture before me is distorted and distended, it is also uncannily, eerily familiar. In a strange repetition of the tumult of the 1860s, we once again live in a country that is deeply divided by partisan politics; and once more, violence and fear are very real manifestations of these divisions.

But there are differences too. Perhaps the greatest difference is that we have been here before. We know where violence leads and the potential damages that can be inflicted. It is difficult to imagine anyone looking at the costs and casualties of the Civil War and wishing to find ourselves in that place again.

As General Joseph Hooker said after the guns fell silent in 1865, "There has been enough blood shed to satisfy any reasonable man, and it is time to quit."

Would it have been easier if the Confederacy had splintered away from the United States a hundred and fifty years ago, developed their own identity, sought their own way forward?

Maybe.

Maybe not.

Alternative history is far from being an exact science, and just like a good choose-your-own-adventure novel, there are far too many unexpected twists and turns to make an educated guess.

What I know is that the nation did not remain divided.

Partly because of Abraham Lincoln, partly because of Anna Ella Carroll, Harriet Tubman, and many other incredible women profiled in this book, and partly because of many other Americans who lived in the Civil War era, this nation decided to stay together as one.

In spite of real differences, in spite of small-mindedness and prejudice and limitations and hate — we stayed together. We fought our messy and complicated and dramatically imperfect way forward to this present moment. And here — in this present moment — is where our choices always lie.

So do we splinter once more and line up along all-too-familiar lines of red against blue, blue versus gray, hunch ourselves into our respective corners, and glare with animosity over fabricated borders? Do we take up arms and add more blood to the battlefields of this country? Or will we take Susie King Taylor's counsel to "not forget that terrible war," and say the cost of previous bloodshed on American soil has been far more than enough? Can we use the memory of past sacrifices to bind our modern nation together?

We, as Americans, are experts at waging war, but perhaps we need more practice waging peace. We are quite good at escalating situations, but we may be less adept at empathizing in situations. If you, like I do, wonder what can be done to bring such a shift to pass, I'm afraid I don't have the answers. I sincerely wish I did.

One thing I do know is that women are an essential piece of the solution, whatever it may be. Nobel Peace Prize winner Leymah Gbowee helped end the Second Liberian Civil War by a joint force of women. Thousands of Palestinian and Israeli women have come together to demand peace for the Middle East. The United Nations has affirmed women's essential role in peacebuilding and conflict prevention. I know this world is more ethical, compassionate, and nonviolent when women are involved in political negotiations at every level.[2]

The other thing I know is that people on every side often need, more than anything else, an opportunity to be heard. They need to be heard even if they don't look like us, think like us, and especially if they disagree with us. They particularly need to be heard if the dominant discourse tends to ignore their voices.

Sometimes, I think one of the most important acts of kindness we can do for one another is to listen — really listen — to each other's stories.

And I believe you just did.

Notes

1. See Gary Younge, "Interview: Eduardo Galeano: 'My great fear is that we are all suffering from amnesia,' " *The Guardian,* July 23, 2013; available at https://www.theguardian.com/books/2013/jul/23/eduardo-galeano-children-days-interview.

2. Women Wage Peace is a collaboration of Israeli and Palestinian women who march and pray together on behalf of peace. See womenwagepeace.org. See also United Nations Report of the Security-General on Women and Peace and Security October 16, 2017.

ACKNOWLEDGMENTS

Writing a volume of history involves a staggering number of people who influence the text, though they remain largely behind the scenes. I am deeply indebted to the staff members, scholars, and experts who contributed to this work. They include:

In Louisiana: The Civil War Museum at Confederate Memorial Hall in New Orleans, Jennifer Navarre at The Historic New Orleans Research Center, Museum at the Cabildo, the guides at the Laura and Whitney Plantations.

In Vicksburg, Mississippi: Bubba Bolm at the Old Court House Museum, Vicksburg Battlefield Museum, Cedar Hill Cemetery, Vicksburg National Military Park, and Duff Green Mansion.

In Savannah, Georgia: Dr. Stan Deaton and the Georgia Historical Society, Massie Schoolhouse, Vaughnette Goode-Walker of Savannah Footprints tour, the Cotton

Exchange Building, Forrest Clark Johnson III, County Historian at Troup County Archives, Georgia.

In Washington, DC: Museum of Health and Sanitation, Clara Barton Home in Glen Echo Park, Lincoln's summer home at US Soldier's and Airmen's home, Ford's Theater, African American Civil War Museum, The National Archives, Arlington House at Arlington National Cemetery, Clara Barton's Office of Missing Persons.

In Maryland: National Museum of Civil War Medicine in Frederick, Antietam Battlefield Museum.

In Pennsylvania: Gettysburg National Military Park and Cemetery.

In Virginia: Chatham House (Lacey House) in Fredericksburg, Fredericksburg Military Museum and Battlefield, The American Civil War Museums at Richmond and Sean Kane at Tredegar. Historians Patrick Schroeder and Frank P. Cauble at Appomattox National Park, and the staff at the Confederate White House Museum in Richmond.

In Astoria, Oregon: Library director Jimmy Pearson and the incredible Civil War collection hidden away in the library's basement.

David Dixon provided essential information on Rachel Brownfield, Sammye Meadows of the Cherokee nation was vital to understanding the impact of the war on native women. Herb Swingle, Dr. Alhaji Conte from the Moorland-Spingarn Research Center, Professor Elizabeth Regine Varon, and James L. Swanson also made valuable contributions. I would like to express a debt of gratitude to all the librarians, historical societies, museums, and guides who interpret and keep memory alive for our nation.

I am indebted to family and friends who read early drafts and provided feedback, including Rachel Hall, Brian King, Jordan Rudd, and Dwight Monson. Lisa Mangum and the rest of the team at Shadow Mountain brought the project to life. My editor, Heidi Taylor, is every author's dream — I couldn't imagine doing this without her support, encouragement, and guidance. Extraordinary research assistant Luis Miguel Arredondo Casas deserves endless gratitude for fielding many a research inquiry, any time of the day or night, with both patience and poise. Meanwhile, my children, Nathan and Aria, put up with the stacks of Civil War books that encroached on every surface of our home, and as always, provide me with the best motivation of all to keep writing my way towards a more beautiful, more equitable world.

PHOTO CREDITS:

Background: pashabo/shutterstock.com

page 15: Harriet Beecher Stowe/public domain

page 23: Lydia Child/public domain

page 45: White Mountain rangers, ca. 1861/ Library of Congress/public domain

page 49: Frances Clayton/Library of Congress/public domain

page 73: Susie King Taylor/public domain

page 95: Belle Boyd/Library of Congress/ public domain

page 102: Rose Greenhow and Daughter/ Library of Congress/public domain

page 112: Pauline Cushman/Library of Congress/public domain

page 125: Harriet Tubman/Library of Congress/public domain

page 135: Anna Ella Carroll/Maryland Historical Society

page 156: Sarah Dawson/public domain

ABOUT THE AUTHOR

Marianne Monson is a writer and professor of English with a strong interest in the relationship between literature and history. She teaches Creative Writing at Portland Community College and regularly speaks at writing conferences.